Current Issues in Victimology Research

Current Issues in Victimology Research

EDITED BY

Laura J. Moriarty

and

Robert A. Jerin

CAROLINA ACADEMIC PRESS
Durham, North Carolina

ISBN 0-89089-861-8
LCCN 98-88619

CAROLINA ACADEMIC PRESS
700 Kent Street
Durham, North Carolina 27701
Telephone (919) 489-7486
Fax (919) 493-5668
E-mail: cap@cap-press.com
www.cap-press.com

Printed in the United States of America

To the Men in my Life —
Craig, Michael, Mark, James, Stephen, and Johnny,
— no aunt could be more proud. LJM

To my Family and Special Friends —
your support makes everything possible. RAJ

Contents

Cases and Statutes

Preface

Research on crime victims is a relatively new phenomena in the criminal justice field. With the birth of victimology in the 1940s and 1950s research focused on victim-offender relationships and victim culpability. It has only been in the last few decades that researchers have started studying the effects of crime upon the victim along with analyzing the services provided to the crime victim. This book seeks to provide an understanding of the impact of the criminal act upon individuals and society through recent research and will provide the criminal justice field with a foundation for grasping the complexities of crime victimization.

The chapters in this book are divided into five sections: fear of crime, campus victimization, victim services and representation, victims' rights versus offenders' rights, and sexual harassment and stalking. Dr. Moriarty served on the 1997 ACJS program committee where she was responsible for the "victimology" section of the program. Nine of the chapters included here were first presented at the 1997 ACJS Annual Meeting in Louisville, Kentucky. The others were invited by the editors. Collectively the chapters represent the most current research in victimology. The field of victimology is expanding, and we are quite pleased to include such a wide variety of topics in our reader.

Part I: Fear of Crime

The three chapters included in this section all focus on fear of crime. Although it has been studied for more than 35 years, fear of crime remains, to a certain extent, an enigma. Some of the well-established relationships are currently being challenged. For example, the elderly have been the most fearful of crime but recent research has not found this relationship to be consistent. The chapters included here test the empirical findings and offer a contemporary perspective on the relationships. In Chapter 1, Anne Sullivan explores fear of crime among multilingual populations (different cultures). In Chapter 2, Bill and Will Pelfrey examine fear of crime at two points in time and discover some interesting and perplexing results. In Chapter 3, Debbie Robinson and David Mitchell ponder if students' fear of crime is justified? They survey the campus to determine the most vulnerable spots on campus for victimization and compare the visual inspection findings with the students' fear of crime results.

Part II: Campus Victimization

The four chapters in this section examine campus victimization. Here we use the term "campus" to mean any school setting, not necessarily only college settings. In Chapter 4, Stephen Cox, Tim Bynum, and William Davidson focus on the behavior of carrying weapons to school and its impact on personal victimization. In Chapter 5, Ron Clarke and Steve Lab examine teacher victimization in both public and private secondary schools. In Chapter 6, Hugh Potter and Alban Wheeler compare campus victimization at one university in the United States and one in Australia focusing on the role alcohol plays in such victimization. Finally, in Chapter 7, Max Bromley provides an overview of campus victimization focusing on legal, statutory, and administrative responses.

Part III: Victims Services and Representation

Four chapters are included in this section. In Chapter 8, Laura Moriarty, Bob Jerin, and Bill Pelfrey compare and contrast victim services in North Carolina and Virginia. In Chapter 9, Rick Tewksbury, Darin Moore, and Nicholas King evaluate prosecutorial victim services in one county in Kentucky. In Chapter 10, Laura Moriarty and Peggy Kenworthy profile child representation models in North Carolina and Virginia. Finally, in Chapter 11, Laura Moriarty, Pat Grant, and Jim Hague explore the role of the church in providing services to victims and offer a hierarchical model of representation.

Part IV: Victims' Rights versus Offenders' Rights

The two chapters in this section focus on offenders' rights in relationship to victims' rights. In Chapter 12, Greg Orvis argues that victim compensation and restoration should be moved from a criminal venue to a civil venue. In Chapter 13, Lloyd Klein provides an overview of state sexual offender notification requirement laws pondering the effectiveness of such laws.

Part V: Sexual Harassment and Stalking

Three chapters are included in this section. In Chapter 14, Bernadette Muscat provides an overview of sexual harassment. In Chapter 15, Lisa Bozenhard examines stalking laws. Finally, in Chapter 16, Toni Dupont-Morales analyzes the female stalker focusing on her victims.

Acknowledgments

This book has been a collaboration of many individuals. We would like to thank the individual contributors for their originality, thoughtfulness, and dedication to the field of victimology. Their efforts have provided a wide-ranging examination of issues in the field.

Additionally, we would like to recognize the support from our institutions: Virginia Commonwealth University and Endicott College including our colleagues and our students. We would also like to thank Carolina Academic Press, especially our editor, Phil Menzies, who has been instrumental in making this book a reality.

Lastly, but most importantly, we would like to recognize the tremendous courage of the survivors of criminal violence. We hope this book provides greater insight into their fight for understanding and justice.

Part I

Fear of Crime

Chapter 1

Assessing Community Fear Across Multilingual Populations

Anne Sullivan

Introduction

Recent research has shown that fear of crime ranks as one of the major concerns of citizens, especially those living in urban areas (Baumer, 1985; Hindelang, Gottfredson, & Garofalo, 1978; Skogan, 1986; Skogan & Klecka, 1977; Toseland, 1982). The fear of crime can greatly reduce the quality of life for residents of high crime areas. In addition, the fear of crime may cause individuals to limit their activities and withdraw into the safety of their homes. As a result, there has been considerable attention focused on the fear of crime. Research has examined the relationship between a number of different factors such as quality of life variables (abandoned buildings, vandalism, traffic, noise, street lighting) and demographic variables (age, gender, income, race, and victimization) and the fear of crime.

Some research has explored the relationship between neighborhood "incivilities" and the fear of crime (Garofalo & Laub, 1978; Hunter, 1978; Skogan, 1990; Skogan & Maxfield; 1981). Baumer (1985) observes, "Signs of incivility are those environmental cues that signify crime indirectly through disorder, decay and disreputable behavior" (p. 242). Examples of community incivilities would include vandalism, drug-related problems, teenagers loitering on street corners, prostitution, and abandoned buildings. The relationship between social disorder and fear is extremely important, since prior research has shown a causal link between social disorder and crime (Kelling & Coles, 1996; Skogan, 1990; Wilson & Kelling, 1982). Skogan (1990) found that social disorder serves as a precursor to crime. Kelling and Coles (1996) observe, "Skogan's research confirms that citizens fear of disorder is neither an unreasonable nor extreme reaction, since disorder does indeed precede or accompany serious crime and urban decay" (p. 26).

Other research has examined the relationship between victimization and fear of crime. For the most part, these studies have shown that those who have been victimized as well as their families and friends experience heightened levels of fear (Skogan & Maxfield, 1981). Skogan and Klecka (1977), however, found that the relationship between victimization and fear of crime varies by type of crime. They examined the effects of robbery, burglary, and assault on crime victims. Only the crime of robbery had a powerful effect on its victims. In fact, burglary and assault victims reported that they were less fearful than nonvictims of walking the streets of their neighborhoods at night.

One possible explanation for these unexpected findings is that the "unknown" produces a higher level of fear and once one has been victimized and survives, the unknown is reduced. Another possible explanation for these findings is that other factors besides victimization affect levels of fear. For example, Skogan and Klecka (1977) examined whether race influences the relationship between victimization and fear of crime. They found that blacks were more fearful of crime than whites and that the effects of victimization upon them were more pronounced.

Lastly, several studies have relied on survey data to analyze fear of crime across different demographic characteristics such as age, race, gender and family income (Hindelang et al., 1978; Skogan, 1986; Skogan & Klecka, 1977; Skogan & Maxfield, 1981; Stinchcombe, Heimer, Dliffe, Schepple, Smith, & Garth, 1978; Toseland, 1982). These studies have examined the extent to which respondents felt safe in their neighborhoods, whether they thought crime had increased or decreased in their neighborhoods in the past few years, whether they had limited their daily activities to avoid victimization, and how well they thought the police were doing relative to responding to local crime problems. In general, this research found that blacks, women, the elderly, and the poor were more likely to report feeling unsafe in their neighborhoods (Hindelang et al., 1978; Skogan, 1986; Skogan & Klecka, 1977; Skogan & Maxfield, 1981; Stinchcombe et al., 1978; Toseland, 1982).

Although there is a rich literature on the demographic correlates of fear, there has been a lack of empirical research examining whether ethnicity is related to fear of crime. This is somewhat surprising given the cultural and ethnic diversity characterizing many American neighborhoods and the current emphasis on community policing. Community policing represents a shift away from reactive law enforcement to a more proactive problem-solving approach. The various programs of community policing endeavor to bring police and citizens together in close working relationships, to reduce fear, and increase citizen satisfaction with the police (Alderson, 1977; Bayley, 1988; Brown, 1985; Davis, 1985; Goldstein, 1987, 1990; Greene & Taylor, 1988; Kelling & Moore, 1988; Sparrow, Moore, & Kennedy, 1990). One of the keys to establishing a successful community policing program lies in listening to and involving local residents in its design and implementation.

The community policing approach encourages citizens to express their views and concerns about local crime problems. The strategies for securing community input and participation vary from one jurisdiction to the next. Some departments sponsor public forums where citizens are able to discuss their concerns directly with local law enforcement officials. In other departments, police solicit input from members of community organizations, such as Neighborhood Crime Watch groups or the Chamber of Commerce. Still, other police departments rely on community surveys to determine what crime problems are most troubling to local residents.

Although police officials have gone to considerable lengths to solicit citizen input, often times, they have not taken into account the cultural and ethnic diversity characterizing American communities. For example, a community is not always homogenous in its composition or values. Consequently, where there is cultural and ethnic diversity whose input gets solicited? Moreover, where there is cultural and ethnic diversity whose concerns get prioritized by the police?

A recent National Institute of Justice report (Brady, 1996) entitled, "Measuring What Matters" addresses some of these very issues. One police executive observed, "The diversity in communities is phenomenal. Our belief now is that every time we go solve a problem, we create another problem for ourselves with another group" (p. 6). In other words, when police are encouraged to use any method to solve a neighborhood problem, certain marginalized ethnic groups within a community may experience discrimination. Therefore, it may be necessary for police to solicit input and participation from all of the ethnic and racial groups within their jurisdictions in order to avoid misunderstanding and miscommunication.

This chapter describes the innovative strategies undertaken by three Massachusetts police departments to solicit input from a cross-section of residents living within their respective communities. All three of these departments have implemented community policing or are in the process of doing so. These departments all relied on community surveys to elicit citizen input. In addition, these departments prepared the surveys in several languages including Spanish, Portuguese, Cambodian, Russian, and Vietnamese. The questionnaires were designed to assess community fear, quality of life, citizen satisfaction with police, and what crimes residents consider most pressing. The use of multilingual surveys gave police officials the opportunity to assess whether different ethnic/racial groups share the same concerns about crime and express similar attitudes about police performance.

Community Data

All three of these police departments are located in communities that have recently experienced a rapid infusion of large immigrant populations from diverse cultures with different languages. These changes have brought escalating tensions, conflicts, and misunderstandings. While all three of these communities have undergone significant changes in their ethnic composition, there are some notable differences between the three municipalities. The following community data was gleaned from two sources, the 1990 Census of Population and Housing and the 1987 Census of Manufactures.

The first community has experienced growth primarily in its non-white Hispanic population. From 1980 to 1990, its Hispanic population increased by 185%. In the past, generations of immigrants settled in this community, drawn by its industrial job base, affordable housing, and ethnic enclaves. In recent years, however, this community has experienced considerable job loss. The decline in manufacturing jobs has led to lower wages and income for local residents.

In contrast, the second community has experienced an influx of many different ethnic groups including Haitians, Brazilians, Central Americans, Koreans, and other Asians. Its minority population rose from 3.8% in 1980 to 11.3% in 1990. The local school system has a large minority enrollment. Approximately 13% of the students are African-American, 12% Brazilian or Cape Verdean, 12% Hispanic, and 4% Asian. These figures underscore the ethnic and racial diversity characterizing this community. Besides changes to its ethnic composition, this community has also lost much of its industrial base, household incomes have declined, and youth crime has increased.

The third community is the most diverse. Over the last decade, this community has become home to a number of different ethnic and racial groups. The community has a large Cambodian and Vietnamese constituency. In addition, a significant number of Russian immigrants have settled in the community. The community also contains a large number of African-Americans and Hispanics. Approximately 80% of the population is white, 7% African-American, 8% Hispanic, 4% Asian, and 1% other. Between 1980 and 1990, the community's black population increased by 743% and its Hispanic population rose by 271%. This community has also seen its industrial base deteriorate and nearly 15% of local families live below the poverty line.

In light of all these changes, all three communities have come to realize that the rapid infusion of large immigrant populations coupled with massive deindustrialization underscores the need for more effective and innovative policing. In order to minimize misunderstandings, police need to become familiar with the traditions and history of new immigrant groups. For example, a significant number of Southeast Asians are refugees who immigrated to the United States from countries where the police were their enemy. Consequently, Southeast Asian immigrants may continue to be suspicious and afraid of police.

As a practical matter, police officials need to take into account the cultural realities of their communities. Along these lines, three Massachusetts police departments have endeavored to solicit input from the various ethnic and racial groups living within their respective communities. As part of their outreach strategy, multilingual community surveys were used to obtain feedback from residents about public safety needs, fear of crime, and police effectiveness in addressing local crime problems.

Method

All three departments employed different data collection methods. In addition, all three departments used different survey instruments. However, there were a number of questions that appeared in all three surveys. These questions included:

- Whether crime had increased, decreased or remained the same in their neighborhood in the past year.
- How safe respondents feel in their neighborhood.
- Whether respondents have limited their activities because of crime.
- Their rating of the performance of local police.
- Their suggestions for improving police effectiveness.

The first community that had seen rapid growth in its non-white Hispanic population administered a survey through a random mailing. The survey contained questions in English and Spanish. A total of 4,000 surveys were distributed and 1,481 were completed and returned. Thus, a response rate of 37% was achieved. The overwhelming majority of respondents were white (97%). Nevertheless, there were some notable differences between whites and Hispanics on several key issues.

The second department translated their survey into several languages including Spanish, Portuguese, and Creole. The survey was distributed through two methods. First, the survey appeared in the local newspaper. Readers were asked to complete the questionnaire and return it to the local police department. The other way that the survey was distributed was through the efforts of community police officers. The officers handed out and collected the surveys from local residents.

A total of 249 surveys were returned. Approximately 17% came from the newspaper while 83% were collected by the community police officers. As with the first community, the vast majority (95%) of the returned surveys were the "English" version. The remaining 5% were in the Portuguese, Spanish, or Creole versions.

The third department worked directly with a multi-ethnic community organization dedicated to improving the quality of life in local neighborhoods through anti-crime initiatives. The survey was prepared in Spanish, Cambodian, and Russian. The police worked with this local organization to insure that the surveys were administered to a representative cross-section of the community's population. For example, the survey was given out to customers at a local Vietnamese market. A total of 4800 surveys were distributed and 1429 were returned. Thus, a response rate of 30% was achieved. The respondents were 65% white, 14% Hispanic, 10% African-American, and 9% Asian. In general, there were a few notable differences between the various ethnic groups relative to police services and fear of crime.

Findings

In the first community, there were significant differences between whites and Hispanics on several key issues. For instance, whites were considerably more fearful than Hispanics that their homes would be burglarized. Approximately 55% of whites compared to 37% of Hispanics indicated that they worried about their homes being burglarized. Along similar lines, whites were far more likely to identify burglary as a serious problem in their neighborhoods. Specifically, 60% of whites compared to 42% of Hispanics responded that burglary is a serious crime problem. Not surprising, a significant percentage of whites (64%) wanted police to concentrate primarily on burglary prevention.

Conversely, the primary concern of Hispanic respondents was reducing drug trafficking in their neighborhoods. The majority of Hispanic respondents (60%) indicated that they were afraid their children were being exposed to drugs while only 40% of whites replied that drug trafficking was a major problem in their neighborhoods. Hispanics were also more concerned than whites about the extent of social disorder characterizing their neighborhoods. For example, 65% of Hispanics worried about strangers loitering near their homes compared to 49% of whites. Similarly, 61% of Hispanics worried about people drinking too much in their neighborhoods compared to 48% of whites.

Approximately 64% of Hispanics responded that they wanted the police to focus primarily on drug trafficking. In addition, 32% of Hispanics wanted police to concentrate on gang activity. In sharp contrast, whites were far less likely to identify drug dealing (40%) or gang activity (18%) as crime problems in need of police attention.

Thus far, the findings suggest that whites and Hispanics have different opinions about the nature and extent of the local crime problem. It should be noted, however, that whites and Hispanics did agree on several important issues. Both whites and Hispanics indicated that hiring more officers would do the most to improve local police services (42% and 33%, respectively). Furthermore, 51% of whites and 59% of Hispanics agreed that police would be most effective patrolling their neighborhoods in cars. Somewhat surprising, only 24% of whites and 22% of Hispanics responded that foot patrols would be effective. Additionally, both whites (21%) and Hispanics (16%) were even less enthusiastic about the effectiveness of bike patrols in their neighborhoods.

In the survey administered in the second community, the respondents generally concurred about what crimes needed the most attention. Although criminal activity varied across neighborhoods, in terms of total responses, residents reported burglary, youth violence, and drug trafficking were the crimes that needed the most police attention. This agreement may be due in part to the relatively low number of respondents in the survey (N=249) or the fact that the sample was not representative of the community's diverse population.

The third police department experienced greater success securing a diverse sample of respondents who were reasonably representative of the community's population. Approximately 76% of the respondents identified stationary patrol in high crime areas as the most important police service. In addition, 65% of the respondents indicated that they wanted more patrol cars in their neighborhoods. Similarly, the majority of respondents (65%) wanted individual police officers assigned to their neighborhoods.

In general, it appears that the respondents shared similar concerns about local crime problems. There were, however, some clear and consistent differences across different ethnic groups. For example, greater support for all police services was found among Hispanic respondents. Hispanics indicated a higher degree of importance on all police services than any of the other ethnic groups. Specifically, 98% of Hispanics identified stationary patrols in high crime areas as the most important police service. They also exhibited higher levels of fear. For example, 74% of Hispanics replied that they were afraid to walk alone in their neighborhood compared to 53% of Asians and 46% of whites.

Asian respondents (82%) were more likely than other ethnic groups to emphasize the need for programs for non-English speaking residents to report crimes to the police. Asians (91%) also were more likely than other ethnic groups to stress the importance of assigning individual officers to their neighborhoods to reduce crime and social disorder.

Conclusions

The purpose of this chapter is to describe the efforts undertaken by three Massachusetts police departments to secure input from a cross-section of citizens living within their respective communities. All three of these police departments should be commended for reaching out to new immigrant groups to solicit their input on local crime problems. Drawing on the collective results, certain practical and valuable lessons emerge which should direct future research and policy development.

First, these findings make it clear that police officials can and should continue to solicit feedback from the various ethnic and racial groups within their communities, especially if the department has moved to community policing. At the heart of the problem-solving approach is the idea that police should listen to and cooperate with residents to identify the crime problems most troubling to them. Working with local residents police can develop tailored solutions for each community problem they face rather than rely on one particular strategy to solve divergent multi-ethnic problems.

In the first community, for example, the police need to determine if the citizens' perceptions are based in reality. If their fears are unfounded the police might want to educate the community about the exact nature and extent of the local crime problem. If citizens' fears are justified then police should formulate a strategy to decrease burglaries in white neighborhoods while developing a different strategy to reduce drug dealing in Hispanic neighborhoods. A program that aims to reduce fear among white citizens regarding burglaries will not necessarily reduce the fears of Hispanic citizens regarding drug trafficking. Therefore, in order to be responsive to all citizens, police may need to develop different strategies that address the unique concerns of each of the constituencies they serve.

Similarly, in the third community police should consider working more closely with Hispanic residents, since they were more concerned about crime than other ethnic groups. In addition, this department might establish a program for non-English speaking residents to report crime. Police may also want to increase their visibility in Asian enclaves since Asian respondents were far more likely than other groups to want individual officers assigned to their neighborhoods.

Second, it is clear that the level of data collection success varied, depending upon the method employed. For example, the second community published the survey in the local newspaper and only a small percentage of readers completed and returned the questionnaire. As a result, the department was not able to secure a cross-section of respondents representative of the community's population. Given that 25% of the residents living in this community speak a language other than English in their homes,

Table 1
Community and Survey Demographics

Community	White	African-American	Hispanic	Asian	Other
Community1	89%	3%	6%	1%	1%
Survey 1	97%	0	3%	0	0
Community 2	88%	6%	2%	3%	1%
Survey 2	95%	0	3%	0	2%
Community 3	80%	6%	9%	3%	2%
Survey 3	65%	10%	14%	9%	2%

it seems reasonable to assume that they probably do not read the local newspaper which is published in English. In the future, perhaps, the survey should be published in non-English newspapers to improve upon the chances of securing a more representative sample.

The data in Table 1 show that the third department achieved the greatest success obtaining a cross-section of respondents representative of the community's population. This department worked in conjunction with a multi-ethnic grassroots organization. This appears to have paved the way for the police to solicit input from a representative sample of residents. Thus, police in other departments may want to work with diverse community organizations as a way of gaining access to and input from new immigrant groups.

At first community outreach initiatives do not necessarily have to focus on crime prevention. For example, a department might sponsor a Police Athletic League for at-risk youth who come from culturally diverse backgrounds. Police would be given the opportunity to interact with young people while simultaneously gaining access to the kids' families.

Another possible community outreach initiative would be the establishment of police/citizen academies. These academies would endeavor to familiarize citizens with police functions and responsibilities. Often times, immigrants arrive in the United States with preconceived ideas about the law enforcement community based on their experience with police in their country of origin. If immigrants are encouraged to participate in these academies, they may learn that the role of police in American society is different from the role of police in their homelands. Furthermore, these academies ideally would expose officers to persons of different nationalities taking into account that police as well as immigrants need to learn about each other's culture.

Through community outreach initiatives police can slowly gain the trust of immigrants. As a result, police and immigrants can then begin work together to address local crime problems through more formal activities such as advisory boards, neighborhood crime watch programs, and police substations.

In sum, collecting data from diverse ethnic and racial groups should be a mainstay of the problem-oriented approach. Specifically, the concerns of all citizens should be taken into consideration by the police relative to identifying and responding to local crime problems. This input, in turn, should then be used to design local community policing programs.

Note: An earlier version of this paper was presented at the 1997 Academy of Criminal Justice Sciences Annual Meeting, Louisville, KY. This paper is utilizing the initial Police Data Bank of Associate Professor Edward J. LeClair, Chair and Founder of the Criminal Justice Program at Salem State College, Salem, MA. Professor LeClair is currently working with fourteen small and mid-sized police departments in Massachusetts and was recently awarded a National of Institute of Justice grant to continue his work. The large quantity of personnel and citizen perception data was acquired during the last four years (1993-1997), however, the trustful relationship that permitted the development of such a rich data source was developed by Professor LeClair over the course of the last fifteen years as he worked with these Massachusetts police departments and their respective chiefs of police.

Discussion Questions

If you were the police chief of a community that had recently experienced a rapid influx of new immigrants, how would you proceed to build trust between your department and newly arrived immigrant?

Why is it as important for police to reduce neighborhood social disorder as it is for them to reduce crime?

If you wanted to assess fear across a community characterized by ethnic diversity, how would you collect data from a representative sample of residents?

Chapter 2

Fear of Crime, Age, and Victimization: Relationships and Changes Over Time

William V. Pelfrey, Sr.
William V. Pelfrey, Jr.

Introduction

While criminology has been struggling with what some have called an "etiological crisis," (Gibbs, 1987; Inciardi, 1980; Schwendinger & Schwendinger, 1982; Voigt, Thorton, Barrile, & Seaman, 1994) with less success than would be expected in explaining the causes of crime, fear of crime has become a major enquiry of criminologists, and with more explanatory success than has been recognized in the study of the etiology of crime. Indeed, fear has been central to criminal justice practices for decades.

The Omnibus Crime Control and Safe Streets Act of the late 1960's made fear of crime a focal concern. Citizens were depicted as being in constant and perpetual fear and unless the "war on crime" were successful, the social system would deteriorate under such fear. In 1973 the National Advisory Commission on Criminal Justice Standards and Goals once again brought fear of crime to the forefront when it stated:

The Commission foresees a time, in the immediate future when:

- A couple can walk in the evening in their neighborhood without fear of assault and robbery.
- A family can go away for the weekend without fear of returning to a house ransacked by burglars.
- Every citizen can live without fear of being brutalized by unknown assaults (1973:1).

Thus the national strategy to reduce crime was actually a strategy to attend to fear of crime. It was at that point that the fear of crime became an

13

important social research issue (Baumer, 1985). Some researchers have maintained that the major crime control initiative of the 1990s, Community Policing, is actually a fear reductions strategy (Trojanowicz & Bucqueroux, 1990).

Fear of Crime and Age

Fear of crime literature abounds in the fields of sociology, criminology, and political science. Public opinion polls routinely question the citizenry regarding their feelings of fear or safety in a defined milieu. As Will and McGrath stated recently (1995, p. 164), fear of crime literature focuses on "who is fearful and when? Second, how can we tell?" Regarding the issue of "who?" much of the early research indicated that the elderly were the most fearful segment of society (Clemente & Kleiman, 1976; Goldsmith & Goldsmith, 1976; Hahn, 1976). Ollenburger (1981, p. 101) stated the dominant view very simply when she said "the elderly have the highest fear of crime." The presumption that the elderly were more fearful seemed so paradigmatic that the major issue to be resolved was variable explanations of this fear level. Efforts to explain reasons for more or less fear among the elderly included social integration explanations but they proved to be equivocal in helping to explain the fear that the elderly seemed to be experiencing. Yin (1982) and Lee (1983), for example, found little evidence that social integration or socialization had a negative effect on fear of crime among the elderly. Kennedy and Silverman (1985a) found that respondents aged 65 and over were less fearful if they lived in a socially homogeneous environment, suggesting support for the social integration model. These efforts to explain the fear experienced by the elderly did not quarrel with the basic premise that the elderly were, in fact, the most fearful age group.

The age relationship to fear of crime was not restricted to the social system of the United States. Research has shown that this social problem transcends borders of countries and geographic areas within countries. Research in Great Britain (Clark & Lewis, 1982; Mawby, 1982) and Canada (Kennedy & Silverman, 1985b) found the elderly to be more fearful of crime within those social systems. Although there was some evidence that social homogeneity and a strong supportive network served to reduce fear among the elderly in other countries as well as the United States (Clark & Lewis, 1982), these were only mitigating or ameliorative effects and did not question the validity of the disproportionate fear within that age category. However, most of the early research has found that personal victimization or knowledge of incidents of victimization result in greatly increased fear among the elderly (Lee, 1983; Norton, 1982).

It was not until recently that researchers questioned the assumption that older adults are the most fearful in our society (Bankston & Thompson, 1989; Ferraro & LaGrange, 1988; LaGrange & Ferraro, 1987). Actually, Yin (1982) was one of the first to question the elder-fear axiom but the research literature did not accumulate in favor of accepting the anomalies of the paradigm until later.

Ferraro bluntly drew a line through many of the prior arguments, issues, and even paradigms related to fear and the elderly by saying (1995, p. 82):

> I think that the overwhelming evidence to date shows convincingly that age differences in fear of crime in adulthood are modest to trivial when we consider those who are 25 years of age or older. Youth and young adults have higher risk and are also more afraid. There really is no victimization/fear paradox by age as described in the literature.

Why the shift in the paradigm related to fear and the elderly? Was the previous research faulty or was there a change in the attitudes of the old fearful and the new fearful? Ferraro suggests that the discrepancies may be due to any of five possible explanations: "measurement, sampling, data collection methods, analytic methods, and social change" (1995, p. 69). The last of these explanations, social change, appears to Ferraro to be an inadequate explanation of the differences. He also comments "we do not have social change analyses which cover the late 1980s or early 1990s but it might be possible that fear of crime increased through the late 1970s and early 1980s and decreased in the last few years" (1995, p. 73). Data collected by the Gallup Poll suggests that fear to walk alone at night ("Is there an area near where you live—that is, within a mile—where you would be afraid to walk alone at night?") decreased from about 45 percent of a national sample responding "yes" in 1981, to 43 percent in 1989, and 40 percent in 1990 (Gallup, 1992). The 1992 Gallup Poll, however, showed an increase to 44 percent of positive responses to the fear question. Similarly, the poll's question about fear in the home ("How about at home at night—do you feel safe and secure, or not?") showed the 1981 levels to be 16 percent responding that they were fearful at home while the 1992 rate was 17 percent fearful (Gallup, 1992). When considering age variations, the Gallup Poll found that those 65 years of age or older were the most fearful (Gallup, 1992). While the data were not divided as precisely as some of the other research reviewed, these poll responses call into question the shift over time of the old as the most fearful.

Measurement of Fear of Crime

While there is ample literature suggesting that "fear of crime" is an amorphous issue, often imprecisely defined (Garofalo & Laub, 1978; Warr, 1984), Ferraro points out that "despite the lack of and confusion over definitions of fear of crime, one finds surprising consistency in the way it has been measured in dozens of studies" (1995, p. 24). He refers to the National Crime Survey question "How safe do you feel or would you feel being out alone in your neighborhood at night?" and the General Social Survey question "Is there any area right around here—that is, within one mile—where you would be afraid to walk alone at night?" Clearly the questions combine the concepts of perceived risk and, therefore the fear, associated with victimization. Ferraro maintains that the two concepts of fear and risk are associated but distinctly different. Risk may be high and fear low or risk may be low and fear high. There are, of course, other concepts bound up in the issues of fear and risk. As other researchers have noted (Liska, Sanchirico, & Reed, 1988; Taylor, Taub, & Peterson, 1986), constrained behavior and avoidance behavior are also proxies of the concept "perception of victimization." Each of the concepts has, arguably, a different method of measurement or multiple methods which may be similar but distinctly different. The key, it appears, in understanding a phenomenon is to measure it as many ways as possible. Risk of victimization is certainly a worthy topic for research, as are levels of constraint and levels of avoidance. The issue most important in comparisons of results, however, is consistency. In that regard, fear of victimization and the factors influencing it are important issues to research even if they are not comprehensive measures of the composite phenomenon.

Literature on Fear and Victimization

The incidence of victimization appears to have been a major issue used to explain when, where, and to whom fear of crime occurs (Gomme, 1988; Kennedy & Silverman, 1985a; Kennedy & Silverman, 1985b; Lee, 1983; Mullen & Donnermeyer, 1985; Norton, 1982; Yin, 1982). Personal victimization or knowledge of an acquaintance victimization (Clark & Lewis, 1982; Lee, 1983; Mawby, 1982; Norton, 1982), are events which logically will influence the fear of crime. Ferraro (1995, p. 54) maintains that "perceived risk is a necessary but not sufficient cause of fear." He goes on to say that perceptions of risk may result in life-style changes or adaptations which might subsequently result in reductions of fear. Others (Liska et al., 1988) maintain that response to risk—constrained behavior—may raise fear, or, as Taylor et al. (1986) posit, have little effect on fear. It appears logical that victimization, as tangible evidence of the perception of risk, would be related to fear but the contradictory nature of the literature suggests that this is an important variable to assess.

A body of recent literature has focused on physical and psychological distress following victimization (Norris & Kaniasty, 1994; Ross, 1993), perception of crime, and fear of crime (Ortega & Myles, 1987), social status (Thompson & Norris, 1992), and race (Parker, McMorris, Smith, & Murty, 1993) but there is still the prevalent theme of age as well as gender (Akers, LeGreca, Sellers, & Cochran, 1987; Bartol & Bartol, 1994; Parker & Ray, 1990; Smith & Hill, 1991; Stanko, 1992).

Smith and Hill (1991) directly considered the issue of the influence of victimization on fear of crime. Victimization was considered an intervening variable with gender, age, and several other exogenous variables in the analysis. The results, consistent with some other research (Lee, 1982; Ortega & Myles, 1987; Skogan & Maxfield, 1981), showed that age and gender "effects are bound up in a sense of vulnerability that reflects not so much objective risk of victimization as subjective estimates of the outcomes of victimization" (Smith & Hill, 1991, p. 233). This result was a validation of the "social vulnerability" model.

Independent of the "sense of vulnerability," Smith and Hill also found that the type of victimization experience itself was related to fear of crime. When they disaggregated the victimization into personal and property, they found that victims of property crime and victims of both personal and property crime were more fearful than those who were victims of only personal crime. This relationship proved valid only for those who lived with others, not victims who lived alone. This finding seems to suggest a different dimension regarding the deleterious effects of personal crime.

Clearly, there is far more fear of crime than victimization. An extensive survey in North Carolina (Pelfrey, Bohm, Dean, Humphrey, Moriarty, Vasu, Willis, & Zahn, 1992; Vasu, Moriarty, & Pelfrey, 1995) found that fear of crime was ten times greater than self-reported victimization. Victimization cannot be the dominant cause of fear, since fear of crime is present among many who have not been victims, but the interaction of victimization, age, and fear is one which bears exploration, especially with a methodology which allows a comparison of the experiences and perceptions of a similar population over time.

The issue being tested here is the relationship between fear of crime, age, and victimization, in two samples of the same population, over time. Specifically, the issues assessed are:

> Is there an association between fear of crime categories—community, neighborhood, home—and age categories, over time?

Is there an association between fear of crime categories—community, neighborhood, home—and victimization categories—any victimization, property victimization, personal victimization—over time?

Is there an association between fear of crime, victimization, and age categories over time?

Obviously the changes over time, if any, are of key concern in this research. We are guided by Ferraro's comment that "we know little about how fear of crime, validly and reliably measured, has changed over time" (1995, p. 124) and his conclusion that limitations of available data "dampens enthusiasm for attempting to delineate change" (1995, p. 124). We were able to access data which, we believe, allows some investigation of the interrelationship of fear, victimization, and age over time. Victimization and fear surveys conducted in Tennessee in 1982 and again in 1992 provide such an opportunity for assessment.

Methodology

This research is based on two similar victimization surveys using systematic random samples of individuals drawn from the population of all Tennessee residents aged 16 and over who had a valid driver's license issued by the State of Tennessee. These surveys were conducted in 1982 (Pelfrey & Dull, 1982) as well as in 1992 (by researchers at the Tennessee Statistical Analysis Center) and asked similar questions regarding fear of crime and victimization for the years 1981 and 1991. The first survey, conducted in Spring, 1982, was sent to 2,000 citizens, aged 16 and above and the Spring, 1992 survey was sent to 2,434 Tennesseans, aged 16 and above. Every *nth* name was selected from the file of Tennessee residents within the Bureau of Motor Vehicles in order to arrive at the desired number. The sampling method, of course, does not attend to those adults who do not hold a driver's license but this procedure is considered a reliable and cost-effective way of providing a systematic random sample of Tennessee citizens. As Maxfield and Babbie state, "in practice, systematic sampling is virtually identical to simple random sampling" (1995, p. 197). Each person in each sample was sent an extensive questionnaire that dealt with a number of issues regarding crime and the criminal justice system as well as questions to determine the demographic categories of each respondent. The questionnaire was pretested by individuals representing different education, income, and age strata in order to enhance internal validity. Questionnaires were mailed in Summer, 1982 and non-respondents were sent a second survey packet approximately six weeks after the first mailing. The 1992 survey was conducted with only one mailing in Spring, 1992 and no follow-up mailing.

The thirteen page questionnaire contained statements designed to measure the citizens' attitudes and opinions toward capital punishment, early release from prison, rationale for corrections, fear of crime, perception of probability of victimization, effectiveness of the criminal justice system, and current issues in criminal justice. The length and complexity of the questionnaire was deemed necessary in order to gather as much information as possible with one instrument.

Of the 2,000 Tennessee residents selected to participate in the 1982 survey, 1,366s or 69% completed and returned the survey instruments. When non-forwardable addresses and deceased persons are deleted from the 2,000 which comprised the sample, the number of potential respondents is reduced to 1,868 and an adjusted return rate, total respondents divided by the total eligible available respondents, is then 73%. The sample used for this survey matched the population characteristics regarding sex, race, education, marital status, and income. In general, the respondents are representative of a cross-section of the population of Tennessee residents. It is possible, therefore, to generalized from these data to the total population of the State of Tennessee.

In 1992, the survey was conducted in Spring and was mailed to 2,434 residents and 943 responded with completed instruments. Two hundred and fifty-six (256) of the surveys were not deliverable and six of the respondents were deceased. Considering the number of "refusals" or eligible respondents who did not respond, an adjusted return rate of 43.4% was lower than desired. This low return rate was probably due to the lack of follow-up mailings.[1] Even though the response rate was lower than expected, the demographics of the respondents were generally consistent with those of the population of licensed drivers in the state and there were no discernable demographic differences in respondents and nonrespondents.

The results of the surveys have been analyzed in a variety of ways. Since the thrust of this study is to assess the relationship between fear of

---

1. Parenthetically, the reason for only one mailing was due to several factors. As expected, cost of subsequent mailings was a consideration as was the time constraint of preparing the survey, getting the results, and analyzing the data prior to the "Southeastern Violent Crime Summit" conducted in July, 1992 under the auspices of the U.S. Department of Justice, Bureau of Justice Assistance. The prevailing reason for only one mailing, however, was the fact that the survey was conducted by the Statistical Analysis Center, Tennessee Bureau of Investigation and it was decided that identifying numbers or codes would adversely affect the responses so no identifiers were used, making it difficult to perform a non-duplicative second mailing.

crime, age, and victimization, only those variables related to these topics were considered.

Measurement of Variables

To measure fear of crime, the questionnaires included three questions often asked in surveys and polls. The first of these questions, "Is there any area within one mile of your home where you would be afraid to walk alone at night." This variable is labeled F1. Another measure of fear is based on responses to the question, "Would you be afraid to walk alone in your neighborhood at night?" labeled F2. Finally, the variable F3 is based on responses to the question "Are you afraid to be in your home alone at night?" These questions were asked in each of the two surveys.

Victimization was based on the response to the following questions: "We are interested in knowing if you were the victim of any of the following crimes during the previous year:"

> Did anyone break into your home and take something or attempt to take something?
> Did anyone steal or attempt to steal a motor vehicle belonging to you?
> Were any other valuable items or property stolen from you that were not mentioned previously?
> Did anyone intentionally destroy property belonging to you?
> Did anyone take something from you by force or threat of force?
> Did anyone threaten or attack you with a knife, gun, club, or other weapons?
> Did anyone threaten or attack you with their fist, feet, or other bodily attack?
> Did anyone have or attempt to have sex with you against your will?

Responses to these questions were collapsed into property victimization (PROVIC) if any answer to the first four items was "yes," personal or assaultive victimization (PERVIC) if any answer to the final four items was "yes," and the inclusive category of any victimization (VIC) if the respondent answered "yes" to any of the victimization questions.

The demographic variable, age, was measured by asking the respondent's age in a straight-forward manner in the last portion of the questionnaires. Age categories were created from the data and, consistent with the comments of Ferraro (1995: 82), the youngest age group was under 25 with the next oldest age group "25 through 29" followed by respondents in their thirties, then forties, fifties, and, finally, those sixty and over.[2]

Analysis

While the response rate for the survey in 1982 was quite strong and the response rate for the survey conducted in 1992 was weak, the demographics of the respondents in the two samples were consistent with the population of Tennessee and with each other. The only major difference in the broad-based demographics of the respondents of the two surveys is the mean age. This characteristic, however, is consistent with the magnitude and direction of the age changes of the population of Tennessee as reported in the 1980 census compared to the 1990 census. Based on the sampling processes and the demographic consistency between the two groups of respondents and the population from which the samples were drawn, we believe that the results of the two surveys may be considered to be representative of the population of the state.

As is shown in Table 1, in 1982 the general fear level (percent responding "yes") for the question "Is there an area within one mile of your home where you are afraid to walk alone at night" labeled F1 in Table 2, was 56.1 percent. In 1992, the percentage of respondents who answered "yes" to the same question was 56.3 percent.

These virtually consistent fear levels are interesting considering the fact that reported crime in Tennessee increased 25 percent in the ensuing ten years (Federal Bureau of Investigation, 1983; Federal Bureau of Investigation, 1993). Using this gross measure of fear within the community with no controlling variables or further refinements in the venue of inquiry, it would appear that the fear level in 1992 was the same as that in 1982. As the locus of inquiry came closer to one's home, however, citizens' fear of crime in 1992 was very different than that of citizens in 1982 (see Table 1).

For questions related to fear within one's neighborhood (F2) and fear in the home (F3), the 1992 fear levels were far greater than those for 1982. In fact, those respondents indicating fear in their neighborhood increased 30.8 percent from 1982 to 1992 and those who indicated fear while in their homes increased 60.4 percent. These increases, along with a closer examination of fear by age categories are important portions of this research.

---

2. We recognize that gender is an important variable in much of the fear of crime literature but felt that to further disaggregate the respondents by gender after dividing them on the basis of age groups, victimization, and fear would have produced extremely small numbers in some cells and produced useless or misleading statistics.

Table 1
Percentage of Respondents Indicating Fear by Age
and Victimization, 1982 and 1992

	1982 (N=1359)			1992 (N=933)		
	F1 (759)	F2 (405)	F3 (131)	F1 (524)	F2 (365)	F3 (139)
Overall fear rates by fear category	56.1	29.9	9.6	56.3	39.1	15.4
Percentage fearful by age group and fear category	F1	F2	F3**	F1**	F2***	F3
Less than 25	56.8	30.7	12.3	50.4	35.6	18.2
25 through 29	57.1	24.8	7.8	58.1	38.7	17.7
30 through 39	53.0	27.8	7.0	58.4	37.4	15.4
40 through 49	48.6	22.4	6.2	49.6	26.8	8.7
50 through 59	55.6	34.4	8.9	50.0	37.8	13.7
60 and Over	62.7	35.7	12.3	64.3	49.2	15.9

F1"Is there an area within one mile of your home where you are afraid to walk alone at night?"
F2"Is there an area in your neighborhood where you are afraid to walk alone at night?"
F3"Are you afraid to be in your home alone at night?"

* Significant at the .05 level
** Significant at the .01 level
*** Significant at the .001 level

Fear by Age Group and Fear Category

Inconsistent with much of the recent research (Bankston & Thompson, 1989; Ferraro, 1995; Ferraro & LaGrange, 1988; LaGrange & Ferraro, 1987) respondents from 1982 and 1992 who were 60 years of age or older *were* the most fearful age group for questions regarding fear within one mile of their homes and fear in their neighborhoods. Chi-square was determined to be the most robust statistic as a test of significance which was suitable to the levels of the data, generally nominal (Kiess, 1996; Neuman, 1995). Chi-square analysis of age groups by fear categories for each of the two surveys showed surprising results, as seen in Table 1.

For each of the first two fear categories, F1 (fearful to walk within one mile of home alone at night) and F2 (fearful to walk in the neighborhood alone at night) in the 1992 data, the analysis showed that the association between the variables age and fear was statistically significant. In 1982, F1 and age were at the verge of significance (p=.05664). In each of four fear categories (F1 and F2 in 1982; F1 and F2 in 1992), the elderly were the most fearful age group based on a comparison of the percentage of respondents expressing fear versus those who were not fearful. In these categories, the youthful respondents, those under the age of 25, were certainly not the least fearful but, as stated earlier, their fear levels were inconsistent with other research focusing on age. For the variable F3, fearful in the home alone at night, the youngest respondents were the most fearful in 1992 and were equal to the oldest category in their fear level in 1982. The chi-square analysis, however, failed to reflect significant association between the variables fear and age group for F3 in 1992 so it is difficult to posit a difference.

A more detailed analysis of the fear and age relationship, over the period of the two surveys was conducted by cross-tabulating each fear category by the year of the survey while controlling for each of the six age groups. This comparison showed no statistically significant association between any of the age groups from 1982 and 1992 for the F1 variable, fear to walk within one mile of home alone at night. For the variable F2, fear to walk in the neighborhood alone at night, the age groups 25 through 29 (chi-square=4.1, df=1, p=.04475) and 60 and older (chi-square=9.69, df=1, p=.0018) both showed statistically significant increases in fear as recorded in the first survey compared to the second. Each of the youngest three age groups—under 25 (chi-square=3.9, df=1, p=.049), 25 through 29 (chi-square=4.4, df=1, p=.036) and 30 through 39 (chi-square=6.3, df=1, p=.012)—showed statistically significant increases in fear levels for F3, fear to be alone at home at night. As shown in Table 1, the increases in percentage fearful in those age groups ranges from a 48 percent increase in the percent fearful for those under 25 years of age to a 126 percent increase in the percent fearful for those 25 through 29.

Fear and Victimization

The fear levels of those who were victims of crime were generally higher than those of non-victims, as Table 2 shows. The differences in fear rates between victims of assaultive crimes within the previous year and those who were victims of property crimes the previous year were surprisingly small except for the F3 variable in the 1982 survey. In that survey, victims of assaultive crimes were more than twice as fearful compared to victims of property crimes. As is shown in Table 2, most of the chi-square analyses showed statistically significant associations in fearfulness of victims and non-victims for victims of any crime (except for F3 in 1982) and victims of property crimes (except for F3 in 1982). Additionally, victims of assaultive crimes in 1982 had significantly higher fear levels than non-victims for the fear variable F3.

The most remarkable observation in the inspection of percentages of respondents expressing fear, as shown in Table 2, is the consistency of the

Table 2
Percentage of Respondents Indicating Fear by Victimization, 1982 and 1992

	1982 Fear Category			1992 Fear Category		
	F1 (759)	F2 (405)	F3 (131)	F1 (524)	F2 (365)	F3 (139)
Overall fear rates by fear category	56.1	29.9	9.6	56.3	39.1	15.4
Percentage fearful by victimization and fear category						
Victim of any crime	60.8**	33.9***	10.7	63.3*	44.1**	21.4***
Non-victims	53.4	27.6	9.0	51.7	35.8	11.6
Victim of assaultive crime	62.4	32.7	22.5***	59.7	44.2	20.9
Non-victims	55.5	29.7	8.6	55.8	38.3	14.7
Victim of property crime	60.7*	34.5**	10.4	64.6*	45.5**	21.9*
Non-victims	53.6	27.5	9.2	51.5	35.4	11.8
Overall Victimization Rates for Respondents		1982 36.6			1992 40.1	

F1"Is there an area within one mile of your home where you are afraid to walk alone at night?"
F2"Is there an area in your neighborhood where you are afraid to walk alone at night?"
F3"Are you afraid to be in your home alone at night?"

  * Significant at the .05 level
 ** Significant at the .01 level
*** Significant at the .001 level

percentages, for those who were victims of assaultive crimes, with the exception of F3, fear to be home alone at night, for 1982 victims.

Fear Levels by Age and Victimization

While independently assessing fear within certain age groups and fear based on victimization is important in understanding the dynamics of these issues, analyzing fear by age groups and victimization in the various categories (F1, F2, and F3) over time was one of the most important purposes of this research. As Table 3 shows, the differences in fear rates within each age group and fear category showed surprisingly few discernable patterns of significance other than the 60 and over age group and the age group 30 to 39. Especially in 1992, these age groups showed significant differences in fear among victims and non-victims.

Assessing the changes over time by age group and victimization for each fear category suggests some strong variations. For the fear category

Table 3
Fear by Age Group, Victimization, and Fear Category
1982 and 1992

		1982 Fear Category			1992 Fear Category		
		F1	F2	F3	F1	F2	F3
Age Group	Victimization						
Less than 25	Victims	56.0	32.7	9.3	53.4	39.2	23.3*
	Non-Victims	57.5	29.1	14.9	47.7	32.2	13.5
25 through 29	Victims	61.0	22.0	NA	45.5	31.8	NA
	Non-Victims	54.3	26.8		65.0	42.5	
30 through 39	Victims	57.3	32.9	13.4**	70.2*	50.9**	22.8*
	Non-Victims	50.0	24.1	2.6	51.1	28.9	10.9
40 through 49	Victims	59.5*	31.1*	8.1	61.7*	25.5	13.0
	Non-Victims	42.6	17.6	5.1	42.5	27.5	6.3
50 through 59	Victims	65.3	43.1	5.9	69.0**	48.3	20.7
	Non-Victims	52.1	31.2	9.9	37.8	31.1	9.1
60 and Over	Victims	71.8*	43.0	19.2*	74.7**	58.5*	24.4**
	Non-Victims	59.2	32.8	9.7	58.7	44.3	11.5

F1"Is there an area within one mile of your home where you are afraid to walk alone at night?"
F2"Is there an area in your neighborhood where you are afraid to walk alone at night?"
F3"Are you afraid to be in your home alone at night?"

Chi-square analyses based on cross-tabulation of Fear (Yes, No), for each fear category, by Victimization (Yes, No) while controlling for age group

* Significant at the .05
** Significant at the .01

NA: No Analyis due to low cell frequency
Note: Only "Victim of any crime" is used as the victimization variable

F1, the youngest victims and non-victims were less fearful in 1992 than in 1982 as were victims in the age group 25 to 29 from 1982 to 1992. For the other age groups, there was consistency in the broadest measure of fear (F1) from 1982 to 1992. For the other fear categories, F2 and F3, victims and non-victims in all age groups showed consistent increases in fear from 1982 to 1992 with the exceptions of non-victims less than 25 years of age in category F3 and those 50 to 59 in F3 where non-victims were slightly less fearful in 1992 compared to 1982 levels.

An unusual and surprising observation is the differences in some categories showing that non-victims were more fearful than victims. This was the case in 1982 for those less than 25 years of age for F1 and F3 and again in 1992 for those 25 through 29 for F1 and F2.

Victims age 60 and over are consistently the most fearful of all other age groups and for all fear categories, except for F2 in 1982. Additionally, the differences in victims' fear and that of non-victims for those age 60 and over are almost all statistically significant.

Conclusion

This research, considering surveys of two independent samples of the same population conducted at an interval of ten years, produced results which both support and contradict recent research on the topic of fear of crime, as it relates to victimization and age. This is not particularly surprising since much of the research heretofore has produced contradictory results. The contributions of this research include within-year assessments of the various categories as well as between-year comparisons and an affirmation of the high fear levels experienced by those age 60 and over, particularly those who have been victims within the preceding year.

In general, fear to walk within one mile of home, alone at night remained at a constant rate from 1982 to 1992. Fear of crime in the neighborhood and fear in the home increased dramatically from 1982 to 1992. These results suggest that gross measures of fear ("Is there an area within one mile of your home where you are afraid to walk alone at night?") are insufficient to measure changes in actual fear over time. The objective is, of course, not to show a higher level of fear but to show the true level of fear. These results suggest that more narrowly defined questions may result in very different answers.

In considering fear of crime by age groups, it was suggested by other research that, if there were an association between the variables, younger respondents would reflect higher levels of fear (Ferraro, 1995; Ferraro & LaGrange, 1988; LaGrange & Ferraro, 1987; 1989) but that was not consistently the case. In the 1982 survey, respondents aged 60 and older had the highest levels of fear for fear to walk within one mile alone at night and fear to walk in the neighborhood alone at night. The same result was shown in the 1992 survey. Respondents under the age of 25 equaled the fear level of older respondents in the 1982 survey question which asked about fear to be in the home alone at night while the youngest respondents exceeded the fear level of the oldest respondents in 1992 for that fear question until victimization was considered. These results suggest that the blanket statements about fear and the elderly as well as those regarding fear and the young should be tempered by the venue at issue. As Ferraro (1995) and others point out, fear and risk are associated with routine activities and social integration and these variables may explain the variance in the present results but, when asked the same questions regarding fear, respondents in the youngest and oldest age groups differed in their responses and these differences were consistent over time.

Consistent with the findings of Smith and Hill (1991), fear of crime and victimization showed a reasonably static association when the victimization was an assaultive one. Victims of property offenses had consistently and significantly higher levels of fear for all fear categories in 1992 and for F1 and F2 in 1982.

The most complex of the associations assessed in this research involved analyzing fear of crime while controlling for age group and victimization. Victimization significantly increased fear in all but one of the fear categories for those aged 60 and over, while those in the youngest age group were not as affected by victimization except for the fear at home category in 1992. In fact, some of the victims in the younger age groups had lower levels of fear than did non-victims, though not statistically significant. Examining the changes over time, it appeared that victims in more age group categories, particularly the older categories, reflected more fear, particularly regarding the fear to walk within one mile of home. An unusual finding, and one which is difficult to explain with the current data, is the significant association of fear, in all categories, with victimization in the age group 30 through 39 in 1992. Other than fear in the home, this age group showed no significant association with fear and victimization in 1982. Only a more focused project would be able to tease out the critical factors influencing that change in fear.

From a methodological perspective, reflecting back to Table 2, and examining the rates of change in the percentage fearful from 1982 to 1992 suggests that several age groups have increased their fear level from 1982 to 1992 when considering the maturation of the group in 1982 and adding ten years to their ages for the 1992 survey. Of course this is not to suggest that the same panel was surveyed in 1982 and 1992 but, if we assume that two samples are representative of the population in 1982 and again in 1992, it is arguable the changes should be studied diagonally based on the aging of each age group, not horizontally, and that some consistent change is occurring with a maturation pattern.

Regardless of a maturation effect, however, it appears that the fear experienced by older respondents is exacerbated by victimization while not the case with younger respondents. The issue may be one of relative resiliency or it may involve younger victims changing their behavior to mitigate their future risk. As suggested by Ferraro (1995), a panel approach to better understanding fear of crime over time may hold the greatest promise for the future. Until then, these results have implication to police organizations employing community oriented strategies to reduce fear as well as ameliorate crime. When older citizens become victims, their quality of life, as measured by fear of crime, may deteriorate more substantially than that of other victims, with the possible inexplicable exception of those 30 through 39 years of age.

This research re-establishes the contention that older citizens are the most fearful outside the homes alone at night while younger citizens are as fearful as the elderly when alone at home at night. Adopting the routine activities model would suggest that for younger citizens to be walking alone at night in their neighborhoods and communities is a rare event so their fear may not be recorded. Indeed, Felson (1987) suggested such an effect when he said "if the routines and routings of young people keep them systematically under informal supervision and away from interesting crime targets, youths will be less likely to commit crimes.... Similarly, potential victims of crime can be guided and channeled in their daily movements so as to minimize their risk" (1987, pp. 927-928). He also discusses the "Great Metropolitan Quilt" which he uses analogously to describe a "special sociocirculatory system" which has the two components of within facilities and between facilities. Within facilities, people walk. Between facilities, people drive. As several researchers have shown, being surrounded by other similar persons depresses the risk and likely the fear of crime (Brantingham & Brantingham, 1982; Felson, 1986; Sampson, 1987). Fear in the home is the major venue for younger citizens, in fact, for citizens under 40 years of age fear in the home increased significantly from 1982 to 1992. Fear to walk in the neighborhood alone at night increased significantly among those 60 and over from 1982 to 1992. National polls which do not control for age may erroneously reflect static fear levels or slight changes over time while certain segments of the population are experiencing significantly higher fear. Conversely, research such as that of Akers et al. (1987), taking into account different types of communities, community structure, and variations, provides considerable specificity and explanations of variances within certain age categories.

While certainly not answering all of the questions pondered by fear of crime researchers, the current research has established rates, levels, and differences for comparison in future research. These data provide insight into the resiliency of some younger citizens to withstand victimization without increasing fear while showing that other older citizens are dramatically affected by victimization. The changes in fear levels over time add dimension to the gross measures used in some national polls and suggest that there are increases in fear levels among certain age groups based on the venue being considered (community, neighborhood, home).

These results help to address the fear issues of Who? Where? and Under what circumstances?

Note: A previous version of this paper was presented at the Annual Conference of the Academy of Criminal Justice Sciences, March, 1995, Boston, MA.

Discussion Questions

Is "fear of crime" a form of victimization? In what ways? Is it too broad a category to address as a public policy issue?

How is fear of crime different from perception of risk? Are the differences substantive or do they describe the same phenomenon?

Discuss the proposition that "routine activities" and the "Great Metropolitan Quilt" as an explanation of different fear levels of different age groups.

Discuss the variances in fear of victims and non-victims, by age group, based on risk and resiliency. Are these viable explanations for different levels of fear of young victims versus old victims? What other explanations might be appropriate?

Chapter 3

A Case Study of Student Fear of Crime on a Small Southeastern University Campus: Is It Justified?

Debra Mitchell Robinson
David L. Mitchell

Introduction

Numerous criminological studies have examined factors and variables in relation to fear of crime, including gender (Stanko, 1992; Warr, 1984), race (Parker, 1988; Parker, Morris, Smith, & Murty, 1993), and location—rural versus urban (Belyea & Zingraff, 1988; Covington & Taylor, 1991; Lee, 1982; Nasar & Fisher, 1992). Included within the variable location as determinants of fear and perception of crime are factors such as accessibility, surveillability, and proximity to activity (Brantingham & Brantingham, 1990, 1991; Jeffery, 1971, 1977; Robinson, 1995, 1996, 1997).

In 1995, the Bureau of Justice Statistics (Reaves & Goldberg, 1996) conducted the largest study ever of police and security services at institutions of higher education in the United States. According to the study, the nation's colleges and universities have far lower violent and property crime rates than the country as a whole. This research indicated that in addressing students' fear of crime on campus, 85% of all campus law enforcement agencies operated a general crime prevention program or unit, about two-thirds of all agencies had a program designed specifically toward date or acquaintance rape prevention, about half of all agencies operated programs aimed at preventing drug and alcohol abuse, and more than one-third of all agencies had a special program or unit for victim assistance (Reaves & Goldberg, 1996).

One of the aspects associated with these crime prevention programs is an emphasis on campus locations associated with crime or criminal activity. In an attempt to make campuses safer, 77% of all campus law enforcement agencies equipped their campuses with special emergency telephones, called "blue light" phones. These special telephones are located at strategic campus locations and are equipped with a direct line when picked up (no need to dial any numbers), connecting the individual using the phone directly with the campus police office (Reaves & Goldberg, 1996).

A study conducted by McConnell (1996) was undertaken on the same university campus as the present study. McConnell's study was conducted to determine levels of fear experienced by students, areas on campus related to students' fear, and the crimes which students feared most. McConnell (1996) found that for each of the fear of crime variables, females reported higher levels of fear than did males, with the majority of all students reporting some level of fear; fear of crime at night was significantly greater than fear of crime during the day; and the students expressed fear of crime in specific locations of campus, including parking lots, jogging paths, classrooms, and the library.

The purpose of this study is to determine the students' perceptions regarding crime on campus and to compare those perceptions to environmental characteristics on campus. An analysis of environmental characteristics of campus was chosen along the lines of C. Ray Jeffery's (1971, 1977, 1990) *Crime Prevention Through Environmental Design* (CPTED) concept. The basic premise of CPTED, which has been used in much research and theory, posits that the frequency of certain types of criminal behavior may be reduced through identification and modification of the environmental conditions under which such offenses occur (see for example, Brantingham & Brantingham, 1990, 1991; Cromwell, Olson, & Avary, 1991; Jeffery, 1971, 1977; Jeffery, Hunter, & Griswold, 1986; Poyner, 1983; Winchester & Jackson, 1982). It is anticipated that, through environmental design, areas may be made safer and the quality of life may be enhanced for individuals living in or using those areas. By focusing on the physical environment, the CPTED model concerns itself with offense areas. "By offense areas we mean where crimes are committed" (Jeffery, 1977, p. 190).

The present research examines fear and perception of students attending a small university located in South Georgia. This university has a current enrollment of approximately 9,600 students, ranging from freshmen to graduate students. A survey was conducted using a questionnaire given to 107 students in five classes during a one week period in the Winter, 1997 quarter. The classes were chosen at random, with each class representing either a freshman, sophomore, junior, senior, or graduate class. This process (McConnell, 1996) was used to ensure a representative sampling of different academic levels, majors, and day versus evening classes. However, as the classes were the units chosen at random, not the students, there is no attempt to generalize the findings to other university campuses.

A major aspect of this study was to determine crime prevention and environmental factors on campus which could then be related to students' fear and perception of crime on campus. The present study asked students to identify areas on campus which they believed to be the most crime-related areas and the campus areas they avoid due to fear of being a victim of crime. After identifying those areas students avoid, a visual walk-through of the entire campus was undertaken to determine environmental characteristics. A checklist was created and used to identify the environmental characteristics of campus, based upon characteristics identified in previous research.

These characteristics include: visibility (Cromwell et al., 1991; Robinson, 1995, 1996, 1997; Winchester & Jackson, 1982), lighting (Brown & Altman, 1981; Jacobs, 1961; Poyner, 1983; Robinson, 1995, 1996, 1997), and density (Bennett & Wright, 1983, 1984; Robinson, 1995, 1996, 1997; Winchester & Jackson, 1982). All of these factors are concerned with the surveillability of an area. According to Jacobs (1961), an area has much surveillability if there are many "eyes on the street." This concept indicates that the more individuals who are engaging in activities within the area and who are capable of viewing others and their activities within the area, the less amount of crime will take place within that area. As such, lighting and density greatly affect the type of surveillance possible within an area. Also, if little activity is present within an area, there is less chance for someone to see illegal behavior occurring within the area, hence less surveillability.

Accessibility (Robinson, 1995, 1996, 1997) is another factor related to the environmental characteristics of an area. Researchers suggested that ease of access, as an environmental characteristic of an area, is related to the amount of criminal victimization occurring in that area (Brantingham & Brantingham, 1975; Cromwell et al., 1991; Rengert, 1991). According to Rengert (1991), if there is an increase in accessibility, there is an increase in potential victimization.

Poyner (1983) defined environmental design in terms of activity support, and activity support was defined as making an area more attractive for human use. As such, aesthetics/incivilities characteristics were identified, including foliage — defined as plants, shrubbery, trees, and so forth on campus. The purpose was not to count the amount of foliage on campus but merely to determine if the foliage present on campus were well-managed and well-groomed, thus making the campus more attractive. In other words, the more attractive an area, the more potential for human use and the more potential targets are available for potential offenders.

These variables explained above are used in the present study as measures collected via the visual walk-through of the entire campus. The results of the student survey and walk-through are presented next.

Survey Results and Findings

The respondents are described as follows: about 15% (n=16) are freshman, 21% (n=22) sophomores, 18% (n=19) juniors, 20% (n=21) seniors, and 27% (n=19) graduate students. The age ranged from 18 to 43 with the average age being 23.46 years. There are more females (67%, n=72) than males (33%, n=35). With regards to residence, almost 19% (n=20) lived on campus, with 90% (n=18) living in dorms and 10% (n=2) living in fraternity houses (the university does not have sorority houses). The remainder of the students, 81% (n=87) lived off-campus, with about half (n=43) living in apartments and half (n= 44) living in houses.

One of the most interesting findings of the student survey was whether students believed there was crime on campus and whether there was a crime problem on campus. With regards to campus crime, 96% (n=103) believe there is crime on campus. Analyzing by gender, of the 35 males, 94% (n=33), and of the 72 females, 97% (n=70) believe there is crime on campus. However, with regards to a crime problem on campus, the overall numbers are fairly evenly distributed with 52% (n=56) of all students believing there is a crime problem on campus and almost 48% (n=51) believing there is not a crime problem on campus.

When examining the numbers related to the question of a crime problem on campus, separating by gender presents an interesting pattern. Of the 35 males, almost 62% (n=22) believe there is a crime problem on campus while 37% (n=13) believe there is not a crime problem on campus. Of the 72 females, 47% (n=34) believe there is a crime problem on campus while almost 52% (n=38) believe there is not a crime problem on campus. Although the overwhelming majority of female students, 97%, believe there to be crime on campus, the majority, almost 53%, believed there is not a crime problem on campus.

The students were also asked questions regarding where most crimes occur, time of day, and how many of each type of crime occurs on campus. Table 1 illustrates the answers to these questions. The questions of where crime occurs on campus and time of day most crime occurs on campus were answered with students indicating, most of the time, more than one answer. As such, there are more than 107 answers. The answers for the question of how many of each type of crime occurs on campus have been computed into averages for each crime, as the answers ranged from 0 to 100. The two most frequently identified categories regarding areas where most crime occurs were dorms and the parking lots, with about 59% (n=63) of the students indicating each. The third most frequently identified category regarding the area where most crime occurs on campus was the streets of campus, with about 35% (n=38) of the students choosing this category. The most frequently identified time of day

Table 1
Crime on Campus: Where, Time and Frequency

WHERE CRIME OCCURS	FREQ	PCT
Classrooms	2	1.87
Dorms	63	58.88
Faculty offices	2	1.87
Departmental offices	2	1.87
Fraternity houses	30	28.04
Football stadium	6	5.61
Library	10	9.35
Student Union—Main campus	6	5.61
Student Union—University Center	1	0.93
Recreational facilities	6	5.61
P.E. Complex	6	5.61
On the streets of campus	38	35.51
Parking lots	63	58.88
Religious student centers	0	0.00
Other	8	7.48

TIME OF DAY	FREQ	PCT
12:01 am to 4:00 am	69	64.49
4:01 am to 8:00 am	4	3.74
8:01 am to 12:00 pm	5	4.67
12:01 pm to 4:00 pm	9	8.41
4:01 pm to 8:00 pm	9	8.41
8:01 pm to 12:00 am	30	28.04

AVERAGE CRIME PER MONTH	OFFENSE/MTH
Aggravated Assault	2.17
Battery—Simple Assault	3.66
Burglary	5.98
Drug/Alcohol Offense	30.12
Murder	0.00
Robbery	4.65
Sexual Assault	4.10
Theft	12.49
Weapons Offense	3.97
Vandalism	8.42
Other	1.24

during which most crime occurs on campus was midnight to 4:00 am, with about 65% (n=69) of the students indicating this answer. The second most frequently identified time was 8:00 pm to midnight, with 28% (n=30) indicating this answer.

The answers to both of these questions indicate that students believe that most crime occurs on campus during the night-time hours at particular locations on campus, corresponding to the same type of data gathered by McConnell (1996). This is an important aspect of the students' perception of crime with regards to crime prevention and will be analyzed later. The most frequently occurring crime on campus, according to the students, was drug/alcohol offense, averaging 30.12 per month. The second

Table 2
Offenders of Campus Crime

OFFENDERS	FREQ	PCT
Students	97	90.65
Faculty	3	2.80
Staff	11	10.28
Relatives of Students	7	6.54
Relatives of Faculty	1	0.93
Relatives of Staff	1	0.93
Friends of Students	50	46.73
Friends of Faculty	2	1.87
Friends of Staff	2	1.87
Local residents	65	60.75
Non-residents of the city or county	19	17.76
Other	5	4.67

most frequently occurring crime on campus was indicated by the students to be theft, averaging 12.49 per month.

The students were also asked who they believed to be the offenders of campus crime. The answers are illustrated in Table 2. The most frequently answered category to the question of who are the offenders of campus crime was students, with 90% (n=97) indicating this answer.

The second most frequently answered category was local residents. The third most frequently answered category was friends of students. This indicates that of the three most frequently identified categories, two involve the students of the university. This information could have important implications for university and student policy made by the administration and campus police department.

The remainder of the student survey involved the students' fear of being a victim of crime while on campus. The first question asked the students if they fear being a victim of crime while on campus. Of the total students, 37% (n=40) indicate they fear being a victim of crime while about 63% (n=67) indicate they did not fear being a victim of crime while on campus. Of the 40 students indicating fear, about 83% (n=33) were female.

The second question asked the students if there were certain areas on campus they avoided because of fear of being a victim of crime. Of the total students, 38% (n=41) indicated yes while about 62% (n= 66) indicated no. Of the 41 students who indicated yes, about 98% (n=40) were females. Both of these questions support McConnell's (1996) study indicating that females report higher levels of fear than do males.

The next question asked those who avoided certain areas to identify those areas avoided because of fear of being a victim of crime. Table 3 illustrates the answers to this question. Again, these results mirror McConnell's (1996) study in finding that students perceive crime to be occur-

Table 3
Places Avoided Because of Fear of Being a Victim

PLACES AVOIDED ON CAMPUS	FREQ	PCT
Parking Lots at Night	25	60.98
Dark Areas when Walking	18	43.90
Wooded or Secluded Areas at Night	10	24.39
Walking on the Streets at Night	4	9.76
Library at Night	4	9.76
Dorms at Night	2	4.88

ring at night (see Table 1) and those students do avoid certain areas of campus during the night-time hours.

One interesting aspect of the results shown in Table 3 is that one of the most frequent answers to an earlier question of where students believe most crime on campus occurs was dorms (see Table 1). However, when asked what areas of campus they avoid because of a fear of being a victim of crime, only 5% of the students answered dorms. This discrepancy may be attributed to an assumption that crimes being committed in the dorms are not the types of crimes to be feared by students.

As students perceive crime on campus to be occurring between certain hours and certain areas of campus are avoided because of fear of being a victim of crime, the next phase of the research study involved a walk-through of campus to determine if the environmental characteristics of campus could be related to the students' fear and perception of crime. A checklist, similar to ones used by Robinson (1995, 1996, 1997), was created to determine environmental characteristics of campus. As with earlier environmental studies, the checklist included surveillability, accessibility and aesthetics/incivilities factors to be determined at each area. The walk-through was completed by the authors and two members of the university police department. The results indicate opinions of the majority of the walk-through team for all categories on the checklist.

In keeping with the results of the student survey, the campus walk-through was completed during the hours of 8:00 pm and 4:00 am. Also in keeping with the student survey results, the areas indicated by the students as those which are to be avoided because of fear of being a victim of crime were the targets of the walk-through. Completing the walk-through in the areas and during the times corresponding to the student survey allowed for ease of comparison between the students' perceptions and fears of crime on campus and the environmental characteristics of campus.

As parking lots in general were identified as the area most students avoided (61%), the walk-through first concentrated on the parking lots on

Table 4
Environmental Characteristics of Parking Lots

SURVEILLABILITY

Lighting:	Dim
Openness of Visibility:	Partially obstructed
Blue Light Phones:	6 of 9 lots
Campus Activity in Vicinity at Night:	Little activity
General Surveillability:	Low

ACCESSIBILITY

Number of Entrance/Exit Points:	Average 2 per lot
Surroundings of Lots:	7 of 9 lots have woods on at least one (1) side
Type of Lot:	Concrete
Type of Traffic Signal:	Stop sign
Proximity to Campus Classrooms and DormsS:	Requires much walking
General Accessibility:	Medium

AESTHETICS/INCIVILITIES

Foliage:	Somewhat kempt
Trash:	Low
General Aesthetics/Incivilities:	Somewhat Attractive

campus. There are nine student parking lots on campus. Each lot was viewed with regards to three categories on the checklist, each category designed to determine particular types of environmental characteristics of the area.

The first category of factors—surveillability—includes lighting (bright, uneven [spotty], dim, dark); openness of visibility, meaning the obstructed view from the street (mostly obstructed, partially obstructed, mostly unobstructed [open]); blue light phones (emergency phones which require only that the user pick up the handset to automatically be connected with the University Department of Public Safety); campus activity in the vicinity at night (much activity, some activity, little activity, no activity); and general surveillability of all lots (high, moderate, low). The second category—accessibility—includes the number of entrance/exit points; surroundings of the lot (woods, buildings, fences, etc.); type of lot (concrete, sand, gravel, etc.); type of traffic signal at entrance/exit points (light, stop sign, yield, etc.); proximity to campus classrooms and dorms (directly adjacent, somewhat close, requires much walking); and general accessibility of all lots (high, moderate, low). The third category—aesthetics/incivilities—includes foliage (well-kempt, somewhat kempt, unkempt); trash, meaning the amount of litter in the lot (high, medium, low); and general aesthetics/incivilities of all lots (mostly attractive, somewhat attractive, unattractive).

Table 4 describes the different factors related to the parking lots in general (see Table 4). The data in this table are a summary of all parking lots

---

Table 5
Environmental Characteristics of Campus

SURVEILLABILITY
Lighting:	Dim
Openness of Visibility:	Partially obstructed
Blue Phones:	Nine (9) phones
Campus Activity at Night:	Little
Density:	Medium
General Surveillability:	Low

ACCESSIBILITY
Number of Entrance/Exit Points:	Many
Volume of Traffic:	Low
General Accessibility:	High

AESTHETICS/INCIVILITIES
Foliage:	Well-kempt
Trash:	Low
Graffiti:	None
Unkempt Buildings:	None
General Aesthetics/Incivilities:	Mostly attractive

---

on campus. The data appear to show that the environmental characteristics of the parking lots coincide with the students' avoidance of the areas. The parking lots are generally not well lit, have very little activity nearby, have few entrance/exit points, are quite a walk from classrooms and dorms, and five of the nine lots have only one blue light phone while one lot has two blue light phones and three lots having no blue light phone.

The remaining answers to the question of what areas students avoid at night refer to campus in general, for example, dark areas and wooded or secluded areas could be interpreted to be anywhere on campus. Also, the streets, library, and dorms are all parts of campus so a second checklist was used to determine the environmental characteristics of the entire campus. Several additional factors were added to the checklist for the purpose of obtaining a better description of the campus environment. Additions are included in each category and are as follows: for the category surveillability—density of buildings (high, medium, low); for the category accessibility—volume of traffic through campus (high, medium, low); and for the category aesthetics/incivilities—graffiti on buildings/sidewalks (high, medium, low, none); and unkempt buildings (many [10 or more], some [5–9], few [1–4], none).

With a walk-through of the entire campus completed, again during the target hours previously identified, the data may be compared to the remaining answers to the question of areas avoided because of fear of being a victim of crime (Table 3). Table 5 shows a summary of the data corresponding to the campus in general (see Table 5).

The data in Table 5 again coincide with the student answers. In general, the campus at night is dim at best. One reason is the use of yellow-hued lighting versus white lighting. There appears to be an aesthetic reason for using the yellow-hued lights but this leaves the areas not as well lit as needed. There also appears to be a pattern to lighting on campus. While the campus grounds are generally not well lit, neither are the buildings. It seems that the general theme for lighting is to have lights surrounding a building put into the ground and shine upwards onto the building. The effect is to illuminate the building while keeping the grounds surrounding the building relatively dark. This presents a problem as one walks to and from a building. As one walks immediately out of a building, it is well lit, but one cannot see well what or who is on the grounds. Also, as one walks from a building to a parking lot, the lighting grows increasingly darker, presenting an uncomfortable aura. This coincides with the students' perceptions of walking in dark or secluded areas.

Another pattern found concerns the foliage which is connected with the lighting of the buildings. The foliage is approximately two feet away from the buildings to allow for the lighting in the ground to shine onto the buildings. This leaves room for an individual to hide. Although the lights are on the ground and shine up, the lights are spaced approximately every ten to twelve feet, thereby leaving some room for a person to hide and not be noticed. Again, this creates an uncomfortable feeling while walking from or to the buildings.

The most surprising finding of the campus walk-through was the number of blue light phones located throughout campus. During the walk-through, nine blue light phones were located, with seven being located in parking lots. This leaves only two blue light phones located throughout the remainder of campus. While examining the blue light phones themselves, it was noted that two of the phones did not have an actual blue light located on top of the light pole. It is usual for these phones to have a blue light which is illuminated at night, indicating the presence of the phone. As such, this leaves only seven of the phones with an illuminated blue light.

There is also little activity occurring during the target hours. Most classes end no later than 10:30 pm. The library closes at midnight during the week. Therefore, there is little official school activity occurring at night. Because of the many buildings, many areas on campus are obstructed to some degree. The surveillability of the campus during the target hours is generally low because of poor lighting on the grounds, the pattern of lighting on the buildings, little activity during the target hours, and obstructed views of many areas on campus. In general, the concept of surveillability corresponds to the students' perceptions and fears of being a victim of crime while on campus. The CPTED model proposes that the structure of environmental characteristics of an area correspond to the usage of an area. If an area is well illuminated, is used to some degree of frequency, and all areas are structured in such a way that individuals within the area can view the events happening in all other locations of the area (the "eyes of the street" concept of Jacobs, 1961), the area is viewed to be less of a crime target. As such, the environmental characteristics of campus do present an explanation for the students' perceptions and fears of being a victim of crime while on campus.

The general accessibility to campus is high as there are no requirements (security gate entrance, security guard passage, etc.) for entrance to campus. Although parking decals are required for all who park on campus, this is not connected with driving or walking through the campus grounds. There are many entrance/exit points located throughout campus creating an ease of accessibility to many different areas of campus. There is also a low volume of traffic during the target hours. Ease of access, together with low volume of traffic on campus, presents an explanation for the students' perceptions and fears as previous research notes that ease of access creates the potential for criminal victimizations while low surveillability (low traffic volume) creates few "eyes on the street."

The aesthetics/incivilities of campus create a mostly attractive campus in general. The foliage is well-kempt, little trash could be found on the grounds, and no graffiti nor unkempt buildings were found on campus. However, as stated previously, the foliage does present a problem under the CPTED model. The foliage, although neat and quite attractive, is sometimes placed in areas which need foliage maintained lower to the ground or placed closer to buildings in an attempt to decrease the amount of space in which a person may crouch and hide. Foliage which is placed in such a way that those passing by cannot possibly see someone crouching behind need to be discarded, regardless of the aesthetic value.

There are also several areas on campus in which the foliage was placed to create a park-like atmosphere as one passes through the area. However, as with other parts of campus, these areas are dim at best and create an aura of uncertainty. Also, during the target hours, these areas have very little activity. One of these areas is located on one side of campus which separates two of the parking lots with classrooms and dorms—thus a major dark and secluded area through which students must walk at night to get to their cars.

Although it is apparent that the aesthetics of campus are an important aspect, according the CPTED model, there are areas on this campus which need to be reconsidered in terms of foliage and lighting. These areas may be aesthetically pleasing while providing for the safety and security of the students if CPTED were used. Again, as with the other categories of factors, the aesthetics/incivilities of campus do present an explanation for the students' perceptions and fears of being a victim of crime while on campus.

Summary

The purpose of this study was to determine if the students of a small, southeastern university perceive crime occurring on campus and if those same students fear being a victim of crime while on campus. The data from this study were then compared to the environmental characteristics of campus as determined by a walk-through of campus using a checklist of environmental factors determined by previous research to be associated with perceptions and fears of crime. One hundred and seven students from a random sample of university classes were asked various questions concerning whether they believed crime occurred on campus, when crime occurred on campus, who committed crime on campus, and if there were areas of campus they avoided because of fear of being a victim of crime while on campus. The data were analyzed and it was determined that certain areas of campus were avoided during particular hours of the day. A walk-through of campus was then completed to determine the physical and environmental characteristics of campus, focusing specifically on the areas and during the times identified by the students.

In terms of the student responses to the questionnaire given, the data show that students do perceive crime on campus and many do fear being a victim of crime while on campus. The data also show that the perceptions and fears coincide with the environmental characteristics of certain areas of campus and during certain times while on campus. Using the Crime Prevention Through Environmental Design (CPTED) model, the areas identified by students as those which they avoid because of fear of being a victim of crime are those areas which have the physical environmental characteristics associated with an increased potential for criminal victimization. This leads to those in the areas having an increased perception and fear of being a victim of crime.

Discussion Questions

Discuss the implications of the findings for university and college student safety policies.

Discuss two alternative strategies for measuring student fear of being a victim of crime and actual crime on campus.

Identify other possible explanations for why, if actual crime rates are low on university and college campuses as compared to the nation as a whole, there is student fear of being a victim of crime on campus.

Part II

Campus Victimization

Chapter 4

Teacher Victimization: Patterns and Reactions

Richard D. Clark
Steven P. Lab

Introduction

Crime and victimization in schools have become major topics of concern among educators, students, parents, and the media in recent years. It is not uncommon to hear horror stories about violence in schools on the evening news. What is portrayed, however, are the most serious and heinous events that are relatively rare in the great majority of schools. The image of schools as a "blackboard jungle," overrun by gangs, drugs, and crime, arises from anecdotal accounts of problems in a few of the largest U.S. cities.

One growing area of concern deals with the victimization of teachers in school. As with the general view of crime in school, it is common to hear war stories about teachers in constant fear of assault at school and needing to carry weapons for protection. Movies, such as the recent "187," often portray teachers as besieged by student violence and turning to desperate solutions to the problem. Unfortunately, there has been little empirical research devoted to this aspect of in-school victimization. What is known about teacher victimization typically comes from highly publicized accounts of isolated incidents or atypical schools in a few major cities.

This chapter reports on a survey of teachers from schools throughout a large Midwestern county. The aim of the survey was to measure the extent of teacher in-school victimization and assess the impact of that victimization on teachers. The data reported here are part of a larger study of school crime. Data on student victimization are used at various times as a point of comparison to the teacher data.

45

Past Research

It is not uncommon for students in American schools to report high levels of fear and victimization. Approximately 40% of high school seniors have reported some type of theft and over 20% have reported being threatened at school or on the way to and from school (Maguire & Flanagan, 1991, p. 303). Moreover, about 12% of eighth graders have reported not feeling safe at school (Ogle, 1990). These findings have led to calls for greater discipline and control within the schools (Ellis, 1992) with the premise being that enhanced pupil controls will reduce violence and disruption thereby enhancing the learning environment.

Equally important for school crime and disruption, however, is teacher victimization. While most school crime studies have focused on student victimization, victimization suffered by teachers has also been identified as a problem (Curcio & First; 1993; North Carolina Center for the Prevention of School Violence, 1994; Quarles, 1989). As noted by Toby (1995, p. 147) "small incident(s) of violence against teachers carry enormous symbolic weight...suggest(ing) that teachers are not in control of the schools where such violence occurs." Additionally, as noted by Bloch and Bloch (1980), teachers who have either been victimized by students, or who work in schools characterized by the presence of disruptive and/or violent students, often suffer psychological problems similar to that suffered by combat soldiers. These problems have forced some teachers into early retirement while others continue although their effectiveness as teachers is diminished.

Perhaps the best known survey of teacher victimization is the Violent School - Safe School study funded by the National Institute of Education (1978). Surveying almost 1,500 junior and senior high schools throughout the U.S., the researchers noted that 12% of teachers reported that they suffered a theft victimization within a typical month, 0.5% of teachers suffered an assault, and 0.6% reported a robbery victimization within the last month. Additionally, 48% of the responding teachers reported that students had swore or made obscene gestures to them in the last month, while 12% reported that students had threatened them in the last month. Twelve percent of the teachers also reported that they hesitated to confront misbehaving students for fear of their own safety. Finally, the researchers noted while risk of teacher victimization was higher in junior high schools, teachers in senior high schools suffered more serious victimizations. Additionally, class size was related to the risk of victimization as was the proportion of students who were low ability, underachievers, or behavior problems. Teachers with larger class sizes, or who had higher proportions of "problematic" students, ran a greater risk of victimization.

Fortunately, many of these victimizations were relatively minor. For example, less than 20% of teachers reported theft losses of more than $10 and one-quarter lost $10 or more in robberies. Similarly, 19% of those assaulted required medical treatment. While many commentators would immediately highlight these seemingly high percentages, it is important to note that the base figures are very low. That is, we are talking about 25% of less than 1% of all teachers who were robbery victims, 19% of the 0.5% who were assaulted, and less than 20% of the 12% who experienced a theft. This does not mean that teacher victimization should be minimized or ignored. Rather, it demonstrates that the problem is not as rampant or as serious as often portrayed.

In a follow-up to the safe School Study, Menacker, Weldon, and Hurwitz (1989) used many of the same questions to assess disruption in four inner city Chicago elementary schools that were located in poor, high crime areas. Based upon data obtained from teachers and sixth and eighth grade students, they noted 15% of the students reported hitting a teacher at least once during the school year, 3% of the teachers reported being physically attacked (with 1% being threatened by a weapon), and 39% of the teachers reported either theft or damage to personal property during the school year. In addition, 18% of the responding teachers reported that they felt "very unsafe" in the school's parking lot while 23% reported that they felt "very unsafe" on other school property. Ninety-eight percent of the teachers reported that the neighborhoods surrounding their schools were dangerous with 48% rating the neighborhood crime problem as very serious. Based upon the reported fear of crime levels and high levels of official crime in the surrounding neighborhoods, Menacker et al. concluded that the school is an "island of relative safety in an ocean of danger" (Menacker et al., 1989, p. 39). This conclusion, however, may have been premised more by the location of the schools they studied rather than by the amount of crime that occurred within the school itself.

Counter to some of these earlier surveys, the 1993 Metropolitan Life Survey of the American Teacher reports fewer problems. Surveying a random sample of 1,000 teachers from public schools across the U.S., they uncovered 11% who reported being the victim of a violent act in or around school, with 95% of those involving a student offender. Despite that percentage, only 1% of the secondary school teachers reported feeling unsafe at school and only 2% claimed to bring something to school for protection (typically mace). These findings are not consistent with the claims of high levels of teacher victimization and fear in American schools, particularly given the fact that only public school teachers (where the problem is supposedly the greatest) were included in the survey.

In conclusion, as noted by Gottfredson and Gottfredson (1985) many teachers suffer thefts or are the butt of jokes or gestures, few however suffer serious harm. Thus teacher victimizations reflect more "day-to-day indignities" rather than "wholesale mayhem and plunder" (Gottfredson & Gottfredson, 1985, p. 4). However, as Toby (1995) notes, while in-school victimizations may be minor indignities, violence is a threat to the educational process, and continued violence and disorder fuels crime and disruption in the school.

Data and Methodology

This chapter reports on the level of teacher victimization and their responses to such victimization in junior and senior high schools. The data were collected through surveys conducted in the Spring of 1994 in Lucas County (Toledo) Ohio. Lucas County is fairly representative of similar sized counties in the United States. Its 1990 population of 462,361 was 82% white, 15% black, and 52% female. A largely urban county, it has a median income of roughly $28,000 and 15% of the population lives below the poverty line. Its unemployment rate ranged from 7.9% for men to 9% for women, with over 10% of the population receiving some form of public assistance. Like many counties its size, its largest employers are involved in manufacturing, retail, health services, and educational services. The 1994 crime rate for City of Toledo (9,130/100,000) was comparable to many other cities of its size.

Lucas County contains ten separate school districts which represent the city of Toledo and its surrounding municipalities/unincorporated areas. In addition, there is a Catholic school system and several private magnet schools. Within the confines of the county there are approximately 40,000 students enrolled in grades 7 through 12. Eight of the ten public school districts (including the City of Toledo), the Catholic school system, and the largest of the private schools agreed to participate in the study. These school districts represent roughly 85% of the junior and senior high school students in the county and are a representative cross-section of the county.

From the public school systems we were able to obtain information from 15 junior high schools and 16 high schools. Of the eligible schools, this represents 88% of the public junior (15 of 17) and senior high schools (16 of 18) in the county. Focusing on the Catholic school system within Lucas County, we were able to secure data from 67% (4/6) of the high schools and 24% of the schools containing grades 7 and 8 (8/33).

Sample Populations

Survey data were collected from the students, teachers, and principal in each school. During the spring of 1994, we anonymously surveyed students in grades 7 through 12 and the teachers in each school. A questionnaire was also sent to each school's principal. The questionnaires were designed to gather respondent demographics, perceptions about school discipline and control, and perceptions about school crime including personal victimization and responses to victimization. All questions on the student and teacher questionnaire were closed-ended and offered the respondent a finite set of answers to choose from. The principal survey included both open and closed-ended inquiries. Respondents were asked to answer all questions in relation to "since the start of the school year." Based upon the dates of the survey, the data represent roughly a six month time frame.

All school teachers and principals received a survey. Teacher surveys that included multiple missing data, erroneous school codes, or inconsistent data were eliminated. A total of 1,045 usable teacher surveys were returned representing an approximate 40% response rate. Principal questionnaires were returned from 44 of the 45 participating schools representing a 98% response rate. Official school records were used to fill out missing response categories where possible. A sample of this magnitude should provide results representative of all teachers. This chapter is a summation of key victimization data for teachers from throughout Lucas County, Ohio.

Measures of Victimization

The analysis uses four measures of teacher victimization at school. These measures are being the victim of a robbery, a theft, a physical assault, or a physical threat at school. Each measure reflects the percent of teachers who reported at least one offense since the start of the school year. In addition, we also use another measure of victimization - indirect or vicarious victimization. This is assessed by two series of questions. The first series asked whether the respondent saw or knew of "other teachers/staff" being victimized at their school. The second series of questions, focusing on behaviors committed by students, asked the respondent how often certain victimizations had occurred at their school.

Results

Direct Victimization at School

Teachers were asked about their experiences as a victim of three types of crimes: robbery, theft, and assaults, with the latter including both di-

Table 1
Teacher Victimization at School

# of Times	Robbery (%)	Theft (%)	Assault (%)	Physical Threats (%)
Never	98.1	56.8	96.4	79.5
Once	0.9	13.8	3.3	9.6
2–3 times	0.8	19.5	0.4	7.7
4–5 times	0.1	4.9	0.0	1.6
6+ times	0.0	5.0	0.0	1.7

rect physical assaults as well as physical threats. Robbery was measured by asking "how many times did anyone take money or other things directly from you by force, weapons, or threat of force at this school." As noted in Table 1 the vast majority of teachers (98%) report never being victimized. Moreover, of those few who were victimized, only 43% report loses of over $10. Theft was probed as having something stolen from "a desk, locker, or some other place at this school." The data show that theft is a more common crime with 43% of the teachers reporting a theft sometime during the school year. However, of the teachers that reported suffering a theft victimization, less than 27% reported losses of over $10. Assault was measured in two different ways. First, we asked the teachers "how many times did a student physically attack or hurt you at this school." Then we asked "how many times has a student threatened to hurt you at this school." Less than 4% of the teachers reported a physical assault by a student, and of these respondents only 28% needed some type of medical care, defined as a visit to a doctor or nurse. More problematically, 20% of the teachers reported they were threatened with physical assault by a student during the school year.

Another way of looking at the extent of teacher victimization is to compare it to student victimization. Since we asked students some of the same questions regarding in-school victimization we were able to make comparisons between teachers and students for the crimes of robbery, assault, and theft. Interestingly, proportionately more students suffered robbery (12% of the students) and assault victimizations (13% of the students) while more teachers suffered a theft victimization (43% of the teachers, 39% of the students). Furthermore, students appeared to suffer more serious victimization than the teachers. For example, 53% of student robbery victims and 37% of student theft victims suffered loses of more than $10, while 33% of student assault victims reported needing medical care. Thus, when compared to students, not only do teachers suffer less frequent victimizations, but their victimizations tend to be of a less serious nature.

Indirect Victimization

In addition to direct victimization, individuals can be effected by indirect or vicarious victimization. As studies on fear of crime have noted, indirect victimization can effect many more people than direct victimization (Lab, 1997). We probed indirect victimization of teachers by asking their knowledge regarding the victimization of other teachers at school. This was assessed by two series of questions. The first series asked whether the respondent saw or knew of "other teachers/staff" being victimized at this school. The second series of questions focused specifically on behaviors committed *by students*, and asked the respondent how often certain victimizations had occurred at this school. The analysis indicated that, in contrast to direct victimization, indirect victimization is more problematic. While only 5% of the teachers knew of other teachers/staff who were robbed at school, 38% reported assaults on other teachers, and 54% report seeing or knowing of thefts from other teachers.

When focusing on behaviors committed by students, we also found higher indirect victimization levels when compared to direct victimization. The results suggest that the proportion of teachers aware of fellow teachers being victimized by students ranged from 72% of teachers who were aware of students stealing from teachers to 15% of the teachers who were aware of student robberies of teachers. In addition, 38% of teachers were aware of assaults on teachers, 61% were aware of threats made toward teachers, 67% knew of swearing or obscene gestures made by students, and 27% were aware of teachers who suffered sexual harassment at the hands of students. When asked how often these behaviors had occurred, teachers reported that the less serious behaviors were the most frequent. For example, when asked if these behaviors occur once a month or more, 32% of teachers reported that they knew of swearing and obscene gestures and 24% reported that they knew of instances involving threats or thefts. However, only 7% knew of actual assaults while 6% knew of sexual harassment incidents, and 4% knew of robberies that had occurred once a month or more.

Influence of School Type

Research has suggested that school type has an influence on in-school victimization. To explore this issue we collapsed our schools into two separate categories, public versus private and junior versus senior high. Using our four victimization measures, we explored the relationship between these school types and teacher victimization. The analyses revealed no differences in victimization of teachers for assault and robbery by either the public vs. private or junior high vs. senior high distinctions. Thus, the

Table 2
Correlations

N=1,045	Robbery	Theft	Assault	Threat
Low Ability	.07*	.22***	.09**	.23***
Under Achievement	-.01	.22***	.03	.15***
Behavior Problems	.12***	.29***	.20***	.35***
Average Class Size	-.02	.01	-.10***	-.11***

*   p<.05
** P<.01
*** P<.001

type of school has no impact upon the percentage of teachers who reported that they were robbed or assaulted. For theft, however, 47% of the teachers in public schools were victimized versus only 23% of teachers in private schools. Similarly, 50% of the teachers in junior highs were victimized compared to only 40% of teachers in high schools. In addition to thefts, teachers in public schools and junior high schools suffer more physical threats. For example, approximately one-quarter of the teachers in public schools and in junior highs reported that they were physically threatened at school. The equivalent percentages for private school and high school teachers was 3% and 18%, respectively.

Thus, the type of school that a teacher works in has an impact upon the probability that he/she will report select types of victimizations.

Influence of Student and Teacher Variables. In addition to measures of across the board victimization, we also looked at the relationship between select student and teacher variables and teacher victimization. Specifically, we looked at the correlation between teacher victimization and the percentage of students a teacher has who are "low ability," "underachievers," or "behavior problems." These percentages were determined by asking each teacher to rate what percentage of their students fell into each specific category. Thus, they are a reflection of each teacher's perceptions of his/her students. In addition, we looked at the teacher's average class size, the teacher's age, sex, number of years teaching, and his/her educational level. There was no relationship between a teacher's age, sex, number of years teaching, their educational level, and their risk of victimization. There was, however, a relationship between teacher victimization and the remaining variables of interest (see Table 2). For example, there was a positive relationship between victimization and the proportion of students a teacher has who are rated "low ability." This relationship was consistent across all four victimization categories. In addition, there was also a positive relationship between the proportion of underachievers a teacher had in his/her classroom and the teacher's chances of victimization. Teachers who taught more underachievers were more likely to lose property to thefts ands/or be threatened. A positive relationship also existed between the proportion of students who were behavioral problems and a teacher's risk of victimization. As was the case for low ability, this relationship was consistent across all four victimization types. Finally, there was an inverse relationship between a teacher's average class size and his/her risk of victimization. Teachers who have smaller average class sizes experienced more assaults and threats than did other teachers.

Since the relationship between class size and victimization was opposite of what was expected, we examined class size via two different variables. First, we looked at class size by type of school (i.e., junior versus senior high). Our rationale for this was that junior high schools tend to have smaller class sizes and therefore the relationship between class size and victimization may in part be driven by higher victimization levels in junior high schools. Interestingly, the only measure of victimization that was influenced by the type of school was being threatened by a student. There was no significant relationship between class size and being threatened for teachers who worked in senior high schools. However, for teachers who worked in junior highs, there was a significant negative relationship between class size and being threatened ($r = -.17$; $p<.01$). As stated, there was no change in the relationship between class size and our other measures of victimization when we controlled for the type of school.

Our second analysis focused on the relationship between class size and our measures of student's scholastic abilities (i.e., low ability, underachievers, behavior problems). We found that there was a negative association between class size and all three of our measures of student performance. Thus, smaller classes are significantly more likely to be populated by either students who are rated as low ability, underachievers, or who have been defined as behavior problems. Thus, we conclude that the relationship between class size and victimization is driven not necessarily by the size of the class, but rather by the type of student within the class.

Finally, one must remember that the relationships presented in the above analyses are correlational in nature. While the relationships discussed are in the theorized direction (i.e., low ability leads to a greater proclivity for disruption), it is possible that the relationships uncovered are due to teacher perceptions rather than actual behavior. For example, while the analysis suggests that teachers working with problem students are more likley to experience victimization at school, it may be that those who experience in-school victimization are more likley to label their students as problematic. Unfortunately, we lack the data to address this question.

Responses to Victimization

Individuals can respond to victimization, both directly and indirectly, in a variety of ways. Perceptions of school safety, fear of victimization, and avoidance behavior are potential responses. The teacher survey included a variety of questions that tap these domains.

Teachers were asked whether they felt it was safe to bring money or other valuables to school and whether it was safe to store these items at school. The results suggested that over half of the teachers (58%) report it is safe to bring valuables to school, but less than half (44%) report it is safe to store these items in one's desk, locker, teachers' lounge, or other such area in the school. Not surprisingly, when compared to students, teachers report higher levels of safety in bringing valuables (58% versus 52%) and in storing valuables (44% versus 35%), respectively.

We also asked a series of questions focusing on the teacher's perceptions of school safety. These questions dealt with perceptions of safety at specific school locations, perceptions of one's overall safety at school, and the perception of overall school safety. Focusing on the perception of safety at specific school locations, we asked teachers to rate specific locations regarding their level of safety. Defining "unsafe" as those who reported feeling either "very" or "fairly" unsafe at each location, the percentage of teachers who report that certain school locations are "unsafe" range from 3% for faculty/staff lounges to 26% for the surrounding neighborhood. It is interesting to note that, with the exception of student restrooms where 17% of the teachers report feeling unsafe, the locations that generate the highest levels of concern are external to the school building. For example, 14% report feeling unsafe at "other places on school grounds," 21% report feeling unsafe in the parking lot, and as noted above, 26% report feeling unsafe in the surrounding neighborhood. Thus, while teachers may have concerns about crime at school, they appear to be more concerned with crime outside of the school.

Most teachers feel safe at school. For example, when asked about perceptions of their personal safety at school, 74% of the respondents reported feeling "very safe" or "safe" at school. Conversely, only 8% reported feeling "unsafe" or "very unsafe" at school. Finally, focusing on overall perceptions of school safety, 66% of the teachers reported that schools are safe while 9% reported that they are unsafe. When compared to students, teachers report higher levels of school safety. For example, only 51% of students reported overall that schools were safe, while 16% reported that schools were unsafe.

Finally, when asked about how often they avoided school due to concerns over school crime, less than 1% of the teachers reported that they missed at least a day of school due to fear of school crime. In comparison,

9% of students reported that they missed at least one day of school due to fear of assault, while 5% of students reported that they missed at least one day of school due to fear of theft.

Discussion and Conclusion

While anecdotal stories regarding crime in the school present alarming scenarios about crime running rampant, in reality, serious teacher victimization is rare. For example, only 2% of the teachers reported they were robbed at school while 4% reported they were assaulted. Both of these percentages were lower for teachers than for students. Moreover, the teachers who suffered either a robbery or an assault, few reported that their victimization was serious in nature. Over one-fifth of the teachers reported that they were threatened at school, and over two-fifths reported that they suffered a theft while at school. Many of these latter victimizations were also of a minor nature. The probability of teacher victimization is in part dependent upon the grade levels taught by the teacher, whether the teacher is employed by a public or private school, and the type of student the teacher has in their class.

While not victimized directly, most teachers report knowing of someone else who has been victimized. The majority of teachers in the county knew of at least one instance where a colleague had suffered thefts, been the subject of swearing or obscene gestures, and/or suffered other physical threats. While many of these instances where infrequent, occurring only once or twice a month, they occurred often enough that most teachers were aware of the existence of the behavior. While vicarious victimization does not directly impact on the individual, it may aid in the development of a climate of fear and distrust among both teachers and students. Such a climate, if it exists, can not be conducive to the well-being of the teachers or the educational and moral development of the students.

The presence of direct and vicarious victimization notwithstanding, fear of crime and avoidance behavior is not an important issue for the teachers in our study. A large majority of teachers report that they feel safe at school and extremely few teachers report that they miss school due to a fear of victimization. This is in contrast to students who report higher levels of fear within the school and who report that they are more likely to miss school due to a fear of victimization. In addition, teachers report that they feel safer in school then they do outside of the school building or off the school grounds. This differs from students who report similar levels of fear whether they are at school or in transit to and from school (Lab & Clark, 1997).

While differing time frames and the methodologies employed do not render the data completely compatible, the results presented herein are consistent with the results from the Violent School - Safe School Study, the Menacker et al. follow-up study, and The Metropolitan Life Survey. While the data do not indicate that teacher victimization is a major problem from a crime control perspective, it is possible, as noted by Bloch and Bloch (1990), that such victimization may have a negative impact upon a teacher's effectiveness as an instructor. It may also be an indication that the faculty and staff have lost control of the institution (Toby, 1995).

Unfortunately, while our data do not address these questions, they do suggest, that in the aggregate, these concerns may be minor. As noted, serious teacher victimization is rare, and while vicarious victimization is a problem, most teachers report that these incidents are also infrequent. As a result, fear of crime among teachers is not prevalent, particularly when teachers are in the school building itself.

How does one ameliorate these findings with the common perceptions about the danger of schools for teachers? Clearly, our results suggest that the perceptions are out of line with reality. Many of the perceptions are probably based on media presentations of relatively isolated incidents occurring in a few schools. In addition, many of these depictions come from inner-city schools located in the largest metropolitan areas, such as New York City, Chicago, Los Angeles, and others. These cities are not representative of most cities in the U.S. and any attempt to extrapolate from these locales to the rest of the country is ill-advised. Both of the more national data (i.e., The Metropolitan Life Survey (1993) and the Safe School Study) and the data for Lucas County provide a more representative view of in-school victimization than found in the mostly anecdotal media presentations.

In conclusion, while we agree that disruptive behavior is not conducive to an educational climate, we find little evidence to support the notion that victimization of teachers is a rampant problem in our schools. We agree with Gottfredson and Gottfredson (1985) that teacher victimizations reflect more of a quality of life issue rather than a crime wave threatening to overrun the schools. While we should continue to strive to make schools as safe a learning environment as possible, it does not appear that teacher victimization is of the magnitude or seriousness often portrayed in more popular forums.

Note: Support for data collection and analysis was provided by Grant #93-IJ-CX-0034 from the National Institute of Justice, Office of Justice Programs, U.S. Department of Justice. The conclusions and opinions expressed herein are those of the authors and do not necessarily reflect the views of the granting agencies.

Discussion Questions

Schools have been referred to as "islands of relative safety in an ocean of danger." What do the authors of this statement mean by this? Does this statement apply equally to both teachers and students?

It has been proposed that by reducing the age of compulsory school attendance we may be able to reduce school crime and disorder. Do you agree with this proposal? What impact would dropping the age of compulsory school attendance from 16 to 15 or 14 have on crime in the neighborhoods? What impact would this have on an individuals' chances for a successful career? How do these concerns balance with the desire for a safe and orderly school system?

Chapter 5

An Exploration of the Relationship Between Carrying Weapons to School and Victimization

Stephen M. Cox
Timothy S. Bynum
William S. Davidson

Introduction

Juvenile violence has become a major social and health problem in the United States. The Office of Juvenile Justice and Delinquency Prevention (OJJDP) reported that the number of juveniles murdered increased 82% between 1984 and 1994 (OJJDP, 1996). An average of seven juveniles a day were victims of homicide in 1994 compared to five per day in 1980. The majority (64%) of juveniles were killed by an acquaintance or a family member. In addition, 49% of all juvenile homicides involved the use of a firearm. For homicides of 15–17 year olds, the percentage rises to 76% that involved a firearm.

OJJDP also reported an increase in the number of juveniles committing violent crimes. In 1994, there were 150,200 juvenile arrests for violent crimes representing a 75% increase over the 1984 rate. For males, the increase was 69% and for females it was 128%. In comparison, the adult arrest rate for violent crimes increased 48% during the same time period. The Office of Juvenile Justice and Delinquency Prevention predicts that if these trends continue, juvenile arrest rates for violent crimes will more than double by the year 2010 (OJJDP, 1996).

The problem of youth violence has also become a major concern in schools (Gaustad, 1991, Johnson & Johnson, 1995b; Mulhern, 1994). Bastian and Taylor (1991) reported that 9% of students participating in the School Crime Supplement of the National Crime Victimization Survey had been a victim of a violent crime or a property crime while at school. Another national survey of 6th through 12th grade students conducted by the National Center for Education Statistics found that 12% of the surveyed students had been a victim of a physical attack, robbery, or bullying while at school and 71% of the students knew of these types of incidents occurring in their school (Nolin, Davies, & Chandler, 1996).

In addition, there were 105 school-associated violent deaths across the nation from 1992 to 1994 (Kachur, Stennies, Powell, Modzeleski, Stephens, Murphy, Kresnow, Sleet, & Lowry, 1996). Forty percent of these deaths (42) occurred as a result of an interpersonal dispute and 94% involved a gun or a knife. Even though school-associated violent deaths account for less than 1% of deaths among school aged children, these numbers were higher than other studies have reported.

Violent incidents and fear of violence can have a profound effect on the educational process. Schools with high rates of crime and violence are less effective in educating students. These schools have lower levels of student achievement, higher rates of absenteeism, and more drop outs (Christie & Toomey, 1990; Lowry, Sleet, Duncan, Powell, & Kolbe, 1995). Even in schools that have a low percentage of students being victimized, a few violent acts can have far reaching detrimental effects for a large number of students. Fear of victimization has been found to inhibit students' educational and psychological development (Asmussen, 1992; Christie & Toomey, 1990). Fear and apprehension affects concentration and academic performance, participation in school activities, and attitudes toward school (McDermott, 1980).

The rise in school-related violence has been attributed to the increase in weapons being brought to school. While students bringing weapons to school is not a new phenomenon, it is occurring more frequently (Gaustad, 1991; National Center for School Safety, 1993). For instance, 35% of 6th through 8th grade students and 48% of 9th through 12th grade students reported that they had seen students bring weapons to school (OJJDP, 1996). Almost one-half of eighth grade students surveyed had seen a weapon (44%), while 38% of the seventh graders and 24% of the sixth grade students had observed a student with a weapon.

Research has suggested two primary reasons students bring weapons to school. First, Webster, Gainer, and Champion (1993) found that students who carried knives and guns were more aggressive than students who did not carry weapons. Students who carried knives were more likely to be males and had been threatened or attacked with a knife. The authors speculated that these students were victims due to their propensity to get into a fight than through random victimization. Gun carrying students were, in fact, found to be more aggressive than knife carrying students. In addition, students who carried guns or knives had been arrested for drug-related charges, held extreme attitudes regarding the use of violence, perceived peer support for violence, and tended to start fights. These results suggested that both gun and knife carrying was more of an aggressive than defensive behavior.

The second reason students bring weapons to school is for protection (National Center for School Safety, 1993; Pearson & Toby, 1992; Webster et al., 1993). These students have either been victimized or have a fear of being victimized and feel that the only way they can avoid this is to carry a weapon. The National Institute of Education (1978) reported that 29% of assault victims brought a weapon to school while only 9% of nonvictims carried weapons. Bastian and Taylor (1991) found that two percent of surveyed students had brought some type of weapon to school for protection at least once during the six month period prior to being surveyed. The weapons being brought to school consisted of guns, knives, brass knuckles, and razor blades. Boys were more likely than girls to carry a weapon to school for protection. In addition, as more schools resort to different types of increased security (e.g., metal detectors, armed security guards, random locker searches, police officers stationed in the school), students' fears of being victimized have increased to the extent that many students feel they are unsafe unless they carry a weapon (Asmussen, 1992; National Center for School Safety, 1993).

While much attention has been dedicated to the level of school violence, characteristics associated with violent acts (e.g., number of incidents, perpetrator-victim relationships, structural characteristics of the school), and the increase in weapons in schools, little research has fully explored the relationship between weapon carrying and victimization. This relationship is important as a significant amount of school violence reduction strategies are primarily aimed at decreasing the number of weapons being brought into schools. Many of these strategies may not be addressing the root causes of the problem.

Victimization and Weapon Carrying

Theory and research suggest that there are two types of victims who bring weapons to school: passive victims and provocative victims (Olweus, 1978). Passive victims are innocent victims who do not provoke attacks and cannot adequately defend themselves. These students believe they are victimized because they are smaller and weaker than other students (Boulton & Underwood, 1992).

There are generally three defensive responses passive students adopt after being victimized at school or as a result of fear of victimization. Besides carrying a weapon to school for protection, students avoid certain places in the school or simply do not attend school (Batsche & Knoff, 1994; Lab & Whitehead, 1992; Pearson & Toby, 1992; Ringwalt,

Messerschmidt, Graham, & Collins, 1992). Johnston, O'Malley, and Bachman (1993 as cited in Batsche and Knoff, 1994) found that 20% of the middle school students in their study avoided certain places at school because they felt unsafe and 8% of the sample did not attend school-related events. In addition, 16% of 8th graders were afraid at school and 7% of 8th grade students skipped school at least once during the previous month because they felt unsafe.

Although we could not find empirical evidence to support our beliefs, a logical assumption would be that the measures a student takes to avoid victimization escalates with fear of victimization. For example, a student with minimal or no fear of victimization will take no precautions. The same student who is later victimized or has an increased fear of victimization will take minor precautions (avoiding perceived dangerous areas of school). As the level of fear increases, the student may skip school or ultimately start carrying a weapon to school for protection.

This is not to say that all students who are extremely afraid of victimization will eventually carry a weapon to school. Highly victimized students who carry weapons for protection do so because they believe that this is the only way to protect themselves from further violence. Studies of gun ownership have found that gun ownership for protection is highest for people who believe that the police and courts cannot effectively deal with crime and they cannot depend on others for protection (McDowall, 1995). Similarly, as passive students become victims, observe other students being victimized, and feel that the protective measures of the school are not working, weapon carrying seemingly becomes their only choice.

In contrast to passive victims, provocative victims are highly aggressive students who actively participate in risk-taking behaviors (Perry, Kusel, & Perry, 1988). Research has found a direct relationship between aggression and victimization (DuRant, Cadenhead, Pendergrast, Slavens, & Linder, 1994; Perry et al., 1988; Sheley, McGee, & Wright, 1995; Webster et al., 1993). Sheley et al. (1995) found that engaging in high-risk behaviors (criminal activity, drug use and trafficking, and gang activity) increased the likelihood of being a victim of violent crime.

This type of relationship between victimization and weapon carrying can be explained using routine activities theory which states that individuals who participate in high-risk behaviors or are involved in situations where the risk of victimization is greater are more likely to be crime victims (Jensen & Brownfield, 1986). Using this approach, students who carry weapons to school participate in several high-risk behaviors, with weapon carrying being one of those behaviors. Victimization occurs as a result of participating in high risk behaviors, therefore, victimization is more of a correlate of weapon carrying rather than a cause.

While there has been research that has supported both views between the relationship of victimization and weapon carrying, little research has directly tested these two approaches. There have been several issues left unanswered by prior research. For example, what is the true relationship between high-risk activities, weapon carrying, and victimization? Does victimization predict weapon carrying for students who participate in high-risk activities? Is there a difference between victims who carry weapons and victims who do not carry weapons? Is there any one type of victimization that increases the probability of weapon carrying? The following study further investigates the relationship between victimization and weapon carrying by addressing these questions. This will be followed by a discussion of the different school policies that have been put in place to decrease the number of weapons in schools.

Methodology

Sample. Data for this study were collected from four middle schools in a large midwestern city. The schools were in the same urban school district but located in different areas of the city. These four schools were selected by research staff and school officials based upon their representativeness of middle schools in the school district. The schools were located in low income residential areas of the city. The principals of these schools believed the area around their school was home to gangs, crack houses, and drug dealers.

Anonymous surveys were distributed and collected during homeroom periods in each school. The surveys were given to all sixth, seventh, and eighth grade students in attendance. The sample consisted of 994 middle school students across the four schools. Slightly more than half (55%) were female and the mean age was 12.6 with a range of 9 to 15 years old. One-third of the students in the sample were sixth graders, 37% were seventh graders, and 30% were eighth graders.

Measures. The student survey contained several items related to weapon carrying. The constructs contained in the survey were: number of times students carried weapons to school, students' self-efficacy, attitude toward school, attitude toward fighting, perception of school safety, self-reported delinquency, the amount of delinquency witnessed at school, and victimization. All of these scales were created by summing the scale items and dividing the sum by the number of items with non-missing responses. Several items were reverse coded to maintain consistency in the direction of the scale.

Carrying a weapon. The students were asked to report the number of times in the past two months that they had brought a gun or a knife to school. The possible responses to these questions were "zero," "one," "two," "three," and "four or more."

Self-efficacy. The scale which assessed students' self-efficacy was comprised of twenty items asking students how difficult it would be to use nonviolent methods to resolve potential conflicts. The responses were coded as "very hard," "hard," "easy," and "very easy." A high scale score indicated that a student felt it would not be difficult to avoid conflicts nonviolently while a low scale score indicated that a student did not feel confident that he or she could avoid a conflict situation by employing nonviolent methods. The scale reliability was tested using coefficient alpha (Cronbach, 1970) and was .80 for self-efficacy.

Attitudes toward school. The construct was based on a six item scale that measured general attitudes toward school (Gold & Mann, 1984). Students were given statements regarding their feelings about teachers, principals, and the school in general and were asked if they "strongly agreed," "agreed," "neither agreed nor disagreed," "disagreed," or "strongly disagreed" with the statement. The scale measured the extent to which the students liked or disliked school. A high scale score represented a positive attitude toward school. The scale reliability was .75.

Attitude toward fighting. The attitude toward fighting scale measured students' belief that fighting was an appropriate way to handle problems. Students were given seven statements regarding the appropriateness of fighting and asked if they "strongly agreed," "agreed," "did not know," "disagreed," or "strongly disagreed" with each item. A high scale score signified a positive attitude regarding fighting and a low scale score meant the student did not believe fighting was an acceptable or appropriate method of handling interpersonal conflicts. The scale reliability was .75.

Perception of school safety. The perception of school safety scale contained five items measuring how safe students felt while they were at school (Clifford & Davis, 1991). For these items, students read a statement regarding a safety issue in their school and reported the extent to which they "strongly agreed," "agreed," "did not know," "disagreed," or "strongly disagreed" with the statement. A high score represented a perception that the school was a safe place while a low score represented a perception that the school was not safe. The scale reliability for perception of school safety was .59.

Self-reported delinquency. The self-reported delinquency scale consisted of six items that focused on school-related misbehavior and were adapted from Elliott, Huizinga, and Ageton (1985). The items included in this scale pertained to school vandalism, being sent to the principal's office for misbehavior, skipping a class, skipping an entire school day, threatening other students, and being suspended. Students were asked to report how many times, "zero" through "four or more," in the past two months they had been involved in these activities. The scale reliability for self-reported delinquency was .82.

Observed delinquency. In measuring the amount of school-related violence students had witnessed in school, students were asked to report the number of times in the past two months they had seen: (1) a fist fight between other students, (2) a student threaten a teacher, (3) a student destroy school property, (4) a weapon that was brought to school by another student, (5) the police remove a student from the school, and (6) students possessing drugs in school. Similar to the questions involving fighting and weapons, the possible responses to these items were "zero," "one," "two," "three," and "four or more." The scale reliability was .73 for observed delinquency.

Victimization. School victimization was measured using four self-report items. Students were asked how many times in the past two months they had been physically assaulted, had something physically taken from them, had something stolen from their school locker, and been threatened by another student. These items were also coded with the responses of "zero" through "four or more" times. The coefficient alpha for this scale was .67.

Results and Discussion

The purpose of this study was to examine the relationship between weapon carrying and victimization in four urban middle schools by testing for differences between weapon carriers and nonweapon carriers who have been victimized, testing for differences between weapon carriers and nonweapon carriers who have not been victimized, and identifying which victimization item may have the most influence on weapon carrying.

The first step in the analysis was to determine the frequency of victimization of the students participating in the survey. The purpose of this step was to compare this sample to other similar studies of school victimization and to determine if victimization was a problem for students participating in this study.

Table 1 presents the frequencies of the four victimization items (see Table 1). The percentages of students who were victimized were higher in our sample than in prior studies. Twenty-two percent of the students had been assaulted at school at least once in the two month period prior to taking the survey. Thirty-five percent had been physically threatened, 47% of the students had an item stolen from their locker, and 27% had been robbed. Overall, 67% of the sample had been a victim of a crime at school at least once in a two month period with 35% of the students reporting to have been victimized four or more times in the same two month period.

Table 1
Frequencies of responses to victimization survey items.

Number of times victimized	Zero	Once	Twice	Three	Four or More
Offense					
Assaulted	768 (78%)	71 (7%)	63 (6%)	38 (4%)	54 (5%)
Physically threatened	647 (66%)	119 (12%)	64 (6%)	41 (4%)	123 (12%)
Items stolen from locker	527 (53%)	180 (18%)	107 (11%)	52 (5%)	128 (13%)
Robbed	724 (73%)	101 (10%)	62 (6%)	48 (5%)	59 (6%)
Ever been victimized	325 (33%)	152 (15%)	98 (10%)	72 (7%)	347 (35%)

Note: All percentages are row percentages.

The second step in the analysis was to determine if the same students who were victimized were bringing weapons to school. Of the 67% of the sample that had been victimized (669 students), 23% (151 students) reported that they had brought a weapon to school in the two month period prior to taking the survey and 77% of the victims (518) reported not carrying a weapon (see Table 2). As expected, only 8% of the students (27) who had not been victimized carried a weapon to school. These percentages suggest a moderate relationship between victimization and weapon

Table 2
Crosstabulation of students carrying a weapon by victimization.

	Ever been victimized		
	Yes	No	Totals
Ever carried a weapon to school			
Yes	151 *(85%)* (23%)	27 *(15%)* (8%)	178 (18%)
No	518 *(64%)* (77%)	298 *(36%)* (92%)	816 (82%)
Totals	669 *(67%)*	325 *(33%)*	994

Note: Column percentages are bolded.
          Row percentages are in italicized.
$r=.18$

Table 3
Comparison of scale means between weapon carriers and nonweapon carriers for students reporting being a victim of a crime in school.

Variable	Weapon Carriers (n=151)	Nonweapon Carriers (n=518)	t value
Self-efficacy	2.70	2.80	2.62*
School attitude	3.55	3.81	3.09*
Attitude toward fighting	2.73	2.27	-6.36*
Perception of school safety	3.02	3.11	1.42
Delinquency	1.86	.67	-14.31*
Observed delinquency	2.66	2.24	-4.74*
Victimization	1.74	.97	-8.30**

*p. value is less than .05.

carrying. If victimization was highly predictive of weapon carrying, we would expect the percentage of victims carrying weapons to be higher than 23% and the correlation between the two items to be greater than .18.

The third step attempted to determine what differences existed between victims who carried weapons and victims who did not carry weapons. This step used t-tests to compare mean scale scores of victims who carried weapons and did not carry weapons. The scales used in this analysis have been found in other studies to be related to weapon carrying (Batsche & Knoff, 1994; National School Safety Center, 1993; Pearson & Toby, 1992; Sheley et al., 1995; Webster et al., 1993).

For victims, there were statistically significant differences between weapon carriers and nonweapon carriers for all of the scale scores except one (perception of school safety). The victims who carried weapons appeared to be students in a high-risk group. These were students who participated in delinquency, were exposed to various delinquent acts, did not like school, had low levels of self-efficacy, and were victims multiple times (see Table 3). Being victimized multiple times was probably related to their involvement in high-risk activities. Perceptions of school safety did not appear to influence students' decisions to carry weapons. This finding lends further support to the argument that random victims and students who are afraid of school crime are not necessarily the ones who resort to carrying weapons for protection.

The same t-tests were conducted for students who reported no victimization. This analysis was conducted to determine which students carried weapons for reasons other than victimization. The results of the t-tests for

Table 4
Comparison of scale means between weapon carriers and nonweapon carriers for students reporting that they have not been a victim of a crime in school.

Variable	Weapon Carriers (n=27)	Nonweapon Carriers (n=298)	t value
Self-efficacy	2.95	2.91	-.51
School attitude	3.58	3.98	2.76*
Attitude toward fighting	3.02	2.28	-4.56*
Perception of school safety	3.05	3.27	1.81
Delinquency	1.61	.36	-5.92*
Observed delinquency	2.80	1.88	-4.53*
Victimization	——	——	——*

*p. value is less than .05.

nonvictims were almost identical to the results for the victims (see Table 4). Weapon carriers had poorer school attitudes, more positive attitudes toward fighting, higher amounts of delinquency, and higher amounts of observed delinquency. No statistical differences were found for self-efficacy and perception of school safety.

The same types of victimized students carried weapons to school as the nonvictimized students. In general, high-risk students were more likely to have carried a weapon to school. However, victimization appeared to increase the likelihood that high-risk students carried weapons. Referring back to Table 2, of those students who reported carrying a weapon (178 students), 85% were victims and 15% reported not being victimized. We tested for differences between these two groups of students (weapon carriers who were victims and who were not victims).

There was only one statistically significant difference between these two groups: self-efficacy (see Table 5). Besides being a victim, weapon carriers had lower levels of self-efficacy than nonweapon carriers. Rather than simply being a correlate of weapon carrying, victimization appeared to be a catalyst that causes high-risk youth to carry weapons to school. In this sense, weapon carrying was increased or moderated by victimization, but only for high-risk youth. The lower level of self-efficacy of weapon carriers might further be attributable to victimization.

While there appears to be a strong relationship between weapon carrying and victimization, it is possible that this relationship is not as strong when controlling for other variables that have been used to explain weapon carrying. To test the strength of victimization to weapon carrying,

Table 5
Comparison of scale means between victims and nonvictims for students reporting that they have carried a weapon to school.

Variable	Victims (n=151)	Nonvictims (n=27)	t value
Self-efficacy	2.70	2.95	2.62*
School attitude	3.55	3.58	.89
Attitude toward fighting	2.73	3.02	1.61
Perception of school safety	2.03	3.05	.20
Delinquency	1.86	1.61	-1.25
Observed delinquency	2.66	2.80	.74*

*p. value is less than .05.

we conducted a multiple regression analysis using victimization, grade in school, gender (boys were coded 1 and girls coded as 2), self-efficacy, attitude toward school, attitude toward fighting, perception of school safety, self-reported delinquency, and observed delinquency as the independent variables. If there was a strong relationship between victimization and weapon carrying, the slope of the victimization scale should be statistically significant.

An additional regression analysis was conducted to determine if any one type of victimization may influence weapon carrying. The same independent variables were entered into the regression equation with one exception, the victimization scale was omitted and the individual victimization items were entered in its place.

Table 6 presents the t-values of the two regression equations (see Table 6). The significant predictors for both equations were: gender, attitude toward fighting, self-reported delinquency, and victimization. These results suggest that males, students who believe fighting is a positive way to resolve interpersonal problems, students who have a high rate of delinquency, and students who are victimized are most likely to carry weapons to school. The number of times students were victimized was the second strongest predictor behind self-reported delinquency.

When substituting the actual victimization items as independent variables for the victimization scale, number of times assaulted was the only item that was statistically significant. Students who were assaulted were more likely to bring weapons to school than students who were physically threatened, had items stolen from their lockers, and who were robbed (although we were unable to determine how many of these students were victims of multiple offenses). Again, the characteristics of students who

Table 6
Regression models predicting number of times
students carried weapons to school.

Variable	t-value	t-value
Grade	.58	1.49
Gender*	-2.05**	-2.13**
Self-efficacy	-.80	-1.74
School attitude	-.80	-.96
Attitude toward fighting	2.70**	2.02**
Perception of school safety	.68	1.21
Delinquency	12.94**	10.34**
Observed delinquency	1.93	1.48
Victimization	4.54**	
Assaulted		2.98**
Physically threatened		1.60
Items stolen from locker		1.27
Robbed		.49
R^2	.32	.32*

Gender was coded as males=1 and females=2.
**p. value is less than .05.

were likely to have brought weapons to school were males, students who believed fighting is a positive way to resolve interpersonal problems, students who had a high rate of delinquency, and students who were assaulted. These findings were consistent with Perry et al. (1988) who suggested that the students who are aggressive and victimized probably are aggressors against weaker students and then are victimized by their stronger, more aggressive peers.

Conclusion

The analyses revealed two distinct findings regarding the relationship between victimization and weapon carrying. First, the students participating in this study were a highly victimized group. The majority of students in the sample (67%) reported that they had been victimized at least once in a two month period. The most commonly reported offense was having something stolen from lockers (47% of the students had something stolen) while the least reported offense was assault, yet this was the distinguishing factor between weapon carriers and nonweapon carriers (23% of the sample was assaulted).

Second, victimization was predictive of weapon carrying for students who participated in high-risk behaviors. While this study was not able to directly test the temporal ordering of the victimization-weapon carrying relationship, victimization appeared to be a moderator for high-risk activities and weapon carrying. That is, not all high-risk students carried weapons. One apparent difference between high-risk students who carried weapons and high-risk students who did not carry weapons was victimization. There were no findings in this study that suggested victimization or fear of victimization caused weapon carrying among students who were not high-risk. In other words, it appears that provocative victims are the ones that carry weapons for protection rather than the passive victims.

Three programmatic implications can be derived from this study. First, since the group most likely to bring weapons to school were students involved in high-risk behaviors, the initial step in any program would be to target these students. These were delinquent students, having poor school attitudes, who likely performed poorly in school. Therefore, decreasing delinquent activity and improving school attachment may decrease the likelihood of participating in high-risk behaviors that lead to victimization. Targeting these students and placing them in traditional education-based programs may indirectly lead to a decrease in weapon carrying. Johnson and Johnson (1995a) stressed that schools must not overlook the factors that cause high-risk students to engage in violence. Allowing students to fail and be socially inept increases the probability that students will resort to violence to deal with their problems.

Third, the second strategy attempts to deal with the problem of high-risk students being assaulted. These students have a positive attitude toward fighting and using violence to resolve conflictual situations. This attitude probably increases their likelihood of being assaulted. Anti-violence programs have become popular in many urban, suburban, and rural school districts. These programs are grounded in social learning theory and attempt to teach students nonviolent methods to resolve interpersonal conflicts. Social learning based programs typically consist of teaching students conflict resolution skills, promoting peer mediation to resolving interpersonal conflicts, and impressing upon all students the problems associated with using violence.

The findings of this study suggest that school-wide violence intervention programs may be more effective in decreasing weapon carrying than individual-level approaches. Conflict resolution programs often target the individual as the level of intervention (Tolan & Guerra, 1994) while school-wide program target multiple facets of violence (Commission on Violence and Youth, 1993). G. Gottfredson (1987) pointed out that implementation of programs in schools with a high number of problems is difficult unless the intervention is also aimed at improving the school as a whole. Research on school environment programs is limited (D. Gottfredson, 1987; Lane & Murakami, 1987), but it has indicated that school improvement programs have been moderately successful in improving the school environment, decreasing the number of suspensions, and decreasing the number of delinquent and drug-related activities in school (G. Gottfredson, 1987). Therefore, a school environmental approach appears to be best suited to decrease the number of assaults taking place in school and decrease students' need to carry weapons for protection.

It is important that school administrators consider all possible effects as they explore different strategies to stop the increase in weapons being brought into their schools. Placing metal detectors at the entrances, posting armed security guards in the hallways, housing police substations, and conducting locker searches may deter some students from carrying weapons, but these measures may do little to prevent high-risk students from bringing weapons to school. Future anti-violence strategies need to focus more on the causes of school violence and less on simple deterrence.

Note: This research was supported by the National Institute of Justice, Office of Justice Programs, U.S. Department of Justice, Grant No. 93-IJ-CX-0046. The contents of this document do not necessarily reflect the views or policies of the National Institute of Justice or the U.S. Department of Justice. Please address correspondence to Stephen M. Cox, Department of Sociology/Criminal Justice, Central Connecticut State University, 1615 Stanley Avenue, New Britain, CT 06050.

Discussion Questions

What is the relationship between victimization and weapon carrying suggested by this research?

What are the programmatic interventions and policy implications of this study?

Many schools have resorted to using metal detectors and armed security guards to decrease the amount of violence and the number of weapons being brought into school. Do you think these are effective strategies for decreasing victimization and violence in school? What are some of the potential indirect effects of using metal detectors and armed security guards?

Chapter 6

The Role of Alcohol in Self-Reported Victimizations: Results from an Australian and an United States University Campus

Roberto Hugh Potter
Alban L. Wheeler

Introduction

Alcohol has been both an accepted part of the university experience as well as an acknowledged problem on campus and among university students and staff. Increasingly over the past two decades our attention has turned to the negative impacts of alcohol consumption in the university and college setting. The correlation between overall alcohol consumption by an individual and particular problems has assumed the status of an empirical generalization. The common wisdom is that increased consumption of alcohol, both in terms of volume and frequency, will lead to increased problem behaviors. Nowhere has this putative link between alcohol consumption and problem behaviors, especially violent and sexual behaviors, been taken as seriously as in the United States' higher educational setting.

Among the cataloged problems associated with alcohol consumption are motor vehicle-related accidents and fatalities, unsafe sexual practices, poor academic performance, and criminal behaviors. Evidence of the role played by alcohol in many of these performance areas is mixed, however. No clear picture of the relationship between individuals' drinking behavior and criminal events among students, staff, nor on campus exists (Bausell, Bausell, & Siegel, 1991; Engs & Hanson, 1988; Gonzales & Broughton, 1986; Rivinus & Larimer, 1993; Schwartz & DeKeseredy, 1997; Wechsler, 1996).

This study examines the involvement of alcohol in two categories of criminal behavior among university students on two continents. We seek to determine what role alcohol played in self-reported incidents of sexual assault and non-sexual physical assaults in an Australian and a U.S. university. These two settings provide a quasi-experimental design in which to examine the role of alcohol in such victimizations where alcohol consumption is legal versus illegal, because of age restrictions on possession and university policies. Our research question thus becomes whether alcohol consumption will be reported to be involved in criminal assaults more often in an environment where alcohol is legally consumed than in an environment where its use is prohibited. Stated more formally, our hypothesis is that alcohol will be involved in more self-reported criminal assaults in the environment where alcohol use is legal than in the environment where it is prohibited.

Like the United States, Australian states and territories reduced the alcohol consumption age limit to 18 during the Viet Nam War era. In the United States, the age at which alcohol is legally consumable has been rolled back from 18 to 21 in all states over the past decade. This is partly due to the association of alcohol consumption with young people and social problems. In Australia, by contrast, the age at which alcohol consumption is legal remains 18. Pubs and other alcohol outlets are integral features of Australian university environments. By contrast, many U.S. universities ban totally the sale, possession, or consumption of alcohol on university grounds. Finally, alcohol content in Australian beer and wine is generally higher than its American counterparts, as well. The blood alcohol content at which a person is considered legally impaired is .05 in all Australian states and territories, whereas in the U.S. the level varies from .08 to .10 across the states. One might argue that Australian students have an even higher awareness of alcohol-related intoxication effects than their American counterparts. These contrasts would appear to offer an excellent quasi-experimental design in which to examine the role played by alcohol in criminal victimization events among university students.

Alcohol and Crime on Campus

During the late 1960's students of crime began to focus attention on the fear of crime, and today it has earned the status of a social problem in its own right (Lewis & Salem, 1986). The public outcry for stronger measures to control crime and criminals has reached almost hysterical proportions, coming at a time when the rates for most types of crime have either stabilized or are even falling.

College and university campuses, once seen as sanctuaries, have become the focus of attention for much of this concern. While it is not possible to establish with a high degree of certainty that crime rates on our campuses are increasing, the perception that they are is obvious. This has caused the US Congress to pass the "Student Right-to-Know and Campus Security Act of 1990," requiring every post-secondary institution receiving federal funds to provide a report showing campus crime statistics and policies to students and staff members. The law took effect in September, 1992, and the *Chronicle of Higher Education* published a summary of the first crime statistics reported in compliance with the Act in its January 20, 1993 issue (Lederman, 1993). Over 2,400 colleges and universities reported nearly 1,000 rapes and more than 1,800 robberies. More than 7,500 violent crimes and 32,127 property crimes were reported.

While crime on campus is a legitimate concern, we think it is equally legitimate to determine whether student crime rates differ significantly from crime rates of the non- student population. Of particular interest to us, is the relationship between alcohol and other mood altering drugs and campus crime. Hanson and Engs (1992) concluded from their analysis of a national sample of over 4000 college students at each of four time periods over the past decade that the drinking behavior and violence related to drinking paralleled the trends of the United States. Sloan (1994) found a weak but statistically significant relationship between the reported rate of drinking and drug related offenses and the reported rate of violent offenses as well as the overall crime rate in a sample of over 400 colleges and universities. However, since Sloan uses aggregate data exclusively, interpretation of this relationship remains problematic.

Much has been written linking alcohol and drug use with sexual assault. Abbey, Ross, and McDuffie (1996) report neither the man nor woman had been drinking in 70% of sexual coercion incidents and in 41% of attempted or completed rapes (as defined by the Koss and Oris Sexual Experience Survey) in their study of 1160 college women. However, these were incidents that had occurred after age fourteen and did not necessarily happen while the women were students. Neither was there any way to determine whether the offender was a student.

We are left with an unclear picture as to the relationship between alcohol/illegal drug consumption and campus crime. Most of the data collected to date have focused on the correlation between alcohol consumption variables and crime rates on campuses or in the overall lives of persons who occupy the social status of student, regardless of the salience of that status to the event. Very rarely does the research address the issue of what role substance consumption played in a particular criminal event. The research question for this presentation is, again, what role does alcohol/illegal drug consumption play in the self-reported victimizations of students at one Australian and one United States university?

The Context of Victimization on
Both Campuses: Official Statistics

Australia

Unlike the United States, Australia has no legal requirement that universities or other tertiary institutions report publicly campus crime figures. Following the British model, all police services in Australia are centralized by State or Territory. Thus, crimes reported to the campus security officers are included along with all other crimes recorded in a particular police management area. In this case, all crimes recorded as occurring at the university were counted as crimes in the city area. It becomes difficult to separate on-campus incidents from those around the town without special software. It might also be noted here that what is "counted" as a criminal event in Australia depends upon the police believing that evidence exists to support the claim of a criminal event occurring. It is not simply enough to allege that a crime has occurred.

Beginning in 1992, one of the authors initiated the "Campus Crimes Survey," which has taken place on an annual basis through 1996 (Potter, 1993–1996). This was done partly in response to the lack of information readily accessible to students and others, as well as to investigate the claims that a wide range of criminal acts occurred (especially crimes against persons) which were never reported to or acknowledged by campus security or state/territory police. Participation in the survey was voluntary, and the number of universities responding ranged from a low of 16 to a high of 31. There are 36 publicly-funded universities in Australia and one private university which were surveyed each year.

By way of summary, the percentage of reported crimes against persons has never exceeded eight percent (7.3%) of the officially recorded criminal acts in these surveys. In fact, the proportion of total reports attributed to crimes against persons fell consistently over the period surveyed. Theft of various types has always accounted for the largest single category of victimizations reported, from just under half to nearly two-thirds of reports. With regard to the two primary categories of victimization considered in this paper, sexual assaults ranged from a low of 6 to 39 reports and physical assaults from 38 to 73 reports. Sexual assaults showed a fluxuating pattern over the years, while physical assaults maintained an increasing growth. By U.S. university performances, there has been relatively little such crime reported at the Australian universities.

Figures for recorded crime over an 11 year period (1983–1994) at the University of New England (UNE) were analyzed by Dr. Alicia Rambaldi (see Potter, Rambaldi, Bailey, & Upton, 1995). Rambaldi noted that there were no "trends or seasonal patterns" in the crime data. She concluded that:

> "The findings indicate that the occurrence of crime on the UNE campus is mainly random, except for theft and vandalism which seem to show a moving average and a seasonal autoregressive pattern respectively... None of the crime series showed a statistically significant trend" (Potter et al., 1995, p. 9).

Overall, both physical and sexual assaults were officially recorded as very rare events. The largest number of recorded sexual assault cases was five (5) in a one year at UNE. One of the security officers pointed out that all occurred in a relatively short period following the first "Reclaim the Night" rally at the university.

Historically, then, officially recorded crimes against persons, especially sexual and physical assaults, were rare events at the University of New England. In the period under consideration here (1995 to mid-1996), there were 1 officially recorded sexual assaults and 10 physical assaults, according to campus security. Interestingly, UNE has the highest total crime rate per 1000 students and staff of all universities in Australia. It is also the university with the largest on-campus resident population. At no point, however, have crimes against persons exceeded five percent (5%) of total recorded crime events.

Alcohol is generally available on the UNE campus. The Bistro is a center of campus life, featuring alcoholic and non-alcoholic beverages, food, and entertainment. In recent years the university sought to position the Bistro as a major venue for concert/dance performances in New South Wales. Alcoholic beverages were also sold in the residence halls at specified times. It was not a violation of university policy to possess alcohol in one's room or office. In addition, alcoholic beverages were available to staff at the Staff Club. Alcohol was not only freely available, but a common aspect of campus life.

We will next examine the context of reported criminal activity at our comparison U.S. university and then turn to the methodology of the comparison.

United States

Like UNE, Morehead State University (KY) has a low reported incidence of overall crime. There was one rape reported in 1994 and 1 reported in 1995. On-campus physical assaults were surprisingly low in those two years, with official sources recording two (2) assaults in 1994 and zero (0) in 1995 (*Crime in Kentucky, 1994* and *1995*). The low official crime figures have earned MSU a reputation as one of the safest campuses in the United States, according to its public relations statement.

Like many U.S. universities, the possession and consumption of alcoholic beverages is prohibited on the MSU campus, including dormitory rooms. Alcohol is not sold in any outlet on the university campus. The nearest bar serving beer and wine is one block away from campus. The county in which MSU is located allows sale of beer and wine only in bars, no spirits are sold by the drink.

On one level, the comparison of these two universities is a serendipitous event. The authors met at a conference on campus violence prevention, returned to their respective universities where the surveys were conducted without each other's knowledge, and then became colleagues at Morehead State University. We believe that the two data sets may be compared in order to generate research directions due to several commonalities between the universities. First, both universities are located in small towns in rural areas. The UNE is more isolated, falling roughly 300 miles from any major city. However, both universities have roughly equivalent on-campus residents and similar demographic profiles and similar proportions of student population living in on-campus housing or within the local area. Both universities offer a similar range of majors, though the Australian degree requires only three years of study. A comparison of the respondents' demographic characteristics and year of study revealed no substantial differences between the two data sets (although the UNE sample had a broader age range). Finally, the consumption of alcoholic beverages is not banned from the UNE campus, as it is from the MSU campus. Nor are the vast majority of the UNE students "under age" for alcohol consumption, as would be the case for MSU students.

In sum, the two campuses under study both officially report crimes against persons to be rare events, specifically sexual assaults and physical assaults. It remains to be seen how different a picture emerges from self-report victimization surveys at the two universities. Our special interest will be the role of alcohol in such incidents reported by the respondents. The alcohol policies on the two campuses provide an interesting comparison point.

Sample and Procedure

Australia

During the first semester of 1996 (March to June), 500 questionnaires were distributed via internal mail to non-first year students with on-campus addresses requesting information about victimizations within the previous 12–18 months. Names and mailing labels for students with on-campus addresses (excluding the university post office boxes) were obtained from the registrar's office. A $k + n$ sampling procedure was employed to produce the sample size of 500 persons. Only one wave of questionnaires was distributed. By the end of the first semester, 48% (n=239) of the questionnaires had been returned. Ten percent (25) of the returned questionnaires were not completed. This resulted in a useable sample of 214 students' experiences, or about a 43% response rate.

The questionnaire was constructed from categories fitting the New South Wales definitions of criminal behavior. The format of the questions reflected previous victimizations surveys such as those employed by the Australian Bureau of Statistics (1993) and the United States Department of Justice. There were 15 categories of victimization about which information was requested. A quick word about the categories of victimization employed is in order. As several of the people who responded wrote, some of the questions asked about behaviors which they did not consider "criminal." Indeed, acts such as people entering a college room without the permission of the inhabitant may not strike one as criminal; however, such behavior may be treated as criminal. And, as we will consider below, even such mundane acts sometimes have detrimental effects for some, yet no impact on others.

United States

The Morehead State University sample was collected by administering a precoded questionnaire to students in lower and upper division classes in four academic disciplines, English, geography, history, and sociology during the spring 1995 semester. The resulting sample of 424 respondents is approximately six percent of the headcount enrollment of the university. The sex composition of the sample is similar to that of the university, 43% male and 57% female. However, upperclass students are over represented and consequently the mean age of the sample, 22 years of age, is older than that of the population from which it was drawn.

Results

The overall victimizations reported by students at the UNE (AUS) and MSU (USA) are presented in Tables 1A and 1B. Given the different categories measured, we will focus on two categories whose definitions were essentially identical. For our present purposes, the results presented in Tables 1A and 1B indicate that most respondents did not report being the victim of a criminal act in the previous year to 18 months. The MSU percentage of non-victims is higher (85.6%) than that of the UNE students (60%). However, when the categories of criminal victimization are collapsed into property- and personal-related crimes, there is a marked difference in reports at the two institutions. Crimes against property account

Table 1A: Victimization Among UNE Students, Location and Reporting

Victims of:	YES N	(%)	Females N	(%)+	Males N	(%)+	On-Campus N	***(%)	Reported N	****(%)
None	81	(41)								
Attempted Trespass	14	(7)	10	(8)	4	(4)	13	(100)	3	(25)
Trespass	62	(29)	34	(28)	28	(31)	64	(97)	8	(12)
Theft of or from vehicle	57	(27)	31	(25)	26	(28)	52	(91)	10	(77)
Vandalism	14	(7)	8	(7)	6	(7)	10	(71)	10	(77)
Attempted Physical Assault	18	(9)	8	(7)	10	(11)	17	(94)	9	(53)
Physical Assault	15	(7)	6	(5)	9	(10)	7	(64)	2	(18)
Weapon Involved	13	(6)	7	(6)	6	(7)	7	(54)	4	(31)
Attempted Robbery	3	(1)	0	(0)	3	(3)	1	(33)	1	(33)
Robbery	6	(3)	3	(2)	3	(3)	3	(50)	0	(0)
Attempted Sexual Assault	3	(1)	3	(2)	0	(0)	3	(100)	0	(0)
Accomplished Sexual Assault*	9	(4)	9	(7)	0	(0)	6	(75)	0	(0)
Rape**	15	(7)	13	(11)	2	(2)	11	(92)	3	(25)
Harrassment/Bullying	69	(33)	40	(33)	29	(32)	59	(88)	15	(23)

+ % based on number in each group, not total   * no penetration involved   ** penetration involved
% where location provided   *% to 'official' office (eg security, college)

Table 1B: Victimization Among MSU Students, Gender, Location and Reporting

Victims of:	YES N	(%)	Females N	(%)	Males N	(%)	On-Campus N	(%)	Reported N	(%)
None	338	(85.6)								
Burglary	32	(7.6)	19	(8.0)	13	(7.1)	18	(7.1)	18	(58.1)
Physical Assault	24	(6.0)	14	(6.2)	10	(5.7)	9	(39.1)	7	(30.4)
Sex Assault	7	(1.7)	7	(3.0)	0		2	(28.6)	0	

Table 2: Categories of Assaults and Alcohol Involvement

	REPORTS				ALCOHOL			
	UNE		MSU		UNE		MSU	
	N*	(%)	N	(%)	N**	Y	N	Y
Physical Assault	24	(20)	24	(38)	7 (50)	7 (50)	4 (21)	15 (79)
Sexual Assault	24	(20)	7	(11)	6 (43)	8 (57)	4 (57)	3 (43)*

* Victims, not incidents
** Victimization, not individuals

for just over half (51%) of reports at MSU and crimes against persons comprise 49% of reports. At UNE, however, property-related crimes account for nearly three-quarters (74%) of reported crimes, with the remaining one-quarter (26%) involving personal crimes.

The categories employed may create a measurement artifact in the data. The UNE students responded to more categories of potential victimization than did the MSU students. As noted earlier, some of the categories represented potentially criminalizable acts which students often did not consider criminal, just rude and inconvenient. Interestingly, the UNE proportions are very similar to the officially reported proportions captured in the 1991–1995 Campus Crimes Surveys (Potter, 1992–1996) in Australia. We now turn to two categories of victimization measured in similar manner on both surveys: Physical assault and sexual assault.

The first column of Table 2 reports the results of physical and sexual assault victimization for UNE and MSU (see Table 2). Focusing on these categories reveals greater similarity between student experiences at the two universities. The UNE figures differ from the MSU figures within two primary categories of crimes against persons. In the "physical assault" category, a higher proportion (38%) of MSU students report victimization than did the UNE students (20%). "Sexual assault" proportions show that the UNE students (20%) reported proportionately more victimizations than did the MSU students (11%). Whether or not this last category was affected by the specificity of the question remains problematic. That is, MSU students were left to define for themselves whether or not they had been sexually assaulted; UNE students responded to three categories of sexual experience defined as criminal in New South Wales. Some UNE students did note that what was defined as a "sexual assault" in the question was simply a matter of ill-mannered behavior in their opinion (similar to the comments regarding "trespassing" behaviors).

The focus of this paper is the involvement of alcohol (and/or illegal substances) in criminal victimizations. This question was asked for physical assault and sexual assault incidents on both studies. Information regarding participants in incidents where alcohol was involved is presented in Table 2. At the UNE, alcohol or illegal substances were involved in half (50%; n=7) of the physical assault incidences where respondents provided this information, and in a slightly higher proportion (57%, n=8) of the sexual assaults. The respective figures for MSU revealed that over three-quarters (79%, n=15) of the physical assault reports and just under half (43%, n=3) of the sexual assault reports featured alcohol consumption. By comparison, then, physical assaults appear to have greater alcohol involvement in the American context than in the Australian, but the alcohol/illegal drug involvement is higher in the Australian university for sexual assaults than at the American university. Our hypothesis thus receives mixed support, depending upon which category of victimization is examined.

The next question to be addressed is whether the victim, the offender(s), or both were using alcohol/illegal substances at the time of the victimization (see Tables 3 and 4). Columns 1 and 2 of Table 3 provide information about the sex of the victims of both physical and sexual assaults where alcohol was reportedly involved. At UNE, males (57%) represented only slightly more physical assault victims than did females (43%). However, females (88%) were overwhelmingly the victims of sexual assault incidents. The student victims at MSU showed a marked tendency for females to be the victims of physical assaults (75%) and the only victims of sexual assaults where alcohol was involved.

At the UNE, victims of physical assaults reported that most often (75%) both they and the assailant had been consuming alcohol. In no cases at the UNE had only the victim been drinking. This is in contrast to the MSU results. Here we find that more often (58%) the victim reported only the perpetrator had been drinking. And, the MSU respondents also reported two cases (14%) in which only the victim had been consuming alcohol. For sexual assaults the results are somewhat similar in trend across the two settings. First, in neither university setting did victims report that they alone had been consuming alcohol/illegal drugs when sexually assaulted. Rather, in both places it was more likely for both offender and victim to be consuming alcohol at the time of the sexual assault event. For the UNE students, the situations in which the offender alone was drinking was equal to those for both drinking.

The offenders in the incidents reported at UNE were overwhelmingly male (91%) regardless of the offense category. The same was true of MSU victimizations, where nearly 88% of the offenders were male when alcohol was involved (all offenders were male in the sexual assaults). One

Table 3: Characteristics of Alcohol-Involved Assaults — Persons

	SEX									
	VICTIM				OFFENDER(S)*					
	UNE		MSU		UNE			MSU		
	F	M	F	M	F	M	C	F	M	C
Physical Assault	3	4	6	2	2	20	0	2	14	—
Sexual Assault	7	1	3	0	1	17	1	0	3	—

	WHO CONSUMED ALCOHOL					
	VICTIM		OFFENDER		BOTH	
	UNE	MSU	UNE	MSU	UNE	MSU
Physical Assault	0 (0)	2 (14)	2 (25)	8 (57)	4 (75)	4 (29)
Sexual Assault	0 (0)	0 (0)	3 (50)	1 (33)	3 (50)	2 (67)

	RELATION TO VICTIM					
	UNKNOWN		CASUAL		CLOSE	
	UNE	MSU	UNE	MSU	UNE	MSU
Physical Assault	2	8	1	8	3	
Sexual Assault	5		1	2	5	1

* Victims may report multiple types of assault.

combination of a male and a female offender in a sexual assault incident was noted in the UNE data.

The relationships of the victim to the offenders when alcohol or illegal drugs were involved varied widely at both universities. For physical assaults at UNE, the largest single category of relationship to offender was "close acquaintance," two of whom were reported to be sexual partners of the victim. Unknown perpetrators were the next most frequent physical assailants. At least two of the perpetrators were other students. At MSU, the relationships between victims and offenders was measured in somewhat different fashion. For physical assaults it was known versus unknown. The relationship between victim and offender was equally split between the two categories. That is, in 50% of the cases the victim knew the offender and in the remaining half they did not.

When the assaults were sexual in nature and alcohol or other illegal substances were involved, the UNE victims were equally divided between unknown assailants and close relationships (one a regular sexual partner

Table 4: Characteristics of Alcohol-Involved Assaults — Places

	PLACE			
	ON-CAMPUS		OFF-CAMPUS	
	UNE	MSU	UNE	MSU
Physical Assault	8	7	8	9
Sexual Assault	11	0	1	3

*Victims may report multiple types of assault

and one casual acquaintance). At UNE the students were also asked to identify whether they knew the assailant to be a member of the faculty or another student. None of the perpetrators were described as faculty members, nor as being other students. The MSU questions were asked in a somewhat similar fashion. Interestingly, all of the three offenders were known to their victims at MSU. Two of the three were casual acquaintances, while the remaining one was a close friend. No measure was made of the "quality" of the close relationship for the MSU survey.

Where the incidents involving alcohol occurred (place) does show a marked difference between the offense categories (see Table 4). At UNE, the students reported that physical assaults involving alcohol or illegal drugs were equally likely to occur on- and off-campus. Sexual assaults were overwhelmingly on-campus events. Of the 12 sexual assault incidents involving alcohol or illegal drugs, 11 occurred in university residence facilities (7 additional sexual assaults on-campus involved no alcohol/illegal drug consumption). All three of the penetrative rapes occurred in the equivalent of dormitories ("colleges"), though two reportedly involved no substances. Just the opposite occurred in the MSU data. All three of the sexual assaults involving alcohol occurred off-campus (and two off-campus sexual assaults involved no alcohol consumption). By contrast, the two additional sexual assaults identified as not involving alcohol consumption by either party occurred in campus dormitories.

Our key findings may be summarized as:

- Alcohol was involved in half (50%) of the reported physical assaults at UNE and three-quarters (75%) of the physical assaults at MSU;
- Alcohol was involved in just over half (57%) of reported sexual assaults at UNE, but in fewer than half (43%) of the sexual assaults at MSU;

- For physical assaults, 75% of reports at UNE involved consumption by both parties, while at MSU over half (58%) of those reporting said only the perpetrator was drinking;
- At both schools, when alcohol consumption was reported, sexual assaults involved alcohol consumption by both perpetrator and victim more often than not.
- At both schools, males were overwhelmingly the offenders when alcohol was involved;
- For physical assaults involving alcohol, the UNE respondents classified the offender as a "close acquaintance" in three-quarters of the incidents, while the MSU respondents were equally split between "known" and "unknown" persons;
- For sexual assaults where alcohol was involved, the UNE victims were equally divided between unknown assailants and close relationships, while the MSU victims all knew their assailant;
- For physical assaults where alcohol was involved, UNE respondents reported they occurred off- and on-campus in equal proportions, while MSU students reported slightly more than half (56%) occurred off-campus; and
- For sexual assaults involving alcohol, UNE students reported they occurred overwhelmingly on-campus (as well as non-alcohol involved sexual assaults), while MSU respondents reported they occurred almost exclusively off-campus (though on-campus events tended not to involve alcohol).

Discussion

Alcohol and Other Risk Factors

Upon returning from the conference where this information was initially presented, the authors were greeted by posters around campus which stated "Friends Don't Let Friends Date Drunk." While this is prudent advice, the results from both universities do not support the notion that alcohol is the primary risk factor in either sexual or physical assaults experienced by these students. As Ted Upton (the former Yeoman Bedell or Security Manager at UNE) liked to say: "The advice your mother gave you about the men you shouldn't date was pretty good." Specifying the advice as risk factors now becomes the issue.

A commonality between the two sets of data is that criminal victimization among university students is relatively rare. Crimes against persons represent very small percentages of the reported victimizations in both settings. This finding, especially with regard to assault-related crimes, is consistent with earlier research regarding experience while enrolled at a university (e.g., Bausell et al., 1991). In the Bausell et al. study, alcohol was strongly associated with assault crimes, especially those which occurred in fraternity/sorority and other off-campus housing settings. Illegal drugs were strongly associated with victimizations again in off-campus settings common to the procurement of such substances. The off-campus settings of many of the criminal victimizations in both countries is also in keeping with earlier research. However, for physical assaults, it appears that location of the crime and the involvement of alcohol are almost equally distributed between on- and off-campus settings. At the UNE, where nearly all of the reported sexual assaults occurred on campus, students were almost as likely to report no alcohol involvement (43%) as alcohol/illegal drug involvement (57%). In the MSU data, alcohol was always reported in off-campus sexual assaults, but not reported to be involved in the on-campus sexual assaults. All of these results are clouded by extremely low number of reports.

At both universities it appears that alcohol consumption by both parties is more strongly associated with an assault event than if only the offender is drinking. Only at MSU was the victim the only person drinking at the time of a physical assault (a similar result was found for robbery events in the UNE sample). However, perhaps contrary to popular thought, no sexual assaults at either university were reported to involve alcohol/illegal drug consumption by the victim alone. We are again left to wonder what role alcohol plays in the genesis of assault events, given that most drinking situations do not apparently result in victimization.

The involvement of alcohol in the crimes reported by the victims is also lower than might be expected from previous correlational research studies. The involvement of alcohol (and illegal drugs) does show a different pattern in the two universities. Physical assaults appear to have more alcohol involvement in the American setting, while alcohol was involved proportionately more often in sexual assaults in the Australian context. In both settings, however, alcohol was not a required component of the victimization event. The manner in which the questions were phrased in both studies did not elicit the amount of alcohol or illegal drugs consumed nor the perceived intoxication level of either victim or offender. This is an area which needs to be addressed in future research efforts. That is, we need to determine whether alcohol is part of a more criminogenic environment generally, or a key contributing factor in the process of the victimization itself.

When the involvement of alcohol/illegal drugs in reported victimization events is analyzed in these two separate educational institutions, the results are quite different from the correlational and sexual experiences research studies. We would argue that the first group are dangerously close to commission of an ecological fallacy. That is, they attempt to generalize from population data to specific events (i.e., offending and victimization) without controlling for whether the alcohol consumption on a university campus is by those who are committing the criminal acts or experiencing the victimizations. In the sexual experiences research tradition, the victimizations often occur prior to the respondents' enrollment in the university. While this is valuable information, it does not address the role of either university responsibility in preventing such victimization or the role that occupying the status of university student plays in the victimization.

It is interesting that the legal availability of alcohol does not appear to significantly affect the levels of victimizations reported to involve the consumption of alcohol (and occasionally, illegal drugs). That is, given two populations of roughly equivalent age, we find similar patterns with regard to the two primary crime categories which are reportedly associated with alcohol consumption in the United States. Alcohol's legal availability appears to have neither an accelerating nor braking effect on the level of assault victimization. Perhaps measures of traffic offenses and related injuries would reveal a different pattern of results, but that is not measured in either study. These findings lead us to question how firm a foundation the association between alcohol consumption and victimization among university students is built.

One seemingly consistent association between alcohol consumption and victimization of university students in the United States has been membership in or association with fraternities/sororities and inter-varsity athletic teams. The results of this comparison raise some important questions regarding the role of such organizations and organizational settings in the genesis of assault behaviors. Part of the philosophical grounding for associating these organizations with assaults relies on the concept of "hyper masculinity," or "masculinity" more generally. It is argued that the emphasis on social stereotypes of masculine and feminine behaviors in these settings increases the likelihood that males will exploit women sexually and that males will assault other males to prove their adherence to masculine norms. Yet we find very similar proportions of students reporting assaultive experiences across two continents in two distinct educational settings which share a common cultural root. One of the differences between the two educational systems is the lack of inter-varsity and Greek social organizations in Australian society. While the "college" system functions somewhere between being simply dormitories on the one hand and fraternity/sorority like housing on the other, it usually exists in a co-educational (on the same floor and utilizing the same facilities) setting rather than one which segregates males from females. This does not deny that norms of masculinity and femininity operate in this environment. Rather, it suggests that the relationship among university experience, alcohol (and to a lesser extent, illegal substance) availability and use, and criminal victimizations (and presumably perpetration) may not be clearcut. Future research in both the United States and Australia should include questions about the broader affiliations which those who occupy the status of university student enjoy, not simply whether they are member of sporting teams or social fraternities/sororities as is most often the case.

The factors which have been shown to be consistently associated with the confluence of alcohol and aggressive violence suggest a line of future research informed by both a routine activities approach (Bora, 1997; Cohen & Felson, 1979; Fox & Hellman, 1985) and a general theory approach (Gottfredson & Hirschi, 1990). Bausell et al. clearly report that victimizations associated with procurement of drugs occur in settings where they might well be expected. Other research reporting over representation of assaultive behaviors in fraternity and athletic residence halls and affiliated parties (e.g., Bausell et al., 1991) also suggest that aspects of the activities commonly associated with those settings need to be examined further. Given that similar rates of victimization are reported in the Australian setting, which does not have these features of campus life, simple notions of hypermasculinity seem weak as an explanation.

Policy Implications for Universities

The results presented here comparing data from two university settings which share a common base culture but different approaches to the consumption of alcohol raise some interesting questions for alcohol-related policy as a factor in violence cessation on university campuses. These questions should be examined in light of a few results. First, criminal victimizations of any type are not the normative experience of students at these two universities. Second, violent victimizations are rare experiences among these students, as well as among students enrolled in Australian and U.S. universities generally. Third, alcohol (and other illegal drugs) do not play either a necessary nor a sufficient role in the explanations of assaultive incidents. That is, alcohol is almost as often not a part of the incident as it is part of the incident. Alcohol does not play "the central facilitating role" attributed to it by writers such as Rivinus and Larimer (1993).

None of these statements should be taken to diminish the central importance of programs to raise students' (or faculty and staff) awareness of the potential dangers associated with alcohol (and other drugs) consumption. Nor should the issue of alcohol involvement in other criminal and anti-social behaviors such as vandalism and verbal abuse be ignored. The MSU students reported that 30% (21 of 69) of those who harassed or bullied them were drinking at the time of the incident.

Apprising students of the potential risk factors associated with the consumption of alcohol, when done in a balanced manner, would seem to be only prudent and an act of citizenship. Portraying alcohol as the ultimate agent of evil, however, will probably cause as many problems as advocates of alcohol control hope to avoid. The responsibility of university policy makers to accurately portray the role of alcohol in the process of criminal victimizations among students should not be taken lightly. There are some areas where care with the research literature needs to be taken.

Consistent with liability issues for universities, a distinction needs to be made between studies which study victimization (generally) and alcohol consumption (specifically) among people who happen to occupy the status of student when the data are gathered and those studies which assess the victimization of students while they are acting as students, either on school grounds or engaged in school-related activities. This latter group of studies should also be examined to determine whether or not the victimization occurred as a result of some activity associated with being a student, compared to victimizations which occurred as a part of the potential life experience of any citizen. For example, the oft-cited works of Koss and associates do not discriminate between the sexual victimization experiences of the respondents *as students* and *prior to university enrollment*. These are important decisions when policy is being made regarding the role of alcohol in campus life. Experiences which have no direct relationship to the student status are not the proper object of university policy. Generalizing from larger population studies, or studies of marital life, is a very shaky basis for addressing university life and student relationships. To talk of "campus crime" or "campus victimization" without restricting our analyses to incidents related to the student status and role during the time they are enrolled in a university seems to be both misleading and disingenuous.

A further distinction needs to be made between empirical studies (either quantitative or qualitative) which explore the relationship between alcohol consumption and campus crimes and theoretical explorations of this relationship. For example, Schwartz and DeKeserdey (1997) further the process of what Altimore (1991) has termed the "social construction of a scientific myth" by concentrating on case studies which support only the theoretical perspective of the authors. There is nothing wrong with case studies, of course. However, Schwartz and DeKeserdey follow the standard procedure of warning readers about the shortcomings of the prior research, and then ignore their own warnings. That is, after the warning, the theory is used to explain what types of findings should be discovered, even though the appropriate research has not been conducted.

Both of these statements betray a philosophical divide among both researchers and practitioners in the area of student life (and university life generally). At the researcher level, we can see a divide between those who adopt a more "grounded" approach, privileging information gathered via systematic research, and those who allow theory to dictate both data collection and interpretation. Among practitioners, especially between faculty and student personnel staff, there is a philosophical divide regarding the role of the university in the personal lives of students (and staff). Much of this divide is around the issue of the intrusiveness of the university into the lives of students beyond the direct campus experience. As with most issues in life, of course, there is no clear-cut divide here, only matters of degree of difference on these issues.

Alcohol appears to be no more and no less involved in criminal assaultive experiences of students at universities on two continents with opposite approaches to consumption of alcohol. Yet, the role of alcohol as a major, if not the central, component of sexual and physical victimizations on U.S. university campuses is almost a statement of fact in the student personnel and journalistic literature. Drawing blanket policies regarding the role of, and subsequent regulation of, alcohol in university life has partly been based on Federal government funding conditions in the United States. It has also been part of the changing composition of university populations during the past three decades and an apparent desire on the part of some university personnel to play a greater role in the lives of people who occupy the status of university student, regardless of the salience of that role to the student.

In sum, the results of victimization surveys at these two universities separated by nearly half the planet show remarkably similar experience with assaultive victimizations among their respective students. The overall numbers of assaults are low. They are almost as likely not to include the consumption of alcohol/illegal drugs as they are to do so. They take place on- and off-campus. Alcohol consumption can be neither ruled in nor ruled out as a causal agent in assault victimizations among these people who occupy the social status of university student. The setting in which victimizations of these sorts occur deserves more detailed attention than we have paid in past research. Whether alcohol is a causal agent in the perpetration or victimization process, or simply an indicator and associate of predictors of low-self control, or the "invariant" effect of age, for example (Gottfredson & Hirschi, 1990), remains an empirical question for the general public as well as for the university environment.

Finally, the continuing role of alcohol as a symbolic target in the control of campus space and students needs to be considered (e.g., Gusfield, 1963). Further, the ambiguous role of adolescence and early adulthood and its use as a period of both danger and promise (Platt, 1977) should also be examined. That is, what role has alcohol consumption played in the attempts by some to return to the doctrine of *in loco parentis* for university students, particularly on-campus residents? These, however, are another research project.

Discussion Questions

In this selection, Potter and Wheeler review a range of studies which examine the putative role of alcohol (and other drugs) on violence in the lives of students. Identify the levels of measurement across the studies and discuss which level provides the "best" information for developing campus violence prevention policies.

Potter and Wheeler argue that the role of alcohol in the victimizations reported in their study are neither necessary nor sufficient to claim alcohol plays a central role in the genesis of violence in the lives of these students. Discuss whether the necessary and sufficient standard is too stringent to apply to an issue such as alcohol and violence on university campuses?

Potter and Wheeler speculate that there is a philosophical divide between sociological/criminological researchers and student services (and some feminist-oriented) writers in the area of violence on university campuses. What might be some of the sources of this disparity? How can any such disparity be overcome in research and policy spheres?

The Potter and Wheeler study points to similarities and disparities in the role of alcohol in violent victimizations of students in two nations. Discuss whether and why the notions of "adulthood" and "adolescence" might be different in two nations sharing similar cultural heritage.

Chapter 7

Campus Crime Victims: Legal, Statutory and Administrative Responses

Max L. Bromley

Introduction

Historically, crime victims have been neglected by the Criminal Justice System and its components. For example, frequently victims are not notified regarding the status of their case or kept informed as to what to expect next (Territo, Halsted, & Bromley, 1998). As a result, they frequently become fearful, anxious and are often less than cooperative during subsequent phases of the criminal justice process. Likewise, victims often feel re-victimized by the police, prosecutors, and the courts when they are treated with little sensitivity.

Fortunately, changes with regard to the treatment of victims of crime have occurred within the last 30 years. These changes have often been initiated by public and private community organizations such as NOVA and MADD, which have been very active in raising public awareness with respect to the rights of crime victims. In addition, several steps have been taken by various levels of government aimed at addressing the needs of crime victims.

Perhaps the first major action affecting crime victims at the federal level of the Criminal Justice System was the passage of the Law Enforcement Assistance Administration Act (LEAA) in the early 1970s. LEAA supported victim assistance programs and ultimately contributed approximately $50 million to victim assistance programs throughout the country (Tomz & McGillis, 1997). Later, in 1982, the President's Task Force on Victims of Crime proposed numerous changes to the way victims were then treated and suggested that government and private groups work collectively to address victim needs throughout the country. One such recommendation led to the passage of the Victims of Crime Act (VOCA) in

93

1984 authorizing millions of dollars for state-level victim assistance programs (Territo et al., 1998).

As a result of various federal initiatives, many states have also enacted victim-related statutes. For example, today 43 states have established victim compensation programs, 49 have passed victims bills of rights, and 22 more states have amended their constitutions to require various services for victims of crime (Tomz & McGillis, 1997).

Most recently, the Congress has recognized that many women who are victims of violence have particular needs not sufficiently addressed by the criminal justice system. This fact is evident in officially documented cases as well as in data derived from victimization surveys. Therefore, in 1994 the United States Congress enacted the Violence Against Women Act that provides funding for efforts on the part of police and prosecutors to improve the delivery of services to women victims.

The last 30 years has seen many diverse efforts aimed at heightening the public awareness of the needs of crime victims and improving services to assist them. The efforts described have been at the general community level. The remainder of this chapter will focus specifically on issues relating to crime victims on college campuses.

A Brief History of Campus Crime and Victimization

Little information regarding campus crime in America before the mid-1900s is available since there was no formal method to document such instances in a systematic fashion. However, some evidence of the campus crime victimization picture is provided in the written histories of various institutions of higher education. While this review is by no means exhaustive, it does provide some basis for a comparison of early college crime and today's campus crime. Several examples of campus crime taken from historical accounts of colleges are as follows.

In Colonial America many students lived on their college campuses. Unfortunately for them these residences closely resembled military barracks in living style, complete with many rigid rules, and strict disciplinary codes. According to Humphrey (1976), even "minor" infractions (some of which would today be considered misdemeanors) were enforced by faculty members.

The enforcement of moral conduct codes was particularly popular at some institutions in the 1800s. Restrictions against having liquor, possessing indecent books, and entertaining company in dorm rooms were strongly enforced on some college campuses (Hollis, 1951; McGrane, 1963). Hollis (1951) notes that strict enforcement policies and military-like living regimes often led to frequent violations on the part of student offenders.

There is some indication of more serious forms of crime victimization on early American college campuses. For example, student vandalism resulted in more than $4,000 in damage to property on the Cornell University campus in 1868 (Bishop, 1962). Four thousand dollars would appear to be a substantial dollar amount given the cost of property at that time. A serious act of interpersonal violence at the University of Georgia was noted by Coulter (1951). In this instance a dorm student attacked a fellow resident with a dagger and had to be removed from the residence.

During the early 1920s, American colleges grew both in size and complexity. Yet, even during this time campus watchmen and college Deans were most concerned with minor student code violations and the protection of property as opposed to crimes of violence (Esposito & Stormer, 1989). More serious forms of disturbances involving students, events often related to alcohol consumption, occurred with greater frequency on campuses during the 1940s and early 1950s (Powell, 1981).

Following World War II the face of American higher education changed dramatically as student enrollment increased substantially. As noted by Smith (1989, p. 10) "As the sizes of institutions grew, and the students came to more closely represent a cross-section of the social and economic classes of the nation, the incidence of campus crime likewise increased." Campus activities during the 1960s and 1970s reflected many of the significant social changes occurring in America during that time. Civil rights and anti-Vietnam War activists often found a supportive atmosphere on the college campus. While much student dissident activity in this era was peaceful in nature, building take-overs, vandalism, arson, and acts of associated violence were not unusual (Powell, Parder, & Nielson, 1994).

While student dissent and its associated crimes had subsided by the mid-1970s, it was during this time that criminal acts on campus including property and violent crimes increased in frequency and severity (Nichols, 1986; Powell, et al., 1994; Sloan, 1992; Smith, 1989). Thus, the victims of serious campus crime began to receive an increasing amount of attention from the media, social scientists, litigators, legislators, campus administrators, and the general public.

Campus Victims: The Media View

There is little question that the media in the 1980s and 1990s have played a significant role in heightening public awareness with regard to campus crime victimization. Serious crimes of violence on campus have been dramatically highlighted by the media in Canada and the United States (Brantingham, Brantingham & Seagrave, 1995; Sloan & Fisher, 1995). Stories of coeds being raped or professors being murdered by irate or mentally deranged students usually makes sensational headlines or lead story lines on the radio and TV daily news. Following acts of extreme violence, universities have been characterized as unsafe places even if the crimes were not committed on campus. For example, a few years ago when a serial murderer took the lives of four women who were university students, the University of Florida was featured in the national media despite the fact that none of the crimes occurred on the campus in Gainesville, Florida.

Within the decade of the '90s, national level media coverage of campus crime had become routine. For example, Castelli (1990) and Matthews (1993) have both written feature articles on the topic for the *New York Times* as did Kalette (1990) for *USA Today*. Ordovensky (1990) wrote a lengthy article on campus crime for *USA Today* entitled "Students Easy Prey On Campus." His article also analyzed the relative safety of over 400 American institutions of higher education.

Perhaps the most widely read and quoted publication in the field of higher education is the *Chronicle of Higher Education*. Not surprisingly, in each of the past six years major stories on campus crime and victimizations have been featured (Lederman, 1993, 1994, 1994b; Lively, 1996, 1997). Data from across the country on campus crime and victimizations are now an annual feature story in the Chronicle.

The Extent of Campus Crime Victimization

Over the course of the last ten years social scientists and campus police officials have attempted to describe the nature and extent of the campus crime problem. Questions such as the following have been investigated: What types of crimes are committed most frequently on campus; what is the nature of serious crimes of violence; how does campus crime compare with community crime; and does the level of community crime effect campus victimization?

One of the major difficulties that must be overcome when attempting to answer these questions is the absence of a complete database with respect to campus crime and victimization. At the present, there is no requirement that campus crime data be forwarded to the FBI for publication in the annual *Uniform Crime Report*. According to Fisher and Sloan (1995), fewer than 25% of this country's colleges report their crime statistics to the FBI.

The *Crime Awareness and Campus Security Act of 1990* (which will be discussed more thoroughly later in this chapter) does require post-secondary institutions to collect and publish data on U.C.R. index crimes, but excludes larceny/theft. In addition, there is no central national repository for this information. The Act is also deficient in that only raw crime numbers are used without population data which limits the utility of the data that is collected (Fisher & Sloan, 1995; Seng, 1995).

The Act did require the Secretary of Education to prepare a report on campus crime statistics for 1992, 1993, and 1994. In January 1997 the report published data received from a sample of over 1,000 post-secondary institutions that participate in Federal Title IV Financial Aid Programs (National Center for Educational Statistics (N.C.E.S.), 1997). The results show that for each of the three years, property crimes far outnumber crimes of violence by a 4 to 1 ratio. Given the fact that larceny, the most frequently reported campus crime (Bromley & Territo,1990; Sigler & Koehler, 1993; Sloan, 1994, 1992; Smith, 1989; UCR, 1997) is not included in the N.C.E.S. data, the true ratio of property to violent victimization is probably even higher than 4 to 1.

A second national report of campus crime statistics was published in 1997 by the International Association of Campus Law Enforcement Administrators (I.A.C.L.E.A., 1997). *The Campus Crime Report 1994–1995* represented responses from 585 (67%) of I.A.C.L.E.A.'s members. This report, unlike the Secretary of Education's publication, included larceny/theft in the database. In this report, larcenies accounted for the vast majority of all on campus crime reported to campus law enforcement officials (I.A.C.L.E.A., 1997). Also, the rates of both reported property crime and violent crime were relatively low (less than 19 per 1,000 and less than 1 per 1,000) respectively). By comparison, FBI statistics for the general community show about 46 per 1,000 property crimes and 7 per 1,000 violent crimes during this same time period (UCR, 1996).

Reaves and Goldberg (1996) found somewhat similar results in a study of 581 campus law enforcement agencies. Their data set of campus index offenses also included larceny/theft. Campuses responding to this survey reported an average of 7 violent crimes and 256 property crimes per year. Approximately 85% of the property crimes reported to the campus police agencies were larceny/thefts (Reaves & Goldberg, 1996).

Other attempts to more adequately describe the extent of campus crime have gone beyond the use of crime data reported to campus police. This would seem to be very important particularly with respect to crimes of violence that are often under reported on college campuses (Cerio, 1989; Roark, 1987). Therefore, it is useful to review some of the findings of campus victimization studies in addition to what is formally reported to the police.

One of the most comprehensive victimization studies to date was conducted by the Towson State University Campus Violence Prevention Center. Their survey of over 1,000 institutions revealed among other things, that most campuses had experienced physical and sexual assault; that about one third had seen an increase in acts of violence; and for the majority of victimizations drugs or alcohol were involved (Bausell, Bausell, & Siegel, 1991; Siegel & Raymond, 1992). The relationship between alcohol or drug use in acts of campus violence has been underscored in other research as well (CASA: 1994; Maloy, 1991; Wechsler, Davenport, Dowdall, Moeykens, & Lastillo, 1994). [Editors' note: However, this relationship is questionable as pointed out in Chapter 6 on this text.]

Numerous studies have also focused on women as victims of violence on campus. Date rape, acquaintance rape, and courtship violence have all been the subject of ongoing research. Koss and her colleagues conducted some of the earliest research in this area that suggested date rape was more widespread then had been previously thought (Koss, Gidycz, & Wisniewski, 1987). These findings have generally been supported by others (Berkowitz, 1992; Cokey, Sherril, Cave, & Chapman; 1988; Ward, Chapman, White, & Williams 1991). Burling (1993) notes that as many as 90% of the perpetrators of campus sexual assaults are acquainted with their victims. Given the prevalence of this form of sexual violence on campus (Gordon & Riger, 1989) and the fact that many crimes of violence against women are not reported (Bachman, 1994), date rape is a very difficult problem for institutions to address.

In addition to date or acquaintance rape, the subject of other forms of courtship violence among students has caught the attention of current researchers. Belknap and Erez (1995) consider this form of violence to be similar to domestic violence in a marital relationship. Recently, Sellers and Bromley (1996) conducted a study of almost 1,000 college students currently involved in dating relationships at a large urban university. Close to 22% of the respondents indicated that they had experienced some form of physical or sexual aggression. While the vast majority of those victimizations were minor forms of violent behavior such as being pushed, grabbed, shoved, or slapped, the findings also show that the use of violence increased with the length of the relationship (Sellers & Bromley, 1996). Belknap and Erez (1995) also reported that students who were cohabitating were most often victimized, a finding that appears to support the assumption that courtship violence is similar to domestic violence.

Legal Actions and Statutory Responses
to Campus Crime

Legal responses to the problem of campus crime victimization have primarily been in two forms: (1) By civil law suits brought against post-secondary institutions for failing to provide adequate security, and (2) by enacting campus crime laws by state legislatures and the Federal government (Bromley, 1993; Fisher & Sloan, 1995). Although the courts have not traditionally involved themselves in policy making or managing the operational functions of post-secondary institutions of higher learning, those days are over (Kaplan, 1990). Recently, there is sufficient evidence to suggest that families of campus crime victims are very willing to bring civil suit against colleges (Bromley, 1993; Bromley & Territo, 1990; Burling, 1991; Fisher & Sloan, 1995; Smith, 1989, 1995).

During the last 25 years, post-secondary institutions have had to defend themselves in civil liability lawsuits brought by the victims of serious crimes. According to Smith (1995) student victims may claim that the institution has failed in one or more duties owed them. Specifically, he notes four types of claimed duties: "A duty to warn about known risks; a duty to provide adequate security protection; a duty to screen other students and employees for dangers; and a duty to control student conduct" (p. 26). In Smith's view, both the courts and the legislatures have been more willing to hold colleges responsible for the first two categories than the latter two.

Holding colleges liable for failing to take adequate steps to protect students is complicated by the "special relationship" theory. Despite the fact that since the 1961 court decision in *Dixon v. Alabama* universities are no longer expected to act in the place of parents ("In Loco Parentis"), there are still important obligations that institutions must assume. According to Burling (1991, p. 2), "a college or university is expected to have an institutional commitment to the welfare and safety of its students. Given this public expectation, most institutions acknowledge their obligation and subsequently exercise care to protect their students by providing appropriate levels of security."

Examples of Civil Lawsuits

Several cases will be briefly described to illustrate typical actions initiated by student victims or their families against colleges. A woman law student was raped in a restroom on the campus of the University of California. In a 1980 ruling on this case, a civil jury awarded the plaintiffs $215,000 in damages for failing to provide adequate security (*Sicilino v. State*). In a similar action a female student was raped and murdered in her on-campus residence (*Duarte v. State of California et al.*). The court found California State University liable partially on the basis of evidence that the university had not revealed to the woman and her family information regarding prior campus crimes.

A 1984 case involving a knife-point rape of a coed in her residence at the State University of New York at Stonybrook further illustrates potential university liability. In *Miller v. New York*, the court found that the institution had failed to provide adequate security based upon the fact that it was standard policy for all campus dorms to be kept unlocked, thus allowing easy access for a rapist to gain entry. Furthermore, the court found that there was some degree of "foreseeability" since other serious crimes in the residence halls had been reported and were well documented. In 1983 a Massachusetts case involving a woman student who had been raped, the courts noted that the college had not fulfilled its obligation to provide adequate security (*Mullins v. Pine Manor College et al.*). The court noted that providing security for students was part of the total package of services students buy. Of particular significance was the finding that the college's Vice President was held to be *personally* liable in his role as supervisor of the security function.

A 1986 lawsuit has provided what may have the greatest impetus for new legislation regarding campus crime and victimization. Following the tragic rape-murder of their daughter Jeanne Clery on the campus of Lehigh University (Pennsylvania), her parents filed a lawsuit against the university for failing to provide adequate security. While the claim was ultimately settled out of court, the family later established an organization called Security on Campus. One of the primary goals of that organization is to push for the enactment of new laws to make information on campus crime and how to prevent it publicly available (Groups Aim Spotlight at Campus Crime, 1990).

Examples of Legislation

To date, over a dozen states and the United States Congress have passed laws dealing with various aspects of campus crime and victimization (Bromley, 1993; Fisher & Sloan, 1995; Griffaton, 1995; Seng, 1995; Tuttle, 1991). While space will not permit review of all such statutes, key segments of several state laws and the federal Crime Awareness and Campus Security Act will be examined. The states will include the following: California, Connecticut, Delaware, Louisiana, Pennsylvania, New York, Washington, Wisconsin, and Florida. The federal law will be discussed after the state laws and elements that may be common to more than one statute will be briefly reviewed. Complete citations for the respective statutes are listed in the reference section for this chapter.

Collection and Distribution of Crime Data

Each of the states identified has a provision in its statute requiring the collection of campus crime data as well as the preparation and distribution of a report containing that information. Some variation was noted, particularly in the distribution of reports. For example, the Connecticut law requires that applicants, students, and employees all be notified in writing about the availability of the report and that a copy be provided upon request. By contrast, the Delaware statute requires that in addition to distributing the report upon request, the campus crime statistics must be published in the campus newspaper or another suitable way. As a third variation, the Louisiana law requires a monthly crime data report to be submitted to the appropriate management board of the institution and be made public at that point. The Florida statute mandates that a report be submitted to the Board of Regents annually which includes the most recent three years of crime data.

Procedures for Victims to Report Crimes and Other Emergencies

The states of Connecticut, Delaware, Louisiana, and Pennsylvania each have provisions in their campus crime laws regarding procedures to be used to report crime victimizations. For example, the Pennsylvania statute calls for a policy that describes "procedures and facilities for students and others to report criminal actions or other emergencies occurring on campus and policies concerning the institution's response to such reports" (Pa. Conn. Stat., 1992, p.450). Both the Delaware (Del. Code Ann., 1993, p. 552) and Louisiana (La. Rev. Stat. Ann. 1993, p. 182) laws require "basic procedures for responding to emergencies or criminal acts and special services for the reporting of emergencies and criminal acts." Connecticut law mandates that "procedures for students, employees, and other persons to report crimes or emergencies occurring on campus..." be established in current security policy for the institutions (Conn. Gen. Stat. Ann., 1993, p. 377).

Services Available to Campus Victims

Several states, including New York, Washington, and Wisconsin, require services to be available for victims of campus crime. The New York statute, which primarily focuses on sex-related offenses, requires a campus committee to annually review security-related policies and procedures including counseling for victims. In Washington, the description of programs regarding counseling, including a directory of services, are required to be part of an overall security report to be given to every student and new employee. Wisconsin requires that every new student receive information regarding the statutory rights of crime victims and the services available at the institution or in the community to assist students who are the victims of sexual assault or sexual harassment. The California law is very comprehensive in its language regarding victim services and mandates that institutional policies state:

> "Services available to victims and personnel responsible for providing those services, such as the person assigned to transport the victim to the hospital, to refer to the counseling center, and to notify the police, with the victims concurrence"(Cal. Educ. Code. Ann. 1994, p. 122).

Also required in the California policy is "a description of campus resources available to victims as well as appropriate off-campus services" (Cal. Educ. Code. Ann. 1994, p. 122).

Policies Regarding Alcohol and Controlled Substances

As mentioned earlier, recent research has documented the correlation between alcohol or controlled substance use and student crime victimization. Therefore, it is not surprising that Connecticut, Pennsylvania, and Washington address the issue in their campus crime statutes. Each statute requires institutions to publish specific policies regarding alcoholic beverages and controlled substances. For example, Washington's law requires information regarding "...policies on controlled substances" be published as a part of their annual security report (Wash. Rev. Code, 1993, p. 474).

The Federal Crime Awareness and Campus Security Act

The most wide-ranging and comprehensive law regarding policies and procedures for the victims of campus crime is the *Federal Crime Awareness and Campus Security Act* passed in 1990 and its subsequent amendment in 1992. The preamble to the law notes the increase in campus crime in general and in crimes of violence in particular. It also states that campus crime data must be shared publicly as well as noting that postsecondary institutions should develop crime prevention measures to enhance campus safety.

The Act has been criticized by some authorities (Burd, 1992; Seng, 1995; Seng & Koehler, 1993). In particular, Seng (1995) suggests that the Act creates a misleading picture of crime on campus by not providing complete information. However, as Sloan and Fisher (1995, p. 4) note, the Act has "partially improved the availability of some campus crime statistics in the United States." Griffaton (1995) suggests that the Act has been successful in increasing the general awareness about campus crime. With the passage of the Act the "wall of silence" around campus crime does seem to be breaking down (Sloan & Fisher, 1995, p. 4).

The Act was significantly amended in 1992. The amendment mandates that institutions establish policies regarding the prevention of sex offenses and stating how such offenses are to be dealt with once reported. Clearly, the intent is to require the establishment of a victim-oriented model for dealing with sex offenses on campus. The following are the specific requirements:

POLICY DEVELOPMENT. Section 485(f) of the Act is amended by adding at the end of the following new paragraph:

"(7) (A) Each institution of higher education participating in any program under this title shall develop and distribute as part of the report described in paragraph (1) a statement of policy regarding

"(i) such institution's campus sexual assault programs, which shall be aimed at prevention of sex offenses; and

"(ii) the procedures followed once a sex offense has occurred.

"(B) The policy described in subparagraph (A) shall address the following areas:

"(i) Education programs to promote the awareness of rape, acquaintance rape, and other sex offenses.

"(ii) possible sanctions to be imposed following the final determination of an on-campus disciplinary procedure regarding rape, acquaintance rape, or other sex offenses, forcible or nonforcible.

"(iii) Procedures students should follow if a sex offense occurs, including who should be contacted, the importance of preserving evidence as may be necessary to the proof of criminal sexual assault, and to whom the alleged offense should be reported.

"(iv) Procedures for on-campus disciplinary action in cases of alleged sexual assault, which shall include a clear statement that-

"(I) the accuser and the accused are entitled to the same opportunities to have others present during a campus disciplinary proceeding; and

"(II) both the accuser and the accused shall be informed of the outcome of any campus disciplinary proceeding brought alleging a sexual assault.

"(v) Informing students of their options to notify proper law enforcement authorities, including on-campus and local police, and the option to be assisted by campus authorities in notifying such authorities, if the student so chooses.

"(vi) Notification of students of existing counseling, mental health or student services for victims of sexual assault, both on campus and in the community.

"(vii) Notification of students of options for, and available assistance in, changing academic and living situations after an alleged sexual assault incident, if so requested by the victim and if such changes are reasonably available.

"(C) Nothing in this paragraph shall be construed to confer a private right of action upon any person to enforce the provisions of this paragraph."

Administrative Responses to Campus Crime Victimization

Perhaps the most critical step to be made in dealing with crime and specifically with sex offenses and other serious acts of violence is recognition by campus administrations that these events really do occur (Belknap & Erez, 1995; Benson, Charlton & Coodhart, 1992; Roark, 1987). To some extent such acknowledgment has been evolving over the last ten years at both the national and state levels. For example, administrative organizations such as the Association of Independent Colleges and Universities in the state of Massachusetts, the American Council on Education, the National Association of State and University Land Grant Colleges, the National Association of Student Personnel Administrators, the National Association of College and University Business Officers, and the International Association of Campus Law Enforcement Administrators have each established guidelines for campuses to follow regarding campus crime and victimization (Bromley, 1995).

The need for victim assistance programs on campuses has been supported by a variety of sources in the campus crime literature. For example, Smith (1989) notes that in developing programs to deal with the crime of rape and its victims, responsibility should be shared campuswide and not assumed only by campus police. Tomz and McGillis (1997) state that colleges have become increasingly involved in providing services to student crime victims and note that this has sometimes been accomplished in conjunction with local community victim assistance programs. The victims of certain crimes such as sexual assault, domestic violence, and hate crimes may have special needs that can best be addressed by victim assistance resources (Belknap & Erez, 1995; Powell et al., 1994

Smith, 1989). Cerio (1989, p. 62) notes that victim service providers should also take into consideration the special needs of non-traditional campus community members such as "gays, lesbians, religious minorities, and the handicapped."

There is some evidence that post-secondary institutions have made advances acknowledging the needs of victims of crime and establishing ways to provide services to them. The United States Department of Justice recently published a monograph highlighting universities cited as examples of "promising practices" in providing total campus security services. Victim assistance programs were among the important services noted at the University of Pennsylvania, Penn State University, University of North Carolina, and the University of Delaware. These programs were mentioned as positive examples now found within the campus setting (Kirkland & Siegel, 1994). In each of these programs, the services were found to be efficiently organized in order to provide easy access for victims (Kirkland & Siegel, 1994). This is obviously a critical component in the potential recovery of the victim as it assists them in dealing with the administrative processes required by the criminal justice system. Two recently published nation-wide surveys of institutions of higher education also report the efforts by campuses to assist crime victims. A report by the National Center for Education Statistics found that 72% of the colleges and universities surveyed "instituted or improved in the last five years victim assistance programs" (NCES, 1997: p. 34). Also in their survey of campus police agencies, Reaves and Goldberg (1996) reported that in over half of the agencies serving populations of 25,000 students or more victim assistance units or programs were available.

Finally, in addition to developing programs to assist persons who have been crime victims, campus administrators must also play an active role in preventing victimizations. Several steps are recommended [1] to administrators to help make their institutions safer communities. First, campuses should require that campus police systematically review criminal activity reports from on-campus as well as those in locations near the campus for at least the prior two years. If a pattern has developed indicating that violent crimes such as rape, assault, robbery, or lewd and lascivious conduct are occurring on or near campus, police should take immediate corrective actions. Even if no pattern is evident, campus community members should be kept informed about the time and location of serious crimes

---

1. Some of this section of the chapter is adapted from an article written by the author appearing in *Violence Against Women News*. Washington, DC: U.S. Department of Justice, January, 1997.

and of procedures teaching how not to become a victim. Second, campus victimization surveys should be periodically conducted in order to determine the number and location of crimes that have not been officially reported, as well as to measure the perception of safety on the part of campus community members. Third, it is important that workshops provide students with information as to how to establish healthy non-violent relationships. Discussing sexual behavior, outlining legal consequences for assaultive behavior, and identifying resources for victims should be topics included in these workshops. Workshops should be conducted on violence prevention, stalking, threats, assaults, domestic violence, and protective court orders. Fourth, the development of self-defense courses for women has been found to be a valuable adjunct to other crime control programs on many campuses. Such a course should be comprehensive in nature and would include awareness, prevention, risk reduction and avoidance, and a hands-on component for all participants. Fifth, as noted earlier, victim assistance programs should be developed on campuses. Available services should include crisis intervention, referrals to various community services, help with criminal and student disciplinary proceedings, assistance with professors and other academic issues, help in locating safe housing, and assistance concerning parents and friends of the victim. Finally, a comprehensive plan for responding to serious crimes should be developed by the institution. Key elements of such a plan should include identifying the specific responsibilities for campus police, student affairs officials, counseling, personnel, and student health officials. The plan should also include a mechanism for communicating with the campus community when a serious crime does occur in order to insure the accuracy of information being circulated.

Conclusion

As institutions of higher education approach the 21st century they will face many challenges. Certainly one of those will be how to deal with campus crime and subsequent victimization. It is quite clear that campuses are no longer free from many of the crime problems facing the communities that surround them. However, the courts, various legislatures, the U.S. Congress, and many of the major organizations associated with post-secondary education have tried to respond by developing guidelines and mandates for action. Campus policymakers must now assume a leadership role and initiate policies and procedures not only to provide services for crime victims, but to also address in a comprehensive fashion ways to reduce campus victimization, based on the nature and extent of their own unique campus crime problems.

Discussion Questions

Briefly discuss the results of the campus crime studies published by the National Center for Educational Statistics (1997), International Association of Campus Law Enforcement Administrators (1997), and Reaves and Goldberg (1996).

List the four types of claimed duties that Smith (1995) says victims of campus crimes may use to bring suits against colleges and universities.

Discuss the importance of the Federal Crime Awareness and Campus Security Act of 1990 and its subsequent 1992 amendment.

Based upon the information provided in this chapter, identify for your institution's President key issues relating to campus crime and steps that need to be taken to assist victims of campus crime.

Part III

Victim Services
and
Representation

Chapter 8

Evaluating Victim Services: A Comparative Analysis of North Carolina and Virginia Victim Witness Assistance Programs

Laura J. Moriarty
Robert A. Jerin
William V. Pelfrey

Introduction

In 1977, the first national study of victim witness assistance programs was conducted by Rosenblum and Blew (1979). Seventy-one such programs throughout the United States were assessed. The key elements of the programs were presented in tabular form and included agency affiliation, financial support, staff size, intended beneficiary, and number of services offered. The authors examined four programs in depth to determine what services were provided to victims. There were eight different types of services found in the four programs reviewed: victim contact, counseling and social services, sensitive crimes prosecution, mediation, restitution, compensation, property return and repair, and involvement in the adjudicatory process. Victim services, per se, included logistical services and facility improvement, witness information, witness notification and management, and witness protection (Rosenblaum & Blew, 1979).

Four years later, Cronin and Bourque (1981) conducted the next national study. Their methodology consisted of first "identifying the potential universe of (victim witness assistance) projects" (Cronin & Bourque, 1981, Appendix A). They did this by consulting with representatives from a variety of national organizations, examining recent publications and directories, and by reviewing LEAA block and discretionary grant awards. They also conducted a postcard survey of 1,799 people including: "heads of criminal justice state planning agencies, regional planning units, and coordinating councils; members of NOVA; all prosecutors and police chiefs in smaller jurisdictions" (Cronin & Bourque, 1981, Appendix A). This detailed procedure resulted in a list of over 400 victim witness assistance projects.

Next the researchers obtained "brief descriptions of these projects from library materials, from state planning agencies, and from the projects themselves" (Cronin & Bourque, 1981, Appendix A). Reviewing the documents and calling the projects resulted in the elimination of projects that were "duplicates, defunct, non-existent, or outside [their] working definition of [the] victim witness assistance effort" (Cronin & Bourque, 1981, Appendix A). This process reduced the initial pool from 480 to 256 projects.

These 256 projects were the sampling frame from which the authors selected a purposive sample. Criteria for site selection included: "client volume, age of project (at least one year old), project size, type of sponsoring agency, nature of service delivery, availability of data, and receptivity to a site visit" (Cronin & Bourque, 19981, Appendix A).

Twenty sites were selected using the criteria listed above. Two and three day site visits were conducted at all twenty locations. Unstructured interviews were conducted with the project director and other key staff personnel, the head of the host agency, the police chief, and the prosecuting attorney or representative of these officials. Agency records were also examined during the site visits.

In addition to the site visits, a mail survey was administered. The main goal of the survey was to collect "descriptive information about each project's service components, population, funding history, and staffing pattern" to augment the information collected from the site visits (Cronin & Bourque, 1981, Appendix A). The mail survey was sent to 318 project sites. The researchers received 237 responses for a return rate of 75%.

Their results revealed two main models of victim witness assistance projects plus a third hybrid. Type I is the victim model, Type II is the witness model, and Type III is a combination of the two victim witness models.

The next national study was conducted by Finn and Lee in 1987 (Finn & Lee, 1987). They conducted their research to determine how best to serve crime victims and witnesses. Their research methodology consisted of reviewing the victim witness program literature to identify the major issues in establishing and operating victim witness programs. They also "sampled the literature on criminal victimization and on providing crisis intervention to victims of traumatic experiences" (Finn & Lee, 1987, Preface).

Next, they conferred with a group of experts to learn what services (at a minimum) should be provided to victims and witnesses. These experts formed an advisory board whose members had experience in "providing victim witness services, establishing and directing victim witness programs, and conducting research on program operations" (Finn & Lee, 1987, Preface).

The authors conducted preliminary research by interviewing 25 program directors and visiting six site locations. To be included in the study, the programs had to "serve victims, provide a wide range of services, have some documentation (e.g., procedural manuals, training materials), have achieved permanence, and have no special features that would make replication difficult" (Finn & Lee, 1987, Preface). In addition, programs selected needed to reflect "geographic diversity and varied sponsorship, staff size, client volume, and funding levels" (Finn & Lee, 1987, Preface). Lastly, the authors wanted programs that "use volunteers, collaborate with the criminal justice system, and provide formal staff training" (Finn & Lee, 1987, Preface).

Out of 200 programs identified in the National District Attorneys Association Directory of Victim Witness Assistance Programs, from the work of Cronin and Bourque, and reviews of project abstracts, 54 programs were identified for possible inclusion in their study. The programs were examined closely and the researchers consulted with their advisory board and experts in the field, ultimately selecting 25 sites for inclusion.

The purpose of their research was to obtain a national picture of victim witness assistance programs. The significant contribution of their research is the comprehensive listing of services provided by these victim witness assistance programs. This research was updated in 1994 (Tomz & McGillis, 1997). The 25 programs were interviewed again finding program variation still existed (See Tomz & McGillis, 1997, Figure 2.1).

The American Association of Retired Persons (AARP) conducted a national survey of 30 U.S. state legislatures regarding treatment and services provided to elderly victims of crime. The study found support for increased services for elderly crime victims expanding current services and implementing victim compensation structures (AARP, 1989).

Roberts (1990) conducted a national survey of 184 victim witness assistance programs in 1985 to find out the organizational structure and functions of such programs. Roberts' methodology consisted of identifying 312 victim witness assistance programs by cross-indexing OVC (Office for Victims of Crime) and NOVA (National Organization of Victim Assistance) membership listings. Roberts sent a detailed four-page questionnaire to the 312 programs identified from the process described above. After adjusting the sample size for bad addresses, the total number of programs included was 305. Roberts received 184 fully completed surveys, resulting in a 60% return rate. The most significant contribution of Roberts' research is his determination of the best features of the programs and the biggest problem areas.

Finally, Sarnoff (1994) conducted a national study to determine the extent to which selected characteristics of state crime victim compensation programs affect the rates at which victims are compensated. He examined the following variables: resources, auspices, philosophies, claims procedures, benefits, and eligibility factors. Overall, Sarnoff found that crime victim compensation programs varied in relationship to their geographical locations and the periods of initiation. He developed systems models based on the data collected and offered recommendations for improving the programs.

State-wide victim witness assistance programs research has been limited (Brown, 1983; Jerin, Moriarty, & Gibson, 1995; Wisconsin Legislative Audit Bureau, 1987) in sheer number of evaluations and the variables assessed. For example, Brown (1983) identified nine victim witness assistance programs in Virginia. He described the programs in terms of geographical location, where the programs are housed (i.e., commonwealth attorney's office), funding, and types of services provided.

Another study conducted in Wisconsin reviewed victim witness assistance programs from a cost- benefit analysis (Wisconsin Legislative Audit Bureau, 1987). The Bureau found that counties provided services to victims to help the prosecution of legal cases. These programs are voluntary and the state had reimbursed up to 90% of the costs associated with the programs. The Bureau concluded that the programs are not operating uniformly because, at that time, the Department of Justice had not issued any administrative rules to govern the programs.

Another study conducted in North Carolina profiled victim witness service delivery (Jerin et al., 1995). These researchers developed an interview schedule based on the work of Finn and Lee (1987) and Roberts (1990). The interview schedule examined the six major service categories identified by Finn and Lee including emergency services, counseling, advocacy and support services, claims assistance, court-related services, and system-wide services. In addition, questions were asked about the needs of the programs, the set-up of the programs, the number and type of personnel involved, and the educational and practical experience of the advocates (Jerin et al., 1995). The interview schedule was administered over the phone to all victim advocates in North Carolina. A total of 62 advocates were interviewed. The most significant contribution of their research is the discovery that service delivery is hindered unless the victim becomes part of the system. In other words, most of the service delivery is being provided to victims who have already found their way into the criminal justice system. Service delivery is the weakest at the first stage of victimization, that is, immediately following the crime.

Other studies, not on a national level, have focused on funding concerns of victims and witness assistance programs (see Anderson &

Woodard, 1985; Cullen, 1991; Curriden, 1990; Herrington, 1985; Rosenblum & Blew, 1979). These authors conclude funding is scarce in such programs and this lack of funding often threatens the very existence of the program.

In conclusion, the literature provided above can be summarized as follows: since their inception, evaluation of victim witness assistance programs have been rare. One reason cited by Weigend (1979) is that victim witness assistance programs often do not have clear cut goals on which to evaluate such programs. When evaluations are conducted, they are often completed on the state level and involve assessing the number of clients served and a list of services provided (Legislative Research Commission, 1993). Often the research is descriptive with little attempt at explaining why certain services should be continued or discarded. Researchers tend to describe the organizational structure and functions of the assistance programs without much emphasis on the programs meeting the states' goals and objectives for the programs.

The purpose of this chapter is to conduct an evaluation of two states' victim witness assistance programs. We compare North Carolina and Virginia in terms of (1) an overview of each program including a descriptive analysis of each states' programs and service providers; (2) a listing of the services provided by each state; and (3) an evaluation of the program compared to each other and compared to what the literature and experts agree are the most critical victim witness services.

It is important to note that the national studies cited above did not include North Carolina in their assessments and when Virginia was included only two victim witness programs were reviewed. As a result, the need for descriptive data regarding both states' victim witness assistance programs is essential. Before an evaluation of the services can be conducted, the reasons for selecting the two states must be presented.

North Carolina and Virginia, two contiguous east-coast states, are remarkably similar in some characteristics and different in others. In 1994, North Carolina was ranked tenth in population amongst all the states and Virginia was ranked twelfth. In terms of population density, North Carolina had 140.5 persons per square mile and Virginia had 161 citizens per square mile. The two states had virtually the same percentages of citizens in the racial categories of white (77%) and non-white (23%). The SAT scores for graduating high school seniors in the two states were similar with North Carolina's slightly lower (405 verbal/455 quantitative) than Virginia's (424 verbal/469 quantitative). The unemployment rates were identical (5%). Per capita income showed some differences with North Carolina's average being $17,488 and Virginia's at $21,634. The employment distribution for the states also reflected differences with 26% of North Carolinians employed in manufacturing and Virginia had the same percentage employed in "service" industries. Generally, however, the two states were similar demographically.

Both North Carolina and Virginia have General Assemblies with a Senate and House of Representatives. In both states, the General Assemblies had a majority of members affiliated with Democrats. Virginia's had a higher percentage of Republican representatives (42%) than North Carolina (31%) and Virginia had a Republican Governor while North Carolina's Governor was a Democrat. An additional similarity which could be meaningful in the comparisons of victim services is the fact that both states' primary victim assistance contracts and funding agencies were located in the State Administering Agency for each state.

Generally, Virginia had a lower crime rate for serious crimes in 1994 than did North Carolina, according to the Uniformed Crime Report (FBI, 1995). North Carolina had a murder rate of 10.9 per 100,000 in 1994 while Virginia's murder rate was 8.7 per 100,000. For the crime of rape, the two states had similar rates with North Carolina's rate 33 per 100,000 and Virginia's 28.5 per 100,000. Robbery rates showed variance with North Carolina having a robbery rate of 181 per 100,000 and Virginia having a rate of 132 per 100,000. Larceny rates in the two states were very similar for 1994. The two crimes which varied the greatest were aggravated assault and burglary. North Carolina had an aggravated assault rate of 429 per 100,000 population in 1994 while Virginia's was only 188 per 100,000. Burglary rates in North Carolina were 1,472 per 100,000 in 1994 yet there were only 638 per 100,000 population in Virginia. As assessment of metropolitan crime rates in the two states showed patterns consistent with the state-wide data presented above. Additionally, as assessment of 1990 crime data showed that the trends in the two states were consistent with each other and that there had been no remarkable differences in increases or decreases in crime rates over time. The crime rates had fluctuated in concert, further suggesting that these two states are comparable.

The similarities between the two states make them likely candidates for comparisons of services. The differences between the two states, particularly the crime rates, may enhance the comparability by establishing expected directions and degrees of differences in the proportion of services for various categories of victim services.

Methodology

A telephone survey using an interview schedule replicating the work of Finn and Lee (1987) was conducted in North Carolina in the Fall, 1993 and in Virginia in the Spring, 1994. The interview schedule was designed from Table 1 of their study which provided a list of services that experts agreed should be part of the victim witness program. Finn and Lee (1987, p.16) identified six major services including emergency services, counseling, advocacy and support services, claims assistance, court-related services, and system-wide services. The experts also identified the specific services include in each area (see Figure 1). All the services were included on the present interview schedule. In addition, questions were asked pertaining to the needs of the program, the set-up of the program, the number and type of personnel involved, and the educational and practical experience of the advocates.

Overview of the Programs

On October 1, 1986 North Carolina enacted the *Fair Treatment for Victims and Witnesses Act* (see G.S. 15A-824 et.seq.). The Act defined the standards of fair treatment for victims and witnesses in the criminal justice system, and enumerated victims' rights including services to be provided to all victims. At the same time, the position of victim/witness assistant was established in each District Attorney's office (see G.S. 7A-347 and 7A-348) to coordinate and manage the delivery of the enumerated

---

Figure 1
Specific Victim Services For Each Cognate

EMERGENCY SERVICES

    Medical Care
    Shelter
    Security Repair
    Direct Financial Assistance

COUNSELING

    24 hour hot-line
    Crisis Intervention
    Follow-up Counseling
    Mediation

ADVOCACY AND SUPPORT SERVICES

    Personal Advocacy
    Employer Intervention
    Landlord Intervention
    Property Return
    Intimidation Protection
    Paralegal/Legal Counsel
    Referral

COURT-RELATED SERVICES

    Witness Reception Area
    Court Orientation — Adult
    Court Orientation — Child
    Notification
    Witness Alert
    Transportation
    Child Care
    Escort to Court
    Victim Impact Statement

CLAIMS ASSISTANCE

    Insurance Claims Aid
    Restitution Assistance
    Compensation Assistance

SYSTEM-WIDE SERVICES

    Public Education
    Legislative Advocacy
    Training

services. [For a detailed explanation of the services provided and the role of the advocate under North Carolina law see Jerin et al., 1995.]

Virginia's victim witness programs got their initial start in 1976 with funding from the Law Enforcement Assistance Administration (LEAA). The first program was prosecution-based and started in the Portsmith Commonwealth Attorney's Office. Today there are 31 judicial districts or circuits in Virginia and all but one has at least one victim witness program. Judicial district 30, representing the most rural and western part of the state, does not have any victim witness programs. No matter where the victim witness program is housed, the Commonwealth Attorneys are the central advising component concerning victim services. As a result, even those programs that are housed in police departments are conceptualized as prosecution-based programs.

There were 64 victim witness advocate programs in North Carolina at the time of this study and 52 in Virginia. Two programs in North Carolina were without a victims' advocate, and as a result, no information was collected because no one in the District Attorneys' offices could complete the interview schedule. In Virginia, 50 program coordinators were interviewed. The Department of Criminal Justice Services provided a list of all the victim programs in Virginia but one program was listed twice and another program did not have a coordinator or advocate. Consequently, 50 programs, not 52, were included in the research.

Description of the Programs

All North Carolina victim witness programs are part of the District Attorneys' office (as mandated by statute) from where they receive their funding. Not surprising, the majority of the victims' advocates feel that they are not independent of this office; however, two felt somewhat independent. Volunteers and interns are not part of most programs (71%) but a small percent (29%) did have one volunteer or intern in the program.

Many needs including more space, computers, office equipment, more training, additional personnel and support staff, and financial needs were listed by the advocates. The advocates were asked to list as many needs as they deemed critical. The following is the rank response of the needs as determined by the percentage of advocates indicating such a need: (1) support staff or increase in personnel (61%), (2) equipment, especially computers (29%), (3) more space (23%), (4) financial needs (8%), (5) training (3%).

In Virginia, seventy-two percent of the programs are part of the Commonwealth Attorneys' office. Half the programs have other support personnel besides the victims' advocate. The number of support staff ranges from 1 to 10 with the average number being 2 support staff personnel.

The program with ten support staff members operated out of a police department and the victim's advocate considered all the police department officers as support staff. Since this doesn't fit the typical definition of support staff, the number ten was excluded before the mean was calculated. More than three-quarters (76%) of the programs had volunteers working in the agency. The number of volunteers ranged from 1 to 10 with an average of two volunteers per program.

Description of Advocates

In North Carolina, most of the advocates are educated beyond high school; however, less than one half (40%) are college graduates. The average number of years of current work experience is four with the range being less than one year to eight plus years. Less than one half (49%) indicate any special training in victimology before employment. Surprisingly, more than one half (55%) do not belong to any victims' organizations; however, more than one third (37%) hold membership in the North Carolina Victims' Assistance Network (NCVAN) and a very small percentage are members of the National Organization of Victims Assistance (NOVA). More than one half (55%) said their previous job was unrelated to their present job with 45.2% indicating their previous job was related to the court process—e.g., administrative assistant/secretary to the District Attorney, legal assistant, etc., with very few having direct prior experience with victim services.

More than one-quarter (28%) of the Virginia advocates have been employed in their current position two years or less. The average amount of time in their current position was 4.1 years. The majority (88%) indicated they worked previously in some field unrelated to victims' advocacy. More than one half indicated their exact job title was "director" of the program and almost one-quarter stated "program coordinator" was their title. The advocates are well educated with 20% having some college credit, 58% college graduates, and 16% receiving a graduate degree. About six percent had only a high school education. The majority (84%) indicated they are members of the *Virginia Network for Victims and Witnesses of Crime, Inc.* with 40% holding membership in NOVA as well.

The advocates were asked to indicate what items they needed to perform their jobs more efficiently and effectively. The most frequently observed category reflected a need for more staff (49%). Others indicated funding (36%), computers/equipment (9%), training (4%), and more space (2%). Respondents were allowed multiple responses.

The advocates majored in many different disciplines while in college. The range includes sociology, social work, American studies, government, psychology, education, human resource management, political science, criminal justice, communications, anthropology and women studies, business, and mental health. The most frequently observed categories are criminal justice and sociology. Criminal justice is the most often cited major for graduate work as well.

Advocates were asked about special training provided before starting their present job. Sixty eight percent indicated training is provided before starting the job. When asked to indicated what kind of advocate training was provided – about three quarters said the training was provided by the Department of Criminal Justice Services.

Summation of Services Available

The services provided by the victim witness assistance programs in North Carolina and Virginia are compiled in Table 1. Examining North Carolina first, it was found that no programs provide medical care, shelter, security repair, or paralegal/legal counsel. However, all the participating programs do provide referral, restitution assistance, witness alert, and assistance with victim impact statements. Compensation, witness fee assistance, notification, property return, and court orientation for children are services provided by over 90% of the programs. Employer intervention, escorts to court, intimidation protection, and personal advocacy are offered by over 80% of the programs. Court orientation for adults is provided by 77% of the programs. Almost 73% of the programs provide transportation. More than half (52%) provide a witness reception area; however, often this area is the advocate's office and not some separate waiting area. The remaining services are provided by less than one half of the programs (see Table 1).

In Virginia, every program provides court orientation for adults and children, and escorts to court. In all but one program, notification and referrals are services provided. In all but two programs, employer intervention and compensation assistance is provided.

At least 90% of the programs provide personal advocacy, crisis intervention, assistance with victim impact statements, and public education. Restitution assistance, witness reception, training, landlord intervention, and property return are services provided by at least 80% of the programs. On-scene comfort, follow-up counseling, transportation, childcare, and witness alert is provided by at least 70% of the programs. Witness fee assistance, intimidation protection, and legislative advocacy are services provided by at least 60% of the programs. The other services including insurance claims aid, mediation, security repair, 24 hour hotline, paralegal/legal counsel, shelter, direct financial assistance, and medical care are provided by less than 40% of the Virginia programs.

Table 1
Rank Order of Services Provided by State

NORTH CAROLINA	VIRGINIA
Referral (100%)	Court orientation – children (100%)
Restitution assistance (100%)	Court orientation – adult (100%)
Witness alert (100%)	Escort to court (100%)
Victim impact statements (100%)	Notification (98%)
Compensation assistance (98 %)	Referral (98%)
Witness fee assistance (98%)	Employer intervention (96%)
Notification (97%)	Compensation assistance (96%)
Court orientation – children (92%)	Personal advocacy (94%)
Property return (92%)	Crisis intervention (92%)
Employer intervention (87%)	Victim impact statement (92%)
Escort to court (82%)	Public education (90%)
Personal advocacy (81%)	Restitution assistance (88%)
Intimidation protection (81%)	Witness reception area (86%)
Court orientation – adult (77%)	Training (84%)
Transportation (73%)	Landlord intervention (80%)
Witness reception area (52%)	Property return (80%)
Public education (45%)	On-scene comfort (76%)
Landlord intervention (40%)	Follow-up counseling (76%)
Child care (27%)	Transportation (74%)
Legislative advocacy (24%)	Child care (74%)
Follow-up counseling (24%)	Witness alert (72%)
Training (23%)	Witness fee assistance (68%)
Mediation (23%)	Intimidation protection (66%)
Crisis intervention (15%)	Legislative advocacy (60%)
Insurance claims aid (11%)	Insurance claims aid (38%)
On-scene comfort (5%)	Mediation (34%)
Direct financial assistance (2%)	Security repair (34%)
24 hour hotline (2%)	24 hour hotline (28%)
Medical care (0)	Paralegal/legal counsel (24%)
Shelter (0)	Shelter (20%)
Security repair (0)	Direct financial assistance (18%)
Paralegal/legal counsel (0)	Medical care (4%)

Analysis

What can be said about the North Carolina and Virginia victim witness assistance programs meeting the needs of victims? The criteria used to evaluate states' victim witness assistance programs comes from the work of Finn and Lee (1987). Using what experts believe are the most important victim witness services as determined by Finn and Lee by examining the number of studies concluding the service is essential or of major importance (see Figure 2), an overall assessment of the services provided by both states can be determined. Figure 2 ranks the services possible in terms of the number of studies that indicated such a service was paramount. For example, four studies were reviewed; all four indicated crisis

Figure 2
Expert Estimation of Most Important Victim Witness Services

Service	Number of Studies Concluding Service is Essential or of Major Importance
Crisis intervention	4
Follow-up counseling	4
Intimidation protection	3
Financial assistance	2
On-scene comfort	2
Referral	2
Restitution assistance	2
Court orientation	2
Notification	2
Witness alert	2
Security repair	1
Personal advocacy	1
Landlord intervention	1
Legal/paralegal counsel	1
Insurance claims aid	1
Compensation assistance	1
Transportation	1
Escort to court	1
Medical care	0
Shelter/food	0
24 hour hotline	0
Mediation	0
Employer intervention	0
Property return	0
Witness fee assistance	0
Witness reception	0
Child care	0

intervention and follow-up counseling were essential services to be provided by victim witness programs. Finn and Lee do admonish that this ranking is somewhat limited because the researchers often asked the questions in different ways and some responses come from the program staff while others come from the victims themselves. Consequently, the comparability among the studies themselves is limited; however, this figure represents the best attempt to determine criteria for evaluating services provided by victim witness assistance programs.

Noting that crisis intervention and follow-up counseling were ranked number 1 by the experts in the cited research, North Carolina falls short in providing these services with only 15% providing crisis intervention and 24% providing follow-up. In contrast, Virginia is much better with 92% providing crisis intervention and 76% providing follow-up counseling. Intimidation protection, ranked third in importance, is provided by more North Carolina programs (81%) than Virginia programs (66%).

The other services ranked by the research seem to be evenly distributed among both states, with the exception of on-scene comfort. Less than five percent of the North Carolina programs provide this service while 76% of the Virginia programs perform this service. The other services including referral, court orientation, notification, witness alert, and restitution assistance are provided by at least 92% of the North Carolina programs and at least 72% of the Virginia programs. Direct financial assistance is provided by only about two percent of the North Carolina programs compared to 18% of the Virginia programs.

Assistance with victim impact statements, not on the list of services considered to be paramount, is provided by 100% of the North Carolina programs and 92% of the Virginia programs.

Conclusion

Each state can be described in terms of services provided. North Carolina is best described as a witness-oriented program (Cronin & Bourque, 1981; Karmen, 1990). The focus of this kind of program is to ensure witnesses attend court proceedings and cooperate. The main beneficiaries of these programs are prosecutors. This is especially true in North Carolina since victims in most cases are not served unless an indictment is returned on their offender by a grand jury. What this means is that most victims of serious misdemeanors, and felonies where a suspect is not apprehended, are never served by the North Carolina victim witness program. In addition, crime victims whose cases are plea bargained may only receive minimal service. The intent of the North Carolina law, to assist crime victims, has not been met and those who are served do not receive any attention from these programs until well after the victimization has occurred.

Examining the crime rates, one would expect a state like North Carolina with high assault and rape rates to certainly provide on-scene comfort to these victims. At the very least, advocates can be contacted if a victim goes to the hospital to provide comfort. However, this does not appear to be the case.

Virginia's programs seem to be the antithesis of North Carolina in many ways. The programs in Virginia are best described as victim oriented (Cronin & Bourque, 1981; Karmen, 1990). A victim oriented program seeks to provide services to the victim immediately after the crime occurs. Virginia is there with crisis intervention and on-scene comfort.

Some reasons may exist for why North Carolina does not provide on-scene comfort or crisis intervention. First, without any notification of the crime, it is difficult for the advocates to provide *any* services. If a person refuses medical attention, and does not go to the hospital or clinic, the advocates may never be aware of the victimization. Second, there may be other agencies that provide on-scene comfort or crisis intervention. For example, there may be rape/assault trauma nurses who provide on-scene comfort and crisis intervention. Third, the advocates in general, are not trained to offer such services. One would expect more emphasis on counseling and social service, evidenced by degrees in social work or psychology; however, the North Carolina advocates are in their current positions more because of prior work experience, i.e., working in the District Attorney's office rather than prior victim experience, that is, working directly with victims or being trained or educated on the subject.

While the Virginia advocates indicate they provide on-scene comfort and crisis intervention, no further questions were asked to detail these services. Further research must be conducted to determine what type of on-scene comfort and crisis intervention is available, how often such services are provided, and how crime victims rate such services: Are they satisfied? Do they need additional services? Research on victim/witness assistance programs must continue however the focus must now shift to the victims served and their opinions regarding the services provided rather than only examining sprogram attributes.

Discussion Questions

Considering the findings of the current research, what, if anything, should be done to ensure that the victim services identified by the experts are being provided to victims?

Do you see any relationship between the services provided (or not provided) and the characteristics of the advocates? How can this be improved?

What problems can you identify with relying on experts to tell us what victims need? How would you go about finding out what victims themselves identify as needs?

What impact does the victims' advocate have on the services delivered?

Chapter 9

Victims' Satisfaction with Prosecutors and Victim Advocates: A Case Study

Richard Tewksbury
Darin K. Moore
Nicholas N. King

Introduction

The criminal justice system has long been under intense scrutiny. Whether it be victims, or simply public, views of various components of the criminal justice system, criminal justice officials are often forced to listen to what society thinks. Despite this, political campaigns to "get tough on crime" and the concepts of restorative justice have displayed the criminal justice system's attempt to respond. Nonetheless, as long as others are responsible for "the business of strangers to be handled mainly as they see fit" (Kelly, 1984, p. 15), it is likely that the public will continue to voice discontent. Thus, it is important to learn specifically what aspects of the criminal justice system attracts the most dissatisfaction, so that further changes can be made to better accommodate victims of crime in their time of need.

To begin, social science research has generally focused mostly on public and victims' perceptions of the police. For example, persons identifying with a conservative ideology have been found to be extremely supportive of both police in general, as well as their local law enforcement agencies (Zamble & Annesley, 1987). Specifically, racial minorities and urban lower-class citizens hold the most negative attitudes toward police personnel, while residents of rural communities and members of the urban middle class express the most positive perceptions of the police (Albrecht & Green, 1977). Overall, factors such as race (Erez, 1984; Hadar & Snortum, 1975; Jacob, 1971), age (Belson, 1975; Courtis, 1970; Smith, as cited in Zamble & Annesley, 1987; Walker, Richardson, Williams,

Denyer, & McGaughey, 1972), and sex (Decker, 1981; Moretz, 1980) have all been found to influence attitudes toward various components of the criminal justice system. Additionally, members of lower class populations, regardless of their race, are more likely to perceive injustice within the entire criminal justice system (Hagan & Albonetti, 1982). However, while research mostly shows society's negative attitudes toward the police, these same attitudes are closely connected to negative perceptions of judges and prosecutors, an extreme cynicism regarding the concept of "equal justice for all," low involvement with the political system, as well as a feeling of political alienation and powerlessness. As can be clearly seen, negative attitudes toward members of the criminal justice system have been present for many years, and such negative views appear to have far-reaching effects.

In spite of the public's view of the police, the courts, and corrections, citizens actually having personal experiences with the criminal justice system (as crime victims) may be more appropriate in identifying problems. One major outgrowth of having been victimized may be the ongoing fear of being victimized again in the future. Additionally, persons having been victimized, and thus forced into the criminal justice system, may come away dissatisfied with police or prosecutors' performance leading to a new, or simply revived negative perception of the legal system.

Similar to research focusing on public attitudes, most research dealing with victims' attitudes toward the criminal justice system focuses primarily on police performance; however, victim-targeted research, instead, measures the influence of personal experiences on victims' perceptions. One study found that neither experiences with police nor the threat of future criminal victimization has any influence on attitudes (Smith & Hawkins, 1973). However, the majority of research (Erez & Tontodonato, 1992; Hylton, as cited in Zamble & Annesley, 1987; Percy, 1980; Scaglion & Condon, 1980a; Sullivan, Dunham, & Alpert, 1987; Tyler, 1990; Zemans, as cited in O'Grady, Waldon, Carlson, Streed, Cannizzaro, 1992) has found that general attitudes toward various components of the criminal justice system are significantly determined by personal experiences with officials from either law enforcement or the judiciary. Additionally, citizens with whom the police are significantly more likely to interact (African-Americans, youth, the indigent, and residents of inner city areas) express far more negative attitudes toward police (Thomas & Hyman, 1977). Finally, the importance of identifying victims' attitudes regarding criminal justice personnel is even more evident as research has shown that future reporting of crimes is affected by victims' fear, perceived helplessness and perceived powerlessness on behalf of the police, and a threat of further victimization by all criminal justice authorities (Kidd & Chayet, 1984).

As the more recent studies point to the significance of personal interaction between victims and criminal justice personnel, it is important to look at the nature of the criminal justice system response to victims. The primary tool to ensure victim satisfaction may be to keep victims informed of their case development (O'Grady et al., 1992); police officers may help foster negative perceptions and dissatisfaction by failing to recognize the importance of communicating with the victim (Thomas & Hyman, 1977). Therefore, a high frequency of communication (Kelly, 1984), as well as both comfort and reassurance (Percy, 1980), is likely to increase crime victims' satisfaction with the criminal justice system.

In order to keep victims informed and increase victim satisfaction, state prosecutors' offices may employ specialized assistant attorneys who concentrate on only one or two types of criminal offenses. This may allow the prosecuting attorney increased opportunities to individually communicate with victims. Additionally, in regards to police, research has shown that victims are much more satisfied with specialized officers than officers responsible for handling a wide array of complaints (Zevitz & Gurnack, 1991).

Another way to help keep the victim informed is through the implementation of various types of victim involvement programs, including communication with victim advocates and programs that directly compensate victims for any financial loss as a result of the crime or related criminal proceedings. However, research has shown that victims frequently complain about the long waits in court they must endure with Victim Involvement Programs due to a massive number of cases and limited advocacy personnel (Davis, Kunreuther, & Connick, 1984). Additionally, not all victims receive equal opportunity to become involved in legal proceedings since victim advocacy services are most often provided to those select victims whose statements are necessary to make a case (Kelly, 1984). Finally, as many cases may be plea-bargained or even dismissed, many victims never benefit from the services offered by advocates. In spite of this, some research has shown that victim participation in the legal process increases their level of satisfaction (Erez & Bienkowska, 1993). However, the majority of studies report the fact that victims do become involved in the legal process (attending court proceedings and being made aware of case outcomes) bears no influence on their overall satisfaction with sentences imposed by the courts (Hagan, 1982). Further, victims who believe the sentence invoked was too lenient and who are displeased with the overall case disposition will remain dissatisfied regardless of the quality of services or the understanding and sympathy they receive from criminal justice personnel (Erez & Tontodonato, 1992).

Victims having gone through such victim compensation plans occasionally express further dissatisfaction due to administrative delay and inconvenience, bureaucratic indifference, and receiving an inadequate award

(Elias, 1984). Despite this, Doerner and Lab (1980) found that some victims who received compensation expressed much more favorable attitudes toward the police than those who failed to receive compensation. Unfortunately, these favorable attitudes failed to "spill over" to other components of the criminal justice system (Doerner & Lab, 1980).

Perhaps the reason many victims remain dissatisfied with criminal justice personnel may be the different ways in which people structure their attitudes, or their actual expectations, of what the criminal justice system should be doing. Research has shown that age, race, and ethnicity play influential roles in how people cognitively structure their attitudes regarding the criminal justice system (Scaglion & Condon, 1980b; Sullivan et al., 1987). Additionally, society tends to expect much more from components of the criminal justice system than they are actually capable of delivering (Blumstein & Cohen, 1980; Percy, 1980), which also affects their level of satisfaction (Brandl & Horvath, 1991). That people perceive situations in different ways, and that some members of society are highly critical of the duties of criminal justice officials may actually prevent the criminal justice system from completely satisfying everyone it encounters.

The majority of past research on crime victims' attitudes primarily focuses on either the police component or the overall criminal justice system; however, it is perhaps most important to look specifically at attitudes toward court personnel. Reasoning behind this is that victims of crime may be less likely to express discontent with the police than with prosecuting attorneys or victim advocates, as court officials have nearly complete control on how an individual is to be charged, prosecuted, and sentenced. As prosecutors are essentially responsible for handling the affairs of others in ways that he or she deems appropriate, such legal proceedings may be subject to the greatest amount of public and victim dissatisfaction. Furthermore, if a victim were to experience delay, intimidation, or even financial loss as a result of involvement with court proceedings, they are less likely to become involved in court procedures in the future, and are likely to share their negative evaluations of the system with others (Kelly, 1984). Therefore, in order to prevent future indifference on behalf of all crime victims, which may hinder advocates' and prosecutors' efforts, it is important to identify victims' first-hand perceptions of the performance and communication skills of criminal court officials. With this in mind, the present research seeks to identify factors related to crime victims' satisfaction (or dissatisfaction) with felony prosecutors and victim advocates.

Methods

Materials. This study took place in Jefferson County, Kentucky. Research was conducted in accordance with the state's prosecuting attorneys' office located in the area which employed a total of 29 full-time prosecuting attorneys, including 14 males and 15 females. Additionally, this office employed 5 victim advocates, all of which were female. Through consultation with officials from the prosecutors' office, a survey instrument was developed to elicit feedback from felony crime victims concerning their perceptions of prosecuting attorneys and victim advocates and the services provided by these professionals. Drawing on the existing literature, the survey focused less on perceived satisfaction of the victim, and more on the relationship between victim demographics and perceptions regarding prosecutors' and victim advocates' overall performance, communication skills, and practices.

Once a victim's case had reached a point of disposition, they received from officials at the prosecutors' office a copy of the survey, along with a postage-paid return envelope. Returned surveys were then mailed to the first author so that analysis could be performed. Data collection spanned fourteen months beginning in November, 1995 and concluding in December, 1996.

Subjects. Respondents of the survey included only victims for which a felony case reached a point of disposition (not necessarily a conviction), so that all respondents experienced all facets of the criminal justice system. A total of 206 victims' responses are considered for the current analysis[1]. This sample includes 56.8% females, 75.7% whites, and 19.4% African American respondents[2]. The age of victims is relatively evenly distributed across categories: 19.8% less than 20 years of age, 28.7% between the ages of 20 and 35, 30.5% between the ages of 36 and 50, and 21% over the age of 50; the mean age for the sample is 37.2. Education of respondents shows that more than three-fourths (76.3%) have at least a high school degree/GED, slightly more than one-fourth (25.8%) hold either a college or post-graduate degree, and only one in five respondents (20%) possess an education level of less than high school completion. Subjects resided in various locations both within and outside Jefferson County. Fully 9.1% reside outside Kentucky, and 7.8% outside Jefferson County but within the state of Kentucky. The offenses experienced by victims have been divided for purposes of analysis into six primary categories:

---

1. The actual response rate is unknown as the survey was administered by the Commonwealth's Attorney's Office, in Jefferson County, Kentucky, who kept no records of how many victims were asked to participate.

2. That the sample is overwhelmingly white can be explained by the racial distribution of Jefferson County in which Whites make up approximately 88% of the population.

survivors of homicide (8.3%), sex crimes (14%), domestic violence (10.2%), child abuse (6.3%), violent crimes (54.9%)[3], and non-violent crimes (22.4%)[4]. These victims' offenders plead guilty in nearly three-fourths of the cases (74.8%) while less than one-fifth (18.9%) were found guilty at trial and very few offenders entered an Alford Plea[5] (1.5%) or were found not guilty at trial (1.0%).

Analysis. The distribution of respondents' satisfaction ratings for both prosecutors and victim advocates were examined. Additionally, respondents were encouraged to offer open-ended responses explaining how and why they did or did not report satisfaction with court officials. Distribution of respondents who reported having specific interactions with, and relations to, prosecutors and victim advocates were also examined. Cross tabulations were performed to examine the relationships between victims' demographic characteristics and their reported satisfaction as well as their reporting of twelve relational aspects with prosecutors and victim advocates. Cross tabulations were also performed to examine the relationship between prosecutors' sex and victims' reporting of twelve specific experiences in the prosecutor/victim relationship. Finally, t-tests of group mean ratings for both prosecutors and victim advocates were performed to examine the relationship between scaled ratings of satisfaction and victims' offense type. The results in the following section reflect this analysis.

Results

Victims' Perceived Relationship with Prosecutors. One central piece of victims' satisfaction with prosecutorial actions is the way that victims perceive the personal and professional qualities of individual prosecutors. Overall, as shown in Table 1, victims overwhelmingly report perceiving positive characteristics of individual prosecutors. Nearly all victims recall having received written communications from prosecutors, and nearly 9 of 10 report having personally spoken with the prosecutor concerning their case. Additionally, the majority of victims believe that the amount of contact they had with the prosecutor was satisfactory. When looking at the specific characteristics of interacting with and relating to the prosecu-

---

3. Violent crimes include the offenses of robbery, assault, arson, attempted murder, and wanton endangerment.

4. Non-violent crimes include burglary, forgery, non-support, theft of labor, and theft.

5. An Alford Plea is another name for the plea "nolo contendre" or "no contest" in which the defendant wishes not to admit complete guilt yet admits to certain facts specified by the prosecution. This plea originated with the case *North Carolina v. Alford* (1970).

tor on their cases, the majority of victims believe they have been involved in a professional relationship, where they were served politely, thoroughly, and in a high quality manner.

Table 1. Prosecutor/Victim Relationship

RELATIONSHIP CHARACTERISTIC	%
SPEAK WITH PROSECUTOR	88.3
LETTER FROM PROSECUTOR	90.3
SATISFIED W/ AMOUNT OF CONTACT	87.4
PROSECUTOR POLITE	87.4
PROSECUTOR EASY TO CONTACT	58.3
PROSECUTOR SYMPATHETIC	59.2
PROSECUTOR EXPLAINS WELL	73.3
PROSECUTOR WELL PREPARED	64.6
PROSECUTOR INTERESTED	52.9
PROSECUTOR IMPOLITE	1.0
PROSECUTOR HARD TO CONTACT	6.3
PROSECUTOR UNSYMPATHETIC	1.0

Based on the high marks victims give to prosecutors, it is not surprising that nearly 8 out of 10 victims (79.6%), when asked to rate the "overall performance" of prosecutors see them as Excellent or Very Good. Less than 3% of crime victims believe that the performance of their prosecutor was Poor or Terrible (see Table 2).

Table 2. Overall Performance Rating for Prosecutors

OVERALL PERFORMANCE	%
EXCELLENT	46.6
VERY GOOD	33.0
GOOD	12.6
FAIR	3.4
POOR	1.9
TERRIBLE	0.5

A more discriminating look at the perceptions of victims toward prosecutors is shown in Table 3. Here, results show that when asked to rate the overall performance of a prosecutor on a scale of 1 (lowest) to 10 (highest), nearly 8 out of 10 victims (76.2%) give a rating of 8 or higher to the prosecutor on their case. The mean rating given to prosecutors is 8.52. A sizable minority of individuals offered comments to explain their perceptions. As shown in Table 4, those who did offer comments typically elaborated on how and why they felt satisfaction. Comments offered commonly included references to an individual prosecutor's caring and politeness and provision of information/explanations. However, a small minority of victims did express dissatisfaction, most commonly through perceptions that the prosecutor had not made one's case a high enough priority.

Table 3. Scaled Rating for Prosecutors

RATING	%
10	37.9
9	25.7
8	12.6
7	5.3
6	4.9
5	2.4
4	0.5
3	2.9
2	1.5
1	1.0

Table 4. Victims' Comments Regarding Prosecutors

COMMENTS	%
WAS GREAT[6]	24.5
CARING AND INFORMATIVE[7]	8.8
LACK OF ATTENTION TOWARD CASE[8]	4.2
DISPLEASED WITH SENTENCE	1.0

Victims' Perceived Relationship with Victim Advocates. In addition to examining the perceptions of crime victims toward prosecutors, questions were also posed regarding contact with, and perceived qualities of victim advocates. Here, it is important to note that less than one-half (39.8%) of responding victims reported having a victim advocate assigned to their cases. The results reported in Tables 5, 6, and 7, therefore, are based solely on these respondents.

---

6. The category "WAS GREAT" includes statements such as "VERY UNDER-STANDING,"VERY NICE," AND "SATISFIED WITH PROSECUTOR.

7. The category "CARING AND UNDERSTANDING" includes statements such as "CONCERNED FOR/WITH VICTIM," AND "KEPT VICTIM INFORMED."

8. The category "LACK OF ATTENTION TOWARD CASE," includes statements such as "NO REAL CONTACT WITH PROSECUTOR," "VICTIM DID NOT UNDERSTAND," "WISH HAD BEEN KEPT INFORMED," "ONLY CONTACT VIA MAIL," and "PROSECUTOR DID NOT FOCUS ON CASE ENOUGH."

Among victims who do report having an assigned victim advocate, more than 80% report both receiving written communications or speaking with an advocate in person, while also expressing satisfaction with the victim advocate's performance. However, where these percentages significantly differ from those regarding prosecutors are in the areas of personal and professional characteristics victims associate with victim advocates. A larger proportion of crime victims perceived their advocates (compared to prosecutors) as both interested in their case and sympathetic to their needs. However, while still generally perceiving advocates in a favorable light, smaller proportions of crime victims perceive advocates as polite, easy to contact, well prepared, and having the ability to fully explain proceedings to them as compared with prosecutors (see Table 5). Unfortunately, only slightly more than one-half of these victims perceive advocates as either well prepared or easy to contact. Consequently, the "overall performance" ratings of victim advocates are slightly lower than are those given to prosecutors. Whereas more than 80% of victims rated prosecutors as Excellent or Very Good, such ratings were given to victim advocates by only 69.3% of victims (see Table 6). However, the more discriminating measure of satisfaction with victim advocates shows a smaller difference, with 76.9% of victims rating advocates 8 or higher on the ten point scale (see Table 7). The mean rating of satisfaction with advocates (8.32), however, is not significantly different than the scaled rating given to prosecutors (8.52).

Table 5. Advocate/Victim Relationship

RELATIONSHIP CHARACTERISTICS	%
SPEAK WITH ADVOCATE	88.5
LETTER/CALL FROM ADVOCATE	87.0
SATISFIED WITH ADVOCATE	89.5
ADVOCATE POLITE	79.0
ADVOCATE EASY TO CONTACT	50.6
ADVOCATE SYMPATHETIC	66.7
ADVOCATE EXPLAINS WELL	63.0
ADVOCATE WELL PREPARED	53.1
ADVOCATE INTERESTED	65.4
ADVOCATE IMPOLITE	0.0
ADVOCATE HARD TO CONTACT	3.7
ADVOCATE UNSYMPATHETIC	0.0

Table 6. Overall Performance Rating for Advocates

OVERALL PERFORMANCE	%
EXCELLENT	41.3
VERY GOOD	28.0
GOOD	20.0
FAIR	5.3
POOR	4.0
TERRIBLE	1.3

Table 7. Scaled Rating for Advocates

RATING	%
10	41.0
9	16.7
8	19.2
7	6.4
6	3.8
5	7.7
4	1.3
3	1.3
1	2.6

An open-ended opportunity to explain one's perceptions of victim advocates provided very few comments. However, the comments that were offered focused on victims' disappointment with the degree of information they were provided and a lack of service or consistency of services provided.

Victims' Perceptions of Prosecutors by Demographics. In order to gain greater understandings of the structure and form of satisfaction and perceived relationships between crime victims and prosecutors and victim advocates, a series of cross tabulations were performed. These statistical tests examine the complexity of the relationships between victims' demographic characteristics and their reported perceptions of prosecutors and victim advocates.

Most importantly, differences across victim demographics are identified for the more discriminating, scaled ratings for prosecutors, focusing on those who gave ratings of 8 or higher for prosecutors. For instance, although not statistically significant, non-whites (83.0%) generally give slightly higher ratings than do whites (79.6%) for prosecutors, whereas a greater proportion of males (84.3%), compared to females (78.6%), rate prosecutors at 8 or higher. In addition, high school graduates (83.0%) tend to rate prosecutors higher than both high school dropouts (80.5%) and college graduates (74.5%). However, the only statistically significant differences are found for age; victims 36 years of age and older (36–50 yrs: 89.1%; 50 yrs and older: 87.8%) give considerably higher ratings than do victims 35 years of age and younger (younger than 20 yrs: 71.8%; 20–35: 70.9%).

When cross tabulating victims' sex, race, age, and education with 12 specific aspects of relationships with prosecutors, victim characteristics showed statistically significant differences with several of the twelve prosecutor/victim relationships. Although not statistically significant, victims' sex appears to be a potentially influential factor for those who considered the prosecutor sympathetic (male: 52.1%; female: 65.5%; p = .065). Differences did reach statistical significance by victims' sex for those perceiving the prosecutor as having the ability to explain things well (male: 65.8%; female: 81.0%; p = .017). Statistically significant differences were reported for respondents by race for those who spoke with the prosecutor (white: 87.6%; non-white: 97.8%; p = .042) and believed the prosecutor did an adequate job of explaining case issues to the victim (white: 70.8%; non-white: 87.0%; p = .027). These results suggest a somewhat greater degree of satisfaction on the part of both female and racial minority crime victims.

While not statistically significant, victims between the ages of 20 and 35 appear most likely to regard the prosecutor as hard to contact (less than 20: 10.3%; 20–35: 12.1; 36–50: 1.8%; older than 50: 2.3%; p = .068). However, statistically significant differences were found for victims by age for those who express prosecutor satisfaction (less than 20: 71.4%; 20–35: 14.3%; 36–50: 100%; older than 50: 100%; p = .003)[9], as well as those who believe the prosecutor was interested in their case (less than 20: 71.8%; 20–35: 41.4%; 36–50: 51.8%; older than 50: 52.3%; p = .033).

Differences approach statistical significance for victims by educational level for those who spoke with the prosecutor (less than high school graduate: 92.7%; high school graduate: 93.1%; college graduate: 82.4%; p = .089) and believed prosecutors were well prepared (less than high school graduate: 63.4%; high school graduate: 71.8%; college graduate: 52.9%; p = .066) and explained things well (less than high school graduate: 82.9%; high school graduate: 76.7%; college graduate: 62.7%; p = .064). Statistically significant differences are seen for respondents' perceptions of the prosecutor's interest in the case (less than high school graduate: 73.2%; high school graduate: 51.5%; college graduate: 41.2%; p = .008) and sympathy for the victim (less than high school graduate: 80.5%; high school graduate: 56.3%; college graduate: 52.9%; p = .012). Finally, differences reached statistical significance for victims by educational level for those who express prosecutor satisfaction (less than high school graduate: 97.5%;

---

9. These victims answered "yes" if they were satisfied with the prosecutors' performance on their case.

high school graduate: 91.9%; college graduate: 82.4%; p = .039). This may suggest that victims with higher educational levels expect more sympathy, interest, case preparation, and in-depth explanations regarding their cases—characteristics many prosecutors apparently do not provide—as well as appear the least satisfied with the prosecutor's overall performance.

Victims' Perceptions of Advocates by Demographics. When looking at whether demographic variables influence scaled ratings for victim advocates, several differences are reported for respondents who give ratings of 8 or higher for victim advocates. Specifically, and in direct contrast to victims' ratings of prosecutors, females are statistically significantly more likely to give victim advocates a higher rating (83.6%) than males (60.0%; p = .030). While not reaching statistical significance, college graduates appear to give universally high ratings for advocates (100%) followed by high school graduates (77.3%) and victims with less than a high school education (70.8%). Also in contrast to prosecutor ratings, victims under 20 years of age (84.0%) generally give higher ratings for advocates than do respondents between the ages of 20 and 50 (20–35 yrs: 72.0%; 36–50 yrs: 76.9%) or over age 50 (71.4%). Finally, both Whites and Non-Whites equally report high ratings for victim advocates (white: 76.9%; non-white: 76.9%).

When cross tabulating victims' sex, race, age, and education with the same twelve aspects of victims' relationships with advocates as was reported for prosecutors, there are few statistically significant differences found. Specifically, differences only approach statistical significance for victims by sex for those who perceived the victim advocate as sympathetic (male: 46.2%; female: 72.7%; p = .088) and having the ability to explain things well (male: 46.2%; female: 75.8%; p = .053). However, there were statistically significant differences for victims by sex for those who received a letter or call from the victim advocate (male: 75%; female: 97%; p = .022) and who considered the victim advocate interested (male: 38.5%; female: 75.8%; p = .016), easy to contact (male: 23.1%; female: 63.6%; p = .013), and well prepared (male: 30.8%; female: 66.7%; p = .027). Furthermore, statistically significant differences were found between victims' sex and their reported satisfaction with advocates' performance (male: 69.2%; female: 96.7%; p = .009). Victims' age also reveals statistically significant differences for those who perceived the advocate as polite (less than 20: 66.7%; 20–35: 100%; 36–50: 55.6%; over 50: 90%; p = .022). These results suggest that male crime victims are less likely to communicate with advocates and less likely to perceive them as sympathetic, interested, easy to contact, well prepared, and having the ability to explain things well. In short, male victims are much less satisfied than female victims with advocates' overall performance.

Victims' Perceptions of Prosecutor by Prosecutors' Sex. When examining the sex of a prosecutor and its relation to characteristics of the victim/prosecutor relationship, several interesting findings are revealed. Differences approached statistical significance for prosecutors' sex and their perceived interest in the case (male: 46.3%; female: 69.7%; p = .062). However, differences reached statistical significance for prosecutors' sex and those victims who recall speaking with a prosecutor (male: 84%; female: 96.6%; p = .001) and who perceive prosecutors as sympathetic (male: 47.6%; female: 69.7%; p = .001), easy to contact (male: 50%; female: 66.4%; p = .019), and polite (male: 80.5%; female: 93.3%; p = .005). These results clearly show that female prosecutors, when compared with male prosecutors, are more likely to be perceived as easy to contact, sympathetic, polite, interested, and the prosecutor with whom victims are most likely to personally communicate.

Victims' Perceptions of Prosecutors and Victim Advocates by Offense Type. In addition to looking at influences of crime victims' demographic characteristics on perceptions of prosecutors and victim advocates, it is possible to determine the presence of relationships between offense type (using dummy variables) and ratings for both prosecutors and victim advocates. This analysis, relying on t-tests of group mean ratings of prosecutors and victim advocates, suggests that the highest satisfaction ratings— for both prosecutors and victim advocates—are provided by victims of child abuse. When comparing satisfaction ratings for prosecutors by victims of other crimes, statistically significant differences show that higher ratings are provided by victims of child abuse (p=.018), and non-violent crimes (p = .007), while lower ratings are provided by victims of homicide (p = .024) (see Table 8). Victims of domestic violence, violent crimes, and sex offenses do not report statistically significant differences in mean prosecutor satisfaction ratings as compared with victims of other offenses. Family members of homicide victims report the lowest mean ratings for prosecutors (8.00) while victims of child abuse give prosecutors the highest ratings (9.30) (see Table 9).

Table 8. Ratings of Satisfaction with Prosecutors by Offense Type

OFFENSE TYPE	MEAN RATING	DEGREE OF SIGNIFICANCE
CHILD ABUSE VICTIM	9.30	
NOT CHILD ABUSE VICTIM	8.46	.018
HOMICIDE VICTIM	8.00	
NOT HOMICIDE VICTIM	8.56	.024
NON-VIOLENT CRIME VICTIM	8.64	
NOT NON-VIOLENT CRIME VICTIM	8.44	.007

Table 9. Mean Ratings for Prosecutor by Offense Type

OFFENSE TYPE	MEAN RATING
CHILD ABUSE	9.30
DOMESTIC VIOLENCE	9.00
SEX CRIMES	8.75
NON-VIOLENT CRIMES	8.64
VIOLENT CRIMES	8.33
HOMICIDE	8.00

When looking at crime victims' perceptions of victim advocates, statistically significant differences in satisfaction ratings are found only between those who are/are not victims of non-violent crimes (p =.043); however, differences approach statistical significance for victims of sex offenses (p = .094). Similar to prosecutor ratings, child abuse victims give the highest mean ratings for advocates (8.80), followed by victims of sex crimes, domestic violence, violent crimes, homicide, and finally non-violent crimes (see Table 10).

Table 10. Mean Ratings for Victim Advocates by Offense Type

OFFENSE TYPE	MEAN RATING
CHILD ABUSE	8.80
SEX CRIMES	8.60
DOMESTIC VIOLENCE	8.36
VIOLENT CRIMES	8.05
HOMICIDE	8.00
NON-VIOLENT CRIMES	7.66

Discussion

Because of the lack of available research concerning crime victims' attitudes toward criminal court officials, this research is at best exploratory. Despite this, valuable information can be seen regarding victims' perceived satisfaction of services rendered by both prosecutors and victim advocates. The data comes directly from victims: predominantly white, female, between the ages of 36 and 50 with at least a high school degree/GED. Offenders who have victimized the sample have most often plead guilty in the cases.

Overall, victims report perceiving positive characteristics for both prosecutors and victim advocates. The majority of victims reported relationships with both prosecutors and victim advocates that produce high degrees of satisfaction, and are characterized as polite, sympathetic, interested, well prepared, and having the ability to explain various aspects of the case to the victim. Both prosecutors and victim advocates receive fairly high ratings by the majority of victims.

Several demographic and situational influences appear significant to victims' perceptions of both prosecutors and victim advocates. For instance, significantly more females, compared to males, perceive prosecutors to be sympathetic and having the ability to explain things well. Also, Non-Whites are significantly more likely than Whites to report having personally spoken with the prosecutor and to believe the prosecutor explains things well. In contrast, female victims are generally more likely than male victims to actually communicate with victim advocates regarding case development, as well as express overall satisfaction with victim advocates' performance, including a higher likelihood of perceiving advocates as interested, well prepared, and easy to contact. Additionally, younger victims are significantly more likely to perceive the prosecutor as interested; however, victims 36 years of age and older appear much more satisfied with their prosecutor's performance. Educational level also makes a difference in victims' perceptions of prosecutors; college graduates are less likely than both high school graduates and those without a high school degree to express overall prosecutor satisfaction with case preparation and performance, and to perceive the prosecuting attorney as either sympathetic to the victim's needs or interested in their case. Furthermore, offense types also influence victims' perception of services rendered by prosecutors and advocates. Specifically, significantly higher satisfaction ratings for prosecutors are provided by victims of child abuse and non-violent crimes. Significantly lower satisfaction ratings are reported by family members of homicide victims. Finally, and possibly the most influential of these results, is the fact that statistically significant differences in various characteristics of the prosecutor/victim relationship are reported across prosecutors by sex. These differences show that female prosecutors (compared to male prosecutors) are most likely to be perceived as easy to contact, sympathetic, polite, interested, and with whom victims are more likely to personally communicate.

Overall, crime victims' general opinions regarding the case handling by both prosecutors and victim advocates is very favorable. However, some alarming findings have come out of this study. Specifically, and possibly most disturbing is the fact that male prosecutors, compared to female prosecutors, are less likely to be perceived as easy to contact, sympathetic, polite, and interested in the victim's case. Further, female prosecutors are much more likely to make verbal or written contact with the victim concerning the development of their case.

Additionally, victim advocates are appearing as both uninterested, unprepared, and difficult to contact in cases involving male victims. Elderly crime victims felt that prosecuting attorneys were not interested in handling their cases, resulting in further dissatisfaction. As a large proportion of total crime victims, both male and elderly citizens are being subject to further victimization as they ultimately feel they are being overlooked by the criminal justice system. Prosecutors are being viewed as lacking in their case preparation and performance by extremely traumatized victims of violent offenses, sex crimes, domestic violence, and family members of homicide victims. Additionally, prosecutors are being perceived as unprepared by victims who hold a college degree; these victims may be more knowledgeable regarding legal system and thus expect more from the justice system. This dissatisfaction with prosecutor case preparation and performance may be eliminated by increased discussions with victims concerning their cases—where victims feel as if their opinions are meaningful.

Each of these findings can, and possibly already have resulted in overwhelming dissatisfaction of the legal system on behalf of the victim. Such victims may no longer have faith in the criminal justice system, and, like past research has shown, decided to quit reporting crimes and cooperating with the legal system. Negative attitudes toward any component of the criminal justice system dramatically effects the function of police, prosecutors, and eventually corrections. Future research is needed to improve the generalizability of the current findings to other prosecutors' offices throughout the United States; however, this study serves as a stepping stone to once again recognizing the victim in criminal cases, and the importance of ensuring their overall satisfaction.

Discussion Questions

How might the criminal justice system reestablish a trust with victims, who have experienced dissatisfaction in the past?

Since female prosecutors receive more favorable ratings than do male prosecutors, should the Commonwealth's Attorney's Office make a point to assign only female prosecutors to those cases with victims having expressed the most dissatisfaction (elderly, college educated, and victims of violent offenses, sex crimes, domestic violence, as well as family members of homicide victims)? Why or why not?

Chapter 10

Child Representation Models: A Descriptive Analysis of Virginia and North Carolina Prototypes

Laura J. Moriarty
Peggy C. Kenworthy

Introduction

A mother dies in child birth; the result of her religious belief to refuse medical treatment. She leaves behind two children, a newly born infant, and a husband. The husband, who is not from the United States, takes the children to a commune in Arizona because he cannot raise the children alone. At the commune, no medical treatment is provided — not emergency treatment nor preventative care. The children are never immunized.

In an effort to find work, the father leaves the children in the care of the elders at the commune while he returns to Europe to find employment. The maternal grandparents find out the children are being cared for by the members of the commune. They immediately seek to gain custody of the children alleging neglect, abandonment, and mistreatment of the children by the father.

The maternal grandparents call social services to report the abuse. During the court proceedings social service was represented by a state attorney, the father was represented by a court-appointed attorney, but who represented the children? A better question is: Do children need separate representation in cases such as this?

In this case, a guardian ad litem represented the children. Although the information given to the guardian ad litem was sketchy at best, she had to investigate the case quickly. The court hearing was in less than 24 hours.

In that timeframe, she was able to establish that the father was a loving parent who did not immunize his children because of his and his deceased wife's religious beliefs. He left the children to look for employment in Europe where he had many contacts. He understood the elders would

141

take good care of his children. Having no other recourse, he left the children to actively pursue employment.

This is a real case where the father retained custody of the children. The maternal grandparents never proved neglect, abandonment, or mistreatment. The court ruled that while it is prudent to have children immunized and receive medical care/treatment when needed, such treatment cannot be legislated when religious beliefs prohibit such action. The court also found that the father had not abandoned the children; he was looking for work and left the children in capable and dependable care.

Think again about the question posed in the scenario, i.e., Do children need separate court representation? The answer is a resounding yes. But, under what circumstances and who will provide the representation? The purpose of this chapter is to answer these questions while focusing on two specific state-wide models of child representation.

Overview

Children need separate court representation when a petition has been filed alleging neglect, abandonment, mistreatment, sexual, and/or physical abuse. This representation allows the court to hear what is in the best interest for the child. Traditionally, social services (i.e., child welfare agencies) are concerned with aggressively seeking out the truth regarding the allegations; however, in many states, there is a mandate to keep the family together. This sometimes causes conflict. The parents or guardians, conversely, are concerned with proving their innocence and their ability to parent. The child, the most important person in the proceedings, is often caught in the middle, with the least amount of opportunity to participate. It may appear that any substantiated case of neglect, abuse, or abandonment should result in the termination of parental rights. However, this is not the case for several reasons, the most important one here being that the child is sometimes better served staying with the parents. These parents may need to attend parenting classes in order to develop better parenting skills but nevertheless loving, inadequate parents often are viewed as better than placing the child into the welfare system where foster care or institutionalization may result. The question therefore remains: What is best for the child? Without separate representation, the child is lost in the process. Having separate representation allows the court to determine how to best serve the child.

We will now examine two state-wide child representation programs: the Virginia Court Appointed Special Advocate (CASA) Program and the North Carolina Guardian Ad Litem (GAL) program. Each will be described, followed by an analysis that compares and contrasts the programs. Although the Virginia program is referred to as the CASA program, it has paid guardian ad litem attorneys. The North Carolina program is called the guardian ad litem program however the guardians are not attorneys and there are no CASA volunteers. The volunteers in North Carolina are called guardians ad litem. The attorney assisting the cases in North Carolina are referred to as guardian ad litem attorneys. [The terminology is somewhat confusing but we hope to clarify the similarities and differences found in the state-wide programs, independent of semantics.]

The Court Appointed Special Advocate Program in Virginia

Virginia's General Assembly officially established the Court Appointed Special Advocate program in 1990 in Virginia Code Sections 9.173.6 through 9.173.13. The CASA program was designed to assist children alleged to be abused and neglected, in need of services, or a child who is in need of supervision. The Virginia statute also gives judges the discretion to appoint a CASA to any other case where such services offered by the program are deemed crucial.

A CASA volunteer is assigned to a case when ordered by the court (Va. Code Ann., Section 9-173.8 (B), Supp. 1996). "The case factors that lead a judge to consider assigning a CASA includes a volatile family situation, age of the child, and the need for victim support beyond what social services or the Court Services Unit can provide" (Criminal Justice Research Center, 1996, p. 13). The volunteer is appointed for the duration of the case or until such time as s/he is relieved from the case by the judge or by the program director.

The duties of the CASA volunteer include investigating, writing reports to the court, and monitoring of the case (Va. Code Ann., Section 9-173.8 (A) (1–3), Supp. 1996). While a guardian ad litem (attorney) is not statutorily obligated to utilize the assistance of the CASA volunteer, the CASA is so obligated under Section 9-173.8 (A) (4), Supp. (1996) to assist the guardian ad litem, if one is appointed by the court.

The role of the CASA volunteer, across the country, has several dimensions. CASA volunteers can be the right hand of the attorney-guardian ad litem, while others work as assistants to social workers or other agency caseworkers involved in the case (Duquette & Ramsey, 1987). In Virginia, the involvement of the CASA volunteer is based largely on the judge's order (Bobby Cosby, personal communication, April 1997). Some judges outline the specific tasks to be fulfilled by the CASA volunteer. While the attitudes of the guardian ad litem certainly affect the relationship between the guardian ad litem and the CASA volunteer, the duties of the CASA have been assigned by the judge; therefore, the CASA is culpable to the judge, not the guardian ad litem (Bobby Cosby, personal communication, April 1997).

The CASA volunteer forms an "independent assessment of the child's conditions and needs" (Virginia Law Foundation, 1996, p.25). The CASA, as an advocate for the child, strives to obtain information that would lead to an informed recommendation, in the best interest of the child. The volunteer is considered a "friend of the court" (Virginia Commission of Youth, 1994, p.12) NOT a party in the case. A friend of the court does not participate formally in the hearing, but is allowed to make informal suggestions to the guardian ad litem and/or the court staff (Virginia Commission Youth, 1994). While the CASA's objective is to discern the best interest of the child, it is the duty of the guardian ad litem to represent the best interest of the child *to the court* (Virginia Commission on Youth, 1994).

The CASA volunteer conducts the investigation in the same manner as the guardian ad litem. The volunteer interviews the child, the parents and/or pertinent family members, neighbors, and anyone else who might have knowledge of the child's circumstance. The CASA volunteer visits the school and obtains records and observations from teachers, doctors, and other agencies involved in the case (Va. Code Ann., Section 9-173.8 (A) (1), Supp. (1996)). The investigation process – which is very time-consuming—is an important element of the CASA's duties. It is imperative that the child's case be adequately and accurately evaluated. As a Court Appointed Special Advocate, the volunteer is given the authority by the court to review and/or copy any records that relate to the child's case (Va. Code Ann., Section 9-173.12, Supp. 1996), and to request an interview with the child's mental health care provider (Va. Code Ann., Section 9.173.12, Supp. 1996; Shepherd, 1995). The CASA is also obligated to submit a written report to the court outlining her/his findings from the investigation, and upon court order, offer recommendations as to the child's disposition (Va. Code Ann., Section 9-173.8 (A) (2), Supp. (1996)).

Who can be a CASA in Virginia? Anyone who is at least 21 years of age and free from a criminal record may apply (Va. Code Ann., Section 9-173.8, Supp. 1996). The prospective volunteer is screened for any past investigations and allegations of child abuse and neglect. All volunteers must be extensively trained (Va. Code Ann., Section 9-173.8 (E), Supp. 1996, p.61).

Guardians Ad Litem in Virginia

The guardian ad litem is a major component of the separate representation model found in Virginia's juvenile justice system. Standards that govern the appointment of attorneys as guardians ad litem are set by the Judicial Council of Virginia in association with the Virginia Bar Association and the Virginia State Bar (Supreme Court of Virginia Brochure, no date). These standards are pursuant to statutes within the Code of Virginia.

The guardian ad litem is appointed upon the discretion of the judge, prior to the hearing for a juvenile who is alleged to be abused and/or neglected, a subject of an entrustment agreement, or a termination of parental rights petition. In addition, a section within the statute includes those children whose parents wish to be "relieved" of their parental responsibilities, authority, and duty.

The Code of Virginia gives a judge the authority to appoint a guardian ad litem when the child's parents are pleading for custody, and the judge perceives the interests of the child are not being addressed during the proceedings. Unlike in abuse and neglect cases, the judge may appoint the guardian ad litem "at any stage in the [custody] proceeding" (Va. Code Ann., Section 16.1–266 (3) (D), 1996, p.134). The court found in *Verrocchio v. Verrocchio* (1993) that appointment of a guardian ad item is an "essential prerequisite" (Va. Code Ann., Section 8.01–9, Editor's Notes, Supp. 1996, p.12) if so doing results in searching for and obtaining the best interest of the child. The appointment of the guardian ad litem in any case lasts throughout the duration of the proceedings, "unless relieved or replaced in the manner provided by law" (Va. Code Ann., Section 16.1–268, 1977, p.137).

A guardian ad litem must be an attorney who is licensed to practice law in Virginia. The attorney must be current in the training required by the state of Virginia, i.e., the role, responsibilities, and duties of guardian ad litem representation. The attorney must be familiar with the court system and have a general background in juvenile law which includes demonstrated competency in the practice of juvenile law.

The administrative offices of the Supreme Court of Virginia maintains a list of attorneys who have met the requirements to be considered guardians ad litem. Currently this list holds approximately 1,000 names and the list is updated quarterly (Bobby Cosby, personal communication, April 1997). The majority of the attorneys who are appointed guardians ad litem in Virginia are sole practitioners (Virginia Commission on Youth, 1994). An attorney must have experience in child representation through working on cases or assisting an attorney serving as a guardian ad litem on at least two cases. The attorney must also have a nomination from a judge. After these requirements are met, seven hours of initial training on the representation of children and six hours of training every two years are required for guardians ad litem (Supreme Court of Virginia Brochure, no date). Judges within several localities in Virginia have "established and imposed their own criteria" (Virginia Commission on Youth, 1994, p.16), which includes training programs for the guardians ad litem who represent abused and neglected children in their judicial districts (Virginia Commission of Youth, 1994).

Guardians Ad Litem in North Carolina

A lay-guardian ad litem (not to be confused with the attorney guardian ad litem found in the Virginia program) is defined as a volunteer who is trained to represent the best interest of the child who is involved in a judicial proceeding as a result of an abuse, neglect, or dependency allegation as part of a team including an attorney advocate. The involvement of the lay-guardian ad litem in a case parallels the duties of Virginia's CASA in many ways. The guardian ad litem is an advocate for the child...the "eyes and ears" for the court (Mary May, personal communication, April 1997). The guardian ad litem gathers information, determines the services appropriate for the juvenile's needs and formulates an opinion as to the best interest of the child. The guardian ad litem must also submit a written report to the court advising the court of the facts of the case and offering recommendations (Cozort & Nelson, February 1996). S/he is a full party to the case and as such is "expected to present the formal findings and recommendations in the court proceeding" (Virginia Commission of Youth, 1994, p.12). The guardian ad litem and the attorney advocate "stand together in the shoes of their child-client, the [attorney advocate] looks to the [guardian ad litem] to assume some of the responsibilities that a client would fulfill in the traditional attorney-client relationship" (Nelson, 1995, p.5).

In one district in North Carolina, the presiding judge has ruled that the guardian ad litem and the attorney advocate will sit together at a separate table in the courtroom (Mary May, personal communication, April 1997). This visually, as well as intelligently, acknowledges and confirms the separate nature of the child's legal representation. It also emphasizes the team relationship between the attorney advocate and the guardian ad litem.

Attorney Advocates – North Carolina

By statute, when a non-attorney guardian ad litem is appointed to handle a juvenile's case, an attorney must also be appointed (N.C. Gen. Stat. 7A-586, 1983, (A)). This mandate is to assure the juvenile will receive all the protections the law has to offer and to provide the guardian ad litem with advice and legal direction.

The attorney advocates are private attorneys contracted with the state (Marilyn Stevens, personal communication, April 1997; Virginia Commission on Youth, 1994; CRS, Inc., 1990). Their performance is monitored and as state employees they are subject to the state's standard personnel management (Virginia Commission on Youth, 1994). Most of the attorney advocates are either in small firms or in solo practice (CRS, Inc., 1990).

The lay-guardian ad litem and the attorney advocate work as a team in support of the best interest of the child. While the duties of the guardian ad litem include investigating, gathering of facts, and forming recommendations, the duties of the attorney advocate focus on legal advice and representation during judicial proceedings (Nelson, 1995). The attorney advocate reviews the petition alleging abuse and neglect and meets with the guardian ad litem to discuss the case. Upon the completion of the guardian ad litem's investigation, the attorney advocate considers the recommendations the volunteer offers for the juvenile. If a settlement is a possibility in the case, both participants determine its scope and feasibility (Nelson, 1995).

The attorney advocate performs all legal activities on behalf of the child, such as legal research, the filing of appropriate motions, subpoenaing witnesses, and preparing witnesses for the hearing. In the hearing, the attorney advocate, utilizing the report written by the guardian ad litem, advocates for the child and advises the court how to meet the needs of the child based primarily on the GAL report. Advising the court of the child's wishes is also a duty of the attorney advocate, especially when the child's wishes and best interest conflict.

The attorney advocate and the guardian ad litem are a team that works together to determine the best interest of the child. According to the statute, the guardian ad litem and the attorney advocate "have standing to represent the juvenile in all actions" (N.C. Gen. Stat. Section 7A-586 (A), as stated in N.C. GAL Training Committee, 1991, pp. 1–3). The attorney advocate does not represent the guardian ad litem; however, s/he does advise the guardian ad litem on legal issues and procedures (Nelson, 1995). The attorney advocate is often called "Attorney Advocate for the Guardian ad Litem" (Nelson, 1995, p.5). This description, according to Nelson, is misleading. The attorney advocate actually represents the child through the guardian ad litem by establishing the methods to accomplish the purposes and goals of the team, which are obtaining the best interest of the child-client (Nelson, 1995).

Comparing and Contrasting the Prototypes

CASA/GAL volunteers. The Court Appointed Special Advocate and the lay-guardian ad litem have comparable duties, roles, and responsibilities outside of the courtroom yet they have different dimensions. They perform investigative work on the case. They interview the child, family, teachers, and anyone else they believe is relevant to the case. Each makes recommendations to the court. Personal conversations with CASAs and lay-guardians ad litem have revealed deep dedication to their work.

The differences begin with the volunteers' perceived standing in the proceedings. From the beginning, the North Carolina lay-guardians ad litem are understood to be equal partners in the advocacy of the child. A guardian ad litem is a full party to the court proceedings (Mary May, personal communication, April 1997). There is a clarification in roles and duties between the lay-guardian ad litem and the attorney advocate. The guardian ad litem does the major portion of the investigation and evaluation while the attorney advocate renders legal advice, attends to the judicial proceedings, and advises as a team, in a joint effort, to determine the best interest of the child. This results in volunteers spending time performing the "leg-work" of the case, i.e., investigating, collecting and evaluating reports, and interviewing. The attorney is utilized for legal expertise and to evaluate, with the volunteer, the child's best interest.

The standing of Virginia's CASA volunteers is dependent upon the orders of the court and the attitude of the attorney-guardian ad litem (Bobby Cosby, personal communication, April, 1997). The judge can order the CASA and the attorney-guardian ad litem to perform specific duties during the course of a case (Bobby Cosby, personal communication, April 1997). If the judge does not offer specifics, the CASA may or may not be perceived as a significant participant in the case by the attorney-guardian ad litem. However, as a recent survey of guardians ad litem reported, most of the GAL attorneys consider their associations with CASA volunteers as "generally good to excellent" (Criminal Justice Research Center, 1996, p.15). Further, judges surveyed in North Carolina and Virginia both acknowledge that the information supplied by and recommendations offered by the volunteers were the most beneficial aspects of their involvement in the case (Criminal Justice Research Center, 1996; Legislative Research Commission, 1996). The most common disadvantage of having a volunteer working on a case, according to judges in Virginia, is their lack of objectivity and over involvement in their cases (Criminal Justice Research Center, 1996). The judges in North Carolina were not asked this question.

To summarize, a significant difference exists between the guardian ad litem in North Carolina and the CASA as to their respective standings in the court proceedings. The guardian ad litem has legal standing, as being a party in the case, to actively participant in the proceeding. The CASA does not have this standing.

Lawyers' Role. The role of the attorney guardian ad litem in Virginia is more prominent than the attorney advocate in North Carolina because of the mandate of the Virginia statute. The attorney-guardian ad litem in Virginia performs similar functions as a CASA volunteer (i.e., investigation, evaluation), in addition to extending legal representation.

The guardians ad litem in Virginia are private attorneys placed on a list after being qualified by the Supreme Court of Virginia. To meet the qualifications, the attorneys must undergo initial training in child representation and attend continuing education seminars every two years. Acquiring a legal expertise is essential in the representation of children; however, a recent survey found "the GAL's [guardian ad litem] role is minimal and that their usefulness in these cases is questionable... because many... GALs come to court hearings to argue the case without ever meeting the child" (Criminal Justice Research Center, 1996, p.16). While this could be interpreted as a lack of dedication or caring on the part of the guardian ad litem, it could also be reflective of the commonality of the cases and high legal expertise of the attorney involved (Department of Criminal Justice Services, 1996).

The lack of time spent on a case (i.e., investigations) is a prevalent criticism of attorney-guardians ad litem nationwide (Poertner & Press, 1990; Edwards, 1993). This was a criticism included in the evaluation of North Carolina's attorney-guardian ad litem system before legislation amended the program in 1983 (Child Watch, Inc., 1981). Nevertheless, due to the insufficient compensation for these cases and high caseloads, it is unrealistic to except attorneys to spend as much time on the investigation process as an unpaid volunteer (Neraas, 1983; Virginia Commission on Youth, 1994). Therefore, the problem might not be with the attorneys, but with the public policy of compensating the attorneys who represent children.

The execution and clarification of duties in North Carolina's program allow attorney advocates to rely heavily on the investigations and recommendations of the volunteer guardian ad litem. This results in less time a paid attorney must work on a case, yet the case receives the necessary attention. A similar process where the guardian ad litem attorney relies more on the lay volunteers to investigate and make recommendations might improve the perception that Virginia cases are not well investigated.

Other program variables. North Carolina's program officially began in 1983. Virginia's program officially began in 1990. When Virginia became "official" there were 10 independent local programs operating in the state. By 1990, there were 37 programs in North Carolina. The difference between the two states is the fact that North Carolina mandated that a guardian ad litem program be established in every judicial district by a certain time. Virginia's program is voluntary. Localities that want to establish a program can with the help of the Department of Criminal Justice Services (DCJS). As of 1997, Virginia has 23 local programs and North Carolina has 53.

As of 1994–95, there were 563 active volunteers in Virginia's programs. They contributed a total of 64,216 hours to the juvenile justice system. North Carolina's program had 3,487 volunteers who gave almost 300,000 hours of time.

The budgets for the programs are very dissimilar. The majority of North Carolina's program budget consists of direct appropriations. Due to the 501 (C) (3) status of approximately 80 percent of Virginia's local CASA programs, the majority of their budgets consists of grants, local government money, and private organizational support.

The regulations of the CASA program in Virginia required each volunteer to undergo 25 hours of training prior to assignment to a case and 12 hours of training and six hours thereafter. North Carolina requires 15 hours of training. The curriculums are very similar. North Carolina also requires courtroom observation as does Virginia's new training regulations.

Conclusion

The two state programs have the same overall purpose: To provide separate legal representation to children who are the subjects of neglect, mistreatment, abandonment, sexual, and/or physical abuse cases. Each state has the best interest of the child as its main goal; however, each state achieves this goal differently.

The North Carolina program seems to be without criticism. However, we observed a potential problem: the reliance on one or two administrative staff members who really support and manage the program. Without such dedication the program would undoubtedly suffer. While such commitment is often viewed as a strength, we see it as a potential problem because what will happen to the program when these people leave? A better approach is to spread the dedication and commitment among many administrative staff members.

The younger Virginia program has some problems. Most disconcerting are (1) the lack of funding including the overall budget and payment to guardians ad litem; (2) the non-reliance on lay volunteers to investigate the cases; and (3) the lack of a real team approach to child advocacy. Personal communications with guardians ad litem, judges, and administrative staff reveal similar concerns; however, such concerns have facilitated discussions and dialogue among the key players. It is possible that the Virginia program will consider making changes, perhaps even using the North Carolina program as a model, in order to provide the best possible child advocacy.

Discussion Questions

Why is it important to have separate child representation in court proceedings where neglect, mistreatment, abandonment, sexual, and/or physical assault has been alleged?

Discuss child representation in your state. Is it more like the North Carolina or Virginia model? How would you improve your state's model?

Do you think Virginia should allow the lay volunteers (people without legal backgrounds) to have a more prominent role in the formal court proceedings thus mandating the attorneys to rely more heavily upon the opinions and conclusions drawn from the volunteers in the disposition of the children they investigate? Why? Why not?

Chapter 11

Victims and the Church: Model Approaches To Building Support

Laura J. Moriarty
Patricia H. Grant
James L. Hague

In recent years, because of the perception that crime rates are increasing, victimization has become a major area of concern for society. According to the Bureau of Justice Statistics (BJS), 38.4 million crimes were committed against individuals 12 years old and older in 1995 (1997). Of those, approximately 9.6 million individuals were victims of violent crimes, including rape, robbery, and aggravated assault. These rates of victimization indicate that an estimated 5 out of 6 people will be victims of violent crime at least once in their lives (BJS, 1997). Consequently, the rise in the rates of victimization has been the catalyst for the increase in professional services by private and governmental agencies (Johnson, 1997; Nice, 1988; Young, 1990). Yet, while the government has provided significant resources for victims, the religious community has not been as forthcoming with its support of this population. Though the attention focused on victims of crimes has led to a new recognition of victimization and the need for religious support systems, this need remains relatively ignored by the religious community.

Research findings indicate that responses from all denominations echo a common refrain that formal church policy and pastoral knowledge of issues of violence is problematic (Johnson, 1995; Kuhl, 1982). Many victims report that church officials lack knowledge, sensitivity, or experience about the problems of victims (Kuhl, 1982). Further, it is reported that the clergy seem least likely to be involved with victims of crime than governmental agencies and when they are involved, it is only on a minimal level (Fortune, 1986; as cited by Johnson, 1997; Johnson, 1997; Kuhl, 1982). Although nonprofit agencies may include religious institutions, there is little evidence that churches are actively involved in the support and assistance of victims. Further, while researchers have acknowledged the importance of the church in aiding victims of crime, little is known about how frequently victims seek help from the clergy and no data exists on how many congregations have programs related to family violence (Martin, 1989). Consequently there is a dearth of information regarding support services provided by churches and their clergy to members of their congregation and the community at large who are victims of crime (Johnson, 1997; Kuhl, 1983; Martin, 1989).

As important entities of the community, religious institutions could provide significant resources for focusing attention on violence and for supporting, encouraging, and assisting victims. In addition, religious institutions may be in the best position to understand the needs of the community and their congregations and to provide support services. Moreover, the research indicates that victims of crime are more likely to seek support from these institutions (Adams, 1994; Kuhl, 1983; Martin, 1989). Further, the Report of the President's Task Force on Victims of Crime (1982) indicated that victims identify the religious community as a vital and largely untapped source of support for crime victims. Although many private or governmental secular organizations aid certain types of crime victims, very few churches and no national Christian ministries, have organized outreach programs for victims of crime and often neglect the needs of crime victims in their midst (Carlson, 1997).

The majority of studies related to the role of the church in assisting crime victims focus on domestic violence and the stigmatization of victims by the church and the community. In addition, research has found that the clerics fail to denounce domestic abuse among its members and further perpetuate abuse by remaining silent (Kuhl, 1983; Martin, 1989). Martin (1989) found that across denominations, clerics do not assume a proactive role in addressing the problems of spousal abuse. Yet, more than one half (54%) of the responding clerics acknowledged that they needed to improve their efforts to address the problem of spouse abuse. Sadly, while studies have shown that victims are more likely to seek the support of clergy as opposed to governmental support services, often these services are not available, especially in cases of domestic abuse (Adams, 1994; Kuhl, 1982; Martin, 1989; Sacco, 1993).

Research on domestic abuse has also shown that these victims are more likely to seek out a minister's help than their abusers, yet this help may not be readily available (Adams, 1994; Kuhl, 1982; Sacco, 1993). Kuhl (1987), researching community responses to battered women, found that 16 percent of the women reported that their ministers knew about the abuse. Of those, 21 percent both saw the results of the violence (e.g., black eye, broken arm) and talked to the woman, 64 percent talked with the woman, and 3 percent witnessed the violence and talked with the woman. On the other hand, when the women were asked about the ministers' response, they indicated that 15 percent believed the women while 4 percent did not. Moreover, 6 percent did not want to get involved, 11 percent were not able to help, and 6 percent made things worse. Finally, 21 percent listened, 20 percent offered information, and only 4 percent intervened. Consequently, although a majority of the clergy talked with the woman and helped by listening and offering information, only a minority attempted intervention (Kuhl, 1982). Therefore, according to Kuhl, clerics believe that the safest approach that provides minimal involvement is to listen and offer information regarding individual problems. Although this approach may be quite effective with more "traditional" mental health problems, persons seeking help for family violence need a more direct approach, according to Kuhl, in order to decrease the potential lethality of the situation.

Literature relating to the role the clergy plays when assisting victims of domestic abuse provides guidelines and a framework for addressing the congregation (Adams & Fortune, 1995). This literature suggests that the clergy has a responsibility to its members to formally denounce domestic violence and to provide counseling and services to the victim and the abuser. In addition, this literature suggests that ministers are accountable to the members and as such should never perpetuate domestic violence by their disregard for or their lack of involvement through intervention. Instead, ministers have a responsibility to address and intervene when cases of domestic violence among their congregation are evident (Adams & Fortune, 1995).

Several research studies have focused on the emotional and psychological effects of violence on victims (Davis & Brickman, 1996; Johnson, 1997; Ruback, 1994). These studies indicate that acts of violence produce adverse emotional and psychological effects that may lead victims to cope by seeking assistance from others, such as friends, family, neighbors, health professionals, clergy, and the criminal justice system (Barnett, Martinez & Keyson, 1996; Davis & Brickman, 1996; Johnson, 1997; Kaniasty & Norris, 1992; Kennedy, 1988; Ruback, 1994). Additionally, although victims of crime experience many psychological effects that include fear, low self-esteem, and depression, many do not seek professional help (Barnett, Martinez & Keyson, 1996; Sacco, 1993). Crime victims typically attempt to cope by taking certain actions either alone (e.g., seeking retribution, or seeking restitution, using self-protective measures) or with assistance from others (Davis & Brickman, 1996; Johnson, 1997; Sacco, 1993). Furthermore, these studies have found that many victims may chose to rely on self-help or assistance provided by their social networks. Victims of crime are more likely to seek support from informal social networks and will usually confide in at least one member of the network immediately after the crime who may be called upon to offer support long before professional help is sought (Barnett, Martinez & Keyson, 1996; Williams & Holmes, 1981 as cited by Davis & Brickman). However, individuals are often uncertain how to respond to victims of crime and these feelings of discomfort may lead to subtle avoidance of victims. Consequently, Wortman and Lehman (as cited by Edleson and Eisikovits, 1996) suggest, based on theoretical and empirical review, that those who care most about the victim may be especially likely to engage in inappropriate support and are incapable of providing the support that is necessary to facilitate healing. As a result, these self-help measures implemented to prevent victimization are ineffective and naturally occurring social resources available for coping with stress may not be enough to alleviate the distress accompanying victimization (Coates & Winston, 1983; Coates, Wortman & Abbey, 1979; Johnson & Merker, 1992; Norris & Johnson, 1988, as cited by Johnson, 1997). In contrast, others assert that the importance of these support sources cannot be underestimated and that coping mechanisms can be enhanced by the active participation of the clergy and their congregations, who can be a source of solace unobtained elsewhere (Davis & Brickman, 1996; OJD, 1982).

Although victims of violent crimes may indicate they want to seek support from the clergy, Martin (1989) found victims often are reluctant to seek such support due to a fear of stigmatization and pastoral response. Moreover, victims might be reluctant to discuss spouse abuse with their pastor as a part of the general pattern of social withdrawal (Martin, 1989). In addition, this reluctance may also be associated with the perceived traditional versus liberal orientation of the clergy and the congregation. However, Johnson (1981) found that while those with inside knowledge and membership of church polices toward domestic violence say individuals largely avoid ministers, because of the anticipated fear of stigma, many persons do first go to a church official for help or assistance with family violence (Bowker, 1982, as cited by Johnson, 1997; Fortune, 1984, 1986).

The victimology literature presented above clearly demonstrates that victims consider the church an important resource for coping with their victimization. However, the literature also indicates that few churches have programs designed specially to deal with the needs of victims. We found several religious publications that explained specific programs in one or two faith communities; however, these programs were narrow in scope and idiosyncratic to the specific unit (religious organization).

In this next section, we propose a model for churches and other religious organizations to use to serve crime victims. We suggest a hierarchical approach to organizing faith communities. The first approach is the simplest for faith communities to invoke while offering victims minimal services. The second approach is more involved with the onerous on the cleric. The third approach is the ideal. It requires a large commitment from both the pastor and the parish but it also offers the most complete services to the victims.

The Hierarchical Model

At the first level, at the very minimum, all churches should provide information regarding services available in the community to assist victims. Educational brochures and pamphlets should be available on a permanent basis in some location of the church. Perhaps a table, where other religious news items are displayed or inserts for church bulletins outlining domestic violence, child abuse, and other victimization statistics and community resources. In addition, the brochures should provide the appropriate support information for various types of victimization that are provided by the church, as well as the appropriate reporting agencies. This is the least intrusive measure but perhaps the most beneficial. It allows victims to gather much needed information without having to confide in anyone.

The church[1] members would be responsible for collecting the information from various community organizations and they should make certain the table has all the available resources. When information pamphlets get low, they should replace them. This level of commitment is very small; however, the potential to serve crime victims in this manner is immense.

The second approach would emphasize the involvement of the religious leader (i.e., pastor, priest, rabbi, and cleric) requiring that the clerics are appropriately trained in counseling and knowledgeable of victim services in the community. Clerics would also need to be willing to counsel and refer victims. Without such a commitment, this approach does not work.

Moreover, clerics could establish within their congregation a system for dealing with offenders that would encourage accountability for their actions and treatment referrals and recommendations. As espoused in the literature, through its silence, the church has traditionally failed to recognize the emotional and/or physical needs of victims while enabling the offender. Therefore, in an effort to accommodate the needs of victims, clerics must accept responsibility for its congregants, which requires focusing on the needs of victims and providing resources to facilitate healing, while not enabling the offender.

Clerics could minister to their congregations by creating an environment that is conducive to promoting disclosure by acknowledging vio-

---

1. Generic term used to refer to any denominations' house/place of worship.

lence, redirecting efforts from offender to the victim, and empowering victims to take charge of their own recovery. Furthermore, clerics could mobilize the religious community to support and advocate for victims. This cooperative effort would develop relationships and alternatives among the local churches to provide services for victims.

The third approach is to get the faith community involved and not rely solely on the pastor, priest, or cleric to provide services to the victims. This approach to victim recovery is viewed as the most beneficial if the community really gets involved. Partnerships should be formed with (1) social organizations that provide counseling services, offer emergency food, and provide financial aid assistance, (2) domestic and homeless shelters, (3) government social service agencies including public welfare, social security, Medicaid/Medicare, workmen's compensation, and legal aid services, and (4) community crime prevention groups organized by local police or sheriff's departments. Working cooperatively with governmental, private, and nonprofit agencies, the faith community could facilitate the healing process for victims. Providing information, resources, and support, the community could assist in the victim's recovery. Members of the community, educated on the available resources, would provide educational information to victims and/or moral support. Community support groups could be established within the church to provide additional support for victims. These groups, facilitated by clerics or their appropriate designees who have been trained in counseling techniques, would focus on the healing process and the restoration of a positive self-identity. In addition, to reduce revictimization, law enforcement agencies and/or victim support groups could provide information that explains appropriate and situation-defined prevention techniques.

In addition to forming partnerships with various community organizations, the church members could be organized to provide the following services to victims: On-scene comfort, post-crime emotional distress, comfort, emergency shelter or food, and childcare.

Organization of the Program

Before a congregation can be organized to provide services to victims, on more than just an ad hoc basis, a survey of the parishioners to determine resources is necessary. Some of the congregation may be doctors, social workers, attorneys, counselors, teachers, homemakers, etc., who have time and talent to offer to develop and maintain a church-based victims program.

Clerics would provide training seminars for members of the congregation on the appropriate forms of assistance and types of referral agencies, how to recognize less visible forms of victimization (i.e., spousal abuse or child abuse), and procedures to facilitate seminars related to victimization. Support groups could be established to provide emotional support among victims. These groups could be setup within the church with regular meetings and could be facilitated by members of the congregation who have been appropriately trained. In addition, teen support groups could be established that are relevant to the issues of victimization experienced by teens. These groups could facilitate discussion among teens who are victims of relationship violence or child abuse, establish safety procedures for those who are victims of violence, and provide information regarding community resources and hotline numbers that are specific to teen problems.

Churches, in partnership with other churches, community organizations, law enforcement, school personnel, emergency service workers, social service personnel, counselors, and private and non-profit governmental agencies could cosponsor conferences to address victimization issues and the community's response to those issues. These conferences would address such issues as family violence law, risk assessment, the effects of violence on children, safety planning, and teen dating violence. Additionally, these conferences would provide information regarding available resources and assistance provided by the different agencies.

Conclusion

Studying the interaction between the clergy and victims of crime is important because of the implications for treating victims who seek ministerial counseling. Counseling by clergy may affect post-victimization decision-making by reducing stress levels and thereby allowing victims to better attend the cues to action that the social environment provides (Sacco, 1993). When such support is available, victims may be better able to adjust to or manage the stigma that victimization often implies (Janoff-Bulman, 1985 as cited by Sacco, 1993). In addition, these services, when provided by ministers may facilitate and enhance the recovery process, especially if additional support services are not as forthcoming. As an integral segment of the community, churches have taken on many tasks to promote the continued health and growth of the community. Although, churches in some cases provide significant services, there are many others that are only minimally involved in the reconciliation and healing process of victimization. On the other hand, it is evident that these services are important and as a result victims are increasingly seeking and requiring additional services from the church. In an effort to provide these services, it is imperative that churches become more involved in the healing and reconciliation of victims. Therefore, the proposed three-tier model provides additional insights for accomplishing this vital and important service.

Discussion Questions

Why is it important to have victim programs offered in a religious setting?

Why do clerics often ignore spouse abuse? Do you think it is important for them to publicly denounce domestic violence? Why/Why not?

Given the hierarchical model presented in this chapter, what level of involvement/commitment do you think is possible for your faith institution? How can you get your community involved?

Part IV

Victims' Rights
versus
Offenders' Rights

Chapter 12

The Evolving Law of Victims' Rights: Potential Conflicts with Criminal Defendants' Due Process Rights and the Superiority of Civil Court Remedies

Gregory P. Orvis

Introduction

There is no question that crime and the damage it does to society is one of the most important questions facing the United States in the twenty-first century. Tabulations of the 1995 National Crime Victimization Survey data revealed crime rates in the United States of 42.5 violent victimizations per 1,000 people aged twelve or older, and almost 300 property crimes per 1,000 households (Rand, Lynch, & Cantor, 1997). Furthermore, the tangible costs of crime victimizations are one hundred and five billion dollars a year, which include property losses, productivity losses, and medical expense outlays. By far, the greater costs are intangible, such as pain, long-term emotional trauma, disability, and risk of death, and have been estimated to be as great as four hundred and fifty billion dollars a year (National Institute of Justice, 1996).

However, the greatest damage of crime victimization this century may have been done to the judicial system. Slowly but surely, the victims' rights movement and its accompanying lobbying groups have pressured the American judicial system to apply civil-like remedies to criminal cases, despite the fact that over two hundred years of common law experience in this country alone proved that this was rather like putting a square peg in a round hole. Whereas the original purpose of the criminal courts in the United States was to protect *society* from criminal deviance, the criminal court system, to its detriment, has been increasingly altered during the last three decades to serve *individual* citizen's interests, which have been traditionally protected under the common law by the civil courts. These alterations have led to longer and more costly criminal proceedings and a confusion as to the boundary between "private law," which deals with relationships between individual citizens and which government has only an indirect interest, and "public law," wherein the government has specific responsibilities (Gardner & Anderson, 1992).

The Common Law Tradition

During the Renaissance, all of Europe except England embraced the rediscovered "Roman" law and its tradition of codification which greatly restricted judicial discretion. England rejected the new legal trend in favor of retaining the common law system that had developed its own "peculiar features of substance, structure, and culture," and, in particular, its reliance on case law and the doctrine of precedent (Friedman, 1984:16). During Henry II's reign in the late tenth century, English law recognized that crimes were more than personal disputes between criminals and victims, but were acts against society and should not be left to personal vengeance (Gardner & Anderson, 1992).

The need to preserve law and order in society created a criminal justice system that evolved under the common law separate from the "private" law that protected individual and which precluded "private" vengeance for crimes. As one legal scholar notes, "Criminal justice is *public* justice; it requires *public* litigation. The plaintiff is "the people" or "the commonwealth" or "the state"...the state sets the process in motion and the state pays the bills" (Friedman, 1984, pp. 158–159). Criminal law evolved to deal "with activities that have been formally forbidden by a society's government" whereas civil law was created to govern "the relationships between individuals in the course of their private affairs," although a tort action may lead to violations of both (Calvi & Coleman, 1989, pp. 8–9). As England created colonies in the "New World," the English brought their common law traditions with them as well as their ideas about criminal justice.

This distinction leads to many procedural differences between criminal justice systems vested in the common law and those of countries that followed the "Roman" or codified law, often referred to as in the "Romano-Germanic" tradition, wherein criminal and civil suits could sometimes be pursued in the same proceeding (Terrill, 1992). Criminal law prosecution under the common law is an adversary system with a more partisan prosecutor and a more impartial judge than the inquisitorial, or non-adversary, system of the Romano-Germanic law, where the victim in some countries can intervene in this cooperative venture and have his civil suit tried along with the criminal suit. However, in these Romano-Germanic countries there is complete discovery of each "side's" case and the judge often leads the examination of the witnesses and the defendant (Glendon, Gordon, & Osakwe, 1985).

In the United States, due process and the protection of the defendant's rights under the Bill Of Rights is better served under the common law adversarial tradition. This is because the very existence of the Bill of Rights draws a dividing line between the government and those accused of crimes. In the seventeenth century under King Charles I, the royal Court of the Star Chamber had abandoned such procedural protection to the detriment of those accused of crimes, usually those in the lower and middle classes, and which included those in the colonies. After the American Revolution and despite the failed Articles of Confederation, the Bill of Rights "reflects deep suspicion, even hostility, to government power" (Samaha, 1996, p. 16). It is not surprising that the adversary system was nurtured under such an atmosphere, with no room left for a third party dispute in the American criminal justice process, even that of a crime victim.

Even before the American Bill of Rights, the common law had a greater quantum of proof to find a person guilty under the criminal law, in that the state had to prove the accused guilty of the crime beyond a reasonable doubt. This quantum of proof is very important, because under the civil law, an individual needs only a preponderance of the evidence to prove their case against a person who has wronged him or her. Furthermore, the rules of evidence in general are much more exacting in the criminal justice process than in the civil justice process under the common law as evolved in the United States (Torgia, 1972).

The Incremental Merging of Criminal and Civil Justice Processes in the United States

The merging of the criminal and civil justice processes in the United States began in the early eighties with the advent of the victims rights movement. In 1982, California voters adopted "Proposition Eight," which included a victims bill of rights and restricted plea bargaining. It is sometimes thought to be the beginning of the victims rights reform movement (Friedman, 1984). The restriction of plea bargaining is especially surprising since supporters of plea bargaining often argue that the fact that ninety percent of criminal cases are settled is good for crime victims and their families because it spares them the stress and possible public humiliation of a trial. This is particularly true in rape, murder, and child molestation cases where demonstrative evidence is often graphic and crossexamination is brutal (Glick, 1983).

Offender restitution, or the concept of transferring money or services from the criminal to the victim as damages predates formal criminal justice systems and dates to the sixties in the United States. However, it was the recommendations of the 1982 President's Task Force on Victims of Crime that began the trend of making it a norm to grant restitution as part of the criminal sentence, and that trend extends to restitution legislation in forty-eight states today. There are many reasons to question the efficacy of restitution, not the least of which is the inability of the criminal courts to administer restitution programs and the inability of these courts to quantify damages from violent crimes and victimless crimes (Doerner & Lab, 1995). There has even been some dispute among federal lower courts about the constitutionality of the restitution provisions of the Victim and Witness Protection Act of 1982, in that the Seventh Amendment guarantees the right of a jury trial in controversies over twenty dollars in dispute between individual citizens (Reid, 1997). Still, the Senate Judiciary Committee recently suggested mandatory victim restitution by those convicted of serious federal crimes except in extraordinary circumstances (Masci, 1995). There are more pragmatic problems with restitution of crime victims by criminals through the criminal courts:

> First, suitable jobs for offenders are difficult to find. Second, judges remain reluctant to impose restitution unless agreements are likely to be enforced. Third, probation and parole officials resent being relegated to the status of "bill collection" agencies. Finally, many appropriate cases slip through the cracks in the system, through a process called "shrinkage" or "funneling," because of unreported crime, unsolved cases, dropped counts, and dismissed charges (Sheley, 1995, p. 158).

Another recommendation of the President's Task Force on Victims of Crime in 1982 was the establishment of a federally financed victim compensation fund. A federal crime victims fund was authorized by Congress in the Victims of Crime Act of 1984. Soon after the Task Force's recommendation, thirty-six states established at least token victim compensation funds, almost all of which came quickly into financial difficulty. As one observer noted, "some contain so little money that state officials try to keep them a secret" (Vetter & Territo, 1984, p. 532). Even with the development of new sources for these funds, such as levying an "abuser's tax" on all convicted offenders, predictions were dire about the future of such funds. Rhode Island bankrupted its funds in the early eighties when it awarded twice as much to victims as it took in on penalty assessments, while in other states, benefits had to be curtailed and victim claimants waited years to receive their approved awards (Karmen, 1984).

Today, the victim compensation funds of forty-four states must be subsidized by federal funds, compensate the victims of only the most violent and injurious crimes, and have complex rules and regulations that *must* be strictly adhered to by the victim applying for the funds (Karmen, 1990). From 1985 through 1994, $1.2 billion dollars was deposited in the federal crime victims fund and collected from criminal fines, forfeited bail bonds, penalty fees, and special assessments by the U.S. Attorney's office, the federal courts, and the federal Bureau of Prisons. The federal Office for Victims of Crime (OVC) administers the fund, with almost half going to state victim compensation programs. Every state administers their own program for victims of state and federal crimes that occur in their state. States grant maximum awards of $10,000 to $25,000 for crime-related expenses such as unpaid medical bills, mental health counseling, funeral costs, and lost wages, but only to the extent that a victim's insurance or other "collateral" sources have not paid out, such as awards from a civil suit (National Criminal Justice Research Services [NCJRS], 1997b). It is interesting to note that these are the very expenses that could be covered by a civil suit award, although without the cost to the taxpayer for supplementing and administering these funds.

Many advocates of victims rights believe that crime victims should play a greater role during the pre-trial proceedings, trial, and the sentencing stage of the criminal justice process. The greatest advances for victims have been in legally prescribed notifications. Forty-one states require advance notification of all court appearances, even ones where they are not a witness, and twenty-seven states require that a victim be notified if the defendant is released on bail. Twenty-seven states give crime victims consultive roles in plea bargaining and twenty-eight states require that the state notify victims when plea bargains are agreed to by the state and the defense (Karmen, 1990). Although there are no statistics on the costs of this additional paperwork, considering that the criminal justice system is one of scarce resources, these costs must be significant.

The federal and many state systems require that the trial judge read prior to sentencing a victim impact statement, in which the victim describes how the crime affected the financial, physical, and mental health of the victim and his/her family. Some jurisdictions even allow the victims to make public statements in the courtroom (Holman & Quinn, 1996). One might remember the New York case a few years ago where a gunman went on a shooting rampage aboard a commuter train, murdering six passengers and wounding nineteen (Roberts, 1995). He was found guilty after a lengthy trial in which the defendant represented himself, and the oral statements read by the victims took much court time and a great deal

of taxpayers' money. Two dozen victims of the Long Island massacre testi-
fied publicly at the defendant's sentencing hearing, including wounded
survivors, relatives of the murdered victims, and two passengers who
were terrorized but neither killed nor wounded (Adler, Biddle & Shentiz,
1995; Thigpen, 1995). As it stands today, recent United States Supreme
Court decisions have upheld victim impact statements as constitutional
and not contrary to the Eighth Amendment, even if potentially inflamma-
tory and in a death penalty case (Doerner & Lab, 1995).

Victims' Rights and the Federal Court System

The federal courts have been slow in their acceptance of victim' rights,
and often were divided in their resolve as to whether to accept them. The
earliest federal court cases on victims' rights were not in agreement even
as to restitution of victims—today a fairly basic right. Whereas one federal court rejected the restitution provisions of the Victim and Witness
Protection Act of 1982 based on the jury requirements of the Seventh
Amendment (*U.S. v. Welden*, 1983), others have held it partially unconstitutional (*U.S. v. Palma*, 1985; *U.S. v. Johnson*, 1987) and other federal
courts have upheld its constitutionality as an exercise of discretion (*U.S. v.
Brown*, 1984; *U.S. v. Atkinson*, 1986). The United States Supreme Court
took a middle ground by limiting restitution orders to the amount of actual damages caused by the crime for which the defendant was actually
convicted (*Hughey v. U.S.*, 1990). Congress altered the holding by statutorily providing that a judge could order restitution based on plea bargains (Crime Control Act of 1990) as well as mandating restitution for
conviction of specified violent federal crimes (Violent Crime Control &
Law Enforcement Act of 1994).

The United States Supreme Court itself was divided over the constitutionality of victim impact statements in the sentencing of death penalty
cases. The court in a 5–4 decision decided that such statements created a
risk that the death penalty would be imposed in an "arbitrary and capri-
cious" manner (*Booth v. Maryland*, 1987). The Supreme Court does not
usually overturn precedent lightly nor soon after it's made, but in the case
of victim impact statements, they did just that in *Payne v. Tennessee*
(1991). The Supreme Court denied that the Eighth Amendment created a
bar to victim impact statements without a showing that the statements
were so prejudicial as to make the process fundamentally unfair, and allowed the states to decide whether such statements should be used or not
in criminal cases. At least forty eight states had already taken the initiative with some form of victim participation in sentencing by that date
(McLeod, 1988).

The Supreme Court often appears inconsistent when balancing state mandated victims rights against the due process rights of defendants. In similar cases in which the defendant's right of confrontation was abrogated by state statutes designed to protect child victims on the witness stand, the U.S. Supreme Court first upheld the Sixth Amendment guarantee to a face-to-face confrontation when the state put a screen between the defendant and the child-victim during trial (*Coy v. Iowa*, 1988) then, a mere two years later, denied that all confrontations have to be face-to-face when a child-victim was allowed to testify via television as provided by state law (*Maryland v. Craig*, 1991).

Victims' Rights and State Legislatures

When it comes to the matter of victims rights, the U.S. Supreme Court appeared to defer to state legislatures, and state legislatures appear to have accepted the mandate. Most legislative activity concerning crime victims has occurred at the state level, establishing victim services that provide financial support, logistical aid, and sometimes personal treatment; changing the criminal justice process to better serve victims needs, both material and psychological; emphasizing special groups of victims for protection and care, such as children and the elderly; creating victims rights; and providing greater penalties for offenders (Elias, 1990). By 1992, thirty-four state legislatures had passed legislation entitled "Victims' Bill of Rights" or "Rights of Crime Victims," and twelve others had laws that could be considered a compilation of victims rights. By the end of 1994, twenty states - Alabama, Alaska, Arizona, California, Colorado, Florida, Idaho, Illinois, Kansas, Maryland, Minnesota, Missouri, New Jersey, New Mexico, Ohio, Rhode Island, Texas, Utah, Washington, and Wisconsin—had constitutional Amendments specifically providing victims' rights (National Victim Center, 1997).

Furthermore, although all states now provide victims rights to some extent, they vary considerably in the definition and scope of these rights. Depending on the state, victims rights may or may not include: (1) right to attend and/or participate in criminal justice proceedings, such as bail or pretrial release hearings, plea agreement entry hearings, post-trial or release hearings, sentencing hearings, probation hearings, temporary relief hearings, change of security status hearings, and commutation or pardon hearings, (2) right to notification of stages or proceedings in the criminal justice process, (3) right to protection from intimidation and harassment, (4) right to confidentiality of victims' records, (5) right to speedy trial, (6) right to a prompt return of victims' personal property seized as evidence from the defendant, (7) right to the defendant's profits from the sale of the stories of the crime against the victim, (8) right to restitution or compensation, and (9) right to notification of other legal remedies (National Victim Center, 1997).

The Danger of Merging Criminal and Civil Justice Processes

The greatest danger of merging criminal and civil justice processes is that you diminish the purpose of both. The philosophy of the American criminal justice system is undermined when the focus is taken from society and put on the individual victim, with "society no longer appeased or vindicated" (Doerner & Lab, 1995, p. 67). Similarly, the public faith in the civil justice system is further shaken when insisting that the civil system cannot protect crime victims rights except by excluding them from having to enforce their individual rights in the civil courts. Furthermore, the logic and wisdom of hundreds of years of common law precedent governing private wrongs are ignored and thus wasted when crime victims' cases are taken from the civil court arena.

Another danger is that the victims rights movement in many states infringe on the rights of those accused of crimes as protected by the Bill of Rights (Reid, 1997). The victims rights movement has been successful in lobbying forty-four state legislatures so that a victims Bill of Rights is included in some format as part of the state constitutions (Karmen, 1990). As Robert Elias (1990, p. 231) notes:

> By implication, some victim protections affect offender rights. Some initiatives specify that victim rights shall not erode defendant's rights, yet lack specific provisions for doing so. Indirectly, offender rights may be affected by victim participation in plea bargaining, sentencing, and parole decisions.

There is an even greater danger to criminal defendants' constitutional rights if Victim-Offender Mediation (VOM) becomes prevalent in the states, and which is the current "fad" among victims rights advocates. The victim becomes the center of the criminal justice process, with the boundaries between public and private authority obscured and the constitutional protections eliminated by relying on "arbitrary criteria" (Weisberg, 1995, p. 60). The danger of victim and crime defendant rights conflicting does not exist in the civil courts, because the constitutional rights of the accused do not apply to civil actions, and thus the constitutional dilemma is avoided completely.

Still many victims rights advocates argue that such rights *should* be gained at the expense of the rights of crime defendants, and that too much time and energy is wasted protecting the criminal. Critics of this victims rights argument raise several objections:

> First, they argue that making convicts suffer more does not make victims suffer any less... Second, they charge that many of these measures do not really empower victims but rather strengthen the government's ability to control its citizens... Finally critics point out that these opportunities to press for institutionalized revenge benefit only a small portion of all victims—only those fortunate ones whose reported cases are solved and are prosecuted vigorously and successfully (Karmen, 1990, pp. 332–333).

The procedures and rules of evidence in criminal courts are very different from and more complex than those in the civil courts, often because of the Bill of Rights and the due process clause of the Fourteenth Amendment. As witnessed in the aftermath of the O.J. Simpson case, public sympathy for crime victims and their families have caused many to question the criminal rules of evidence and procedure, and even the presumption of innocence that is the foundation of our criminal courts. Such short-term public fervor could cause elected legislators to again second-guess hundreds of years of common law in the name of victims rights, with possible disastrous results in the long-term.

Due process is not specified in either the Fifth or the Fourteenth Amendments, but has had almost two hundred years of precedent to establish it, albeit the majority of the precedent has been in the last four decades. Due process is therefore founded on the logic of countless legal and political scholars. On the other hand, victims rights only date back to the nineteen-eighties and are based on current public fervor.

Although both claim to be based on fairness, a defendant's due process is based on the carefully constructed federal constitution and the concept of equity that has evolved over centuries of common law. Victims rights are based on public fear of crime and a desire by state legislators to curry their voters favor on an issue with which they cannot lose. James Madison warned us to avoid a "tyranny of the masses." It makes no sense to abandon common and constitutional law with hastily made decisions; thus deserting the logic of separating criminal and civil cases that has evolved over the centuries.

Reform of the Civil System as a Better Remedy to Wrongs Caused by Victimization

The problems with reforming the civil law judicial system, created to redress citizens' private disputes with other citizens, are far outweighed by the problems of ad hoc adapting and reconfiguring the criminal law judicial system, which has specifically evolved under the common law to protect society as a whole and not to compensate the individual victim. In fact, the problems with reforming the civil law system so that it better enforces victims rights are primarily financial. The costs of legal aid, lengthy civil litigation, and enforcement of civil judgements, are often insurmountable obstacles to the criminal victim seeking justice from the civil courts today.

Probably the greatest problem with redressing such wrongs in the civil courts are the financial costs of civil litigation. As one judicial scholar has correctly noted, "the resources required to initiate and sustain civil litigation prevent poor people from fully utilizing the judicial branch of government as a forum for dispute processing" (Smith, 1991, p. 59). It is a financial hardship for most victims to pursue justice in the civil courts today. The highest violent crime rates fall on victims from families earning less than seven thousand, five hundred dollars a year and households victimized by burglaries the most have an annual income of less than fifteen thousand dollars (Bureau of Justice Statistics [BJS], 1994).

However, the dispute resolution structure already exists and legal service programs exist to help the poor in the civil courts, although the programs have suffered from political opposition, with their budgets cut tremendously because of government fiscal austerity and the political perception of these programs being used to pursue unpopular social welfare policies (Smith, 1991). In the long run, it would cost less to reform the existing civil court structure than to "tack on" various victims rights programs to a criminal justice system that has not evolved to nor was ever created to redress a crime victim's private dispute with the criminal. In fact, legal aid programs for the poor would no doubt benefit with increased political and economic support if the legal aid lawyers were perceived as crime victims' advocates by both the public and the government officials who hold the "purse-strings."

The substantive law framework for redressing the wrongs against victims by criminals also exists in the American civil law. Intentional violent and property crimes have their civil law counterparts in the form of intentional torts against persons and property. Furthermore, a person who does not exhibit ordinary care or is reckless as to the welfare of others is held at fault by the civil law for the damages done to those others (Calvi & Coleman, 1989). Negligence is often the grounds for a civil lawsuit, although proof of criminal negligence is much more exacting then proof of civil negligence, which is generally true when comparing proof of crimes with proof of their civil counterparts.

Still, civil cases take longer than criminal cases and are therefore more expensive because civil procedural laws, like the laws of evidence in civil cases, are less restricting than criminal procedural laws. Even small claims courts that are structured for fast hearings take a month or more between the filing of a civil case and its trial, whereas cases in other civil courts may take as long as several years for trial (Glick, 1983). However, there are ways to streamline the civil court process for crime victims.

One difficulty of proof in the civil law, as well as in the criminal law, is the proof of the intent of a tortfeasor. The common law developed the concept of "strict liability" under certain conditions when others are endangered, wherein the tortfeasor is responsible for the damages, even thought there is no proof of "fault" (Calvi & Coleman, 1989). Certainly making another a victim of a criminal act could be another condition where strict liability could apply legally. Unlike civil actions, criminal actions are bound by the "speedy trial" requirements of the Sixth Amendment of the Constitution, and therefore are likely to be tried before their civil counterpart. The doctrine of collateral estoppel could be modified in favor of the crime victim in civil actions as it already works in favor of the crime defendant in criminal actions, so that any fact established at the criminal trial would not have to be reproved at the civil trial (Samaha, 1996). Both of these legal concepts could be easily and logically expanded under the common law governing civil actions, thus simplifying what would have to be proven at trial.

An adaptation of the civil law concept of "default judgement" would simplify a civil action for a crime victim even more. One definition of "default" is the "failure to perform a duty or obligation" which allows a judgement to be entered without trial against the offending party (Lusk, Hewitt, Donnell, & Barnes, 1978, p.s 1332). It could certainly be argued that a criminal failed to perform his citizen's obligation not to criminally victimize a fellow citizen, hence breaching the "social contract." Therefore, a successful criminal action could act as a default judgement against the criminal in civil court, leaving only the damages to be determined by the civil court judge or jury.

Garnishment could be one of several routine measures available under the civil law to enforce judgements in favor of criminal victims. Under civil statutes, garnishments "are used to reach bank accounts, wages due, or accounts receivable; however, under some statutes, one can reach goods in storage, the redemption value of pawned goods, and other similar assets" (Lusk et al., 1978, p. 275). Furthermore, the court structure for collecting such debts and garnishments already exists in the civil courts for over two hundred years in the United States, so very little adaptation would have to be made by the civil court system.

A major argument against civil litigation is that the offender has no funds from which the victim may collect a civil court's judgement. This "myth" of uncollectability ignores the fact that an offender has many present and future sources of income. Such sources of income include: (1) wages, (2) benefits (i.e., pension payments and annuities), (3) unearned income (i.e., dividends, interest, and gifts), (4) trust fund income, (5) tax refunds, (6) government entitlements, (7) personal property (i.e., cars, jewelry, etc.), (8) real property (i.e., home, land, etc.), (9) bank accounts, (10) all debts owed to the offender, (11) financial holdings (i.e., stocks, bonds, etc.), (12) partnership interests, and (13) future interests in real and personal property through wills and trusts. Furthermore, there is the possibility of insurance coverage because current court decisions make it often difficult to delineate between coverage and non-coverage in civil actions (NCJRS, 1997a).

Conclusion

Many victims rights advocates argue that having victims play a more important part in the criminal justice system is both "empowering" and therapeutic (Adler, et al., 1995; Thigpen, 1995). Others worry that victims might be worse off if they see a defendant get a light sentence despite their best efforts (Thigpen, 1995). Still others argue that the pain and suffering of victims should play little role in determining punishment in the criminal justice process, although those factors are highly significant in figuring compensation for torts in the civil law process ("Victim Justice," 1995).

It is also questionable whether crime victims have more confidence in the criminal justice system when they are "empowered" with rights. The proportion of crimes reported to law enforcement authorities nationally was thirty-three and a half percent in 1974 (BJS, 1992). However, according to the 1995 Victimization Survey, victimizations reported to the police have decreased five percent since that time (Rand et al., 1997). If crime victims are supposed to be more confident in the criminal justice system since the advent of the victims' rights movement of the eighties, then these statistics do not support this proposition. In fact, one scientific study found no effect when victims provide impact statements and their satisfaction level with the criminal justice system (Davis & Smith, 1994). Furthermore, several studies have found that very few victims exercise their "victims' rights," although whether this was because of ignorance, apathy, or alienation is unclear (Kelly, 1990).

Although there are no statistics on the costs of modifying the criminal justice systems to accommodate victims so far, it is likely to be a significant amount. The money and effort would be better served in changing and streamlining the already existing civil court system to better serve crime victims' needs. Furthermore, crime victims would be more "empowered" because they, instead of the prosecutor, would decide whether to bring suit or settle a case (NCJRS, 1997a). It would be better for society to accommodate crime victims rights in a court system designed to resolve disputes between individuals, rather than awkwardly attaching duties and structures to serve individual needs to a court process created and evolved to serve societal needs. However, legal aid and faster litigation processes must be made available to crime victims if the civil courts are ever going to be a viable option for satisfying victims' needs.

Discussion Questions

Have the courts gone too far and too fast in legitimizing victims' rights assertions during judicial hearings? Do the positive effects on crime victims' psyches out balance the negative impacts on crime defendants' due process rights?

Are civil court remedies for crime victims indeed superior to criminal court remedies, as the author maintains? What are the political, economic, and social problems associated with the civil court remedies listed by the author as compared with the present trend of criminal court remedies?

Chapter 13

Do Ask, Do Tell: Assessing Implications of Community Notification Requirements within Sexual Offender Legislation

Lloyd Klein

Introduction

Community corrections remains a hot topic as we progressively move through the last portion of the decade. Crime is an ever-present cutting edge issue affecting both criminal justice authorities and neighborhood residents. Community crime control measures are a constant feature of media and citizen-based demands for public safety. The resultant citizen safety concerns are the nexus of a systematic outcry demanding a more efficient community corrections protocol.

The community is not altogether irrational in their perception of this threat. Bernstein (1996) paints a bleak picture of a Fertile, Minnesota prison inmate who is instrumental in maintaining "The Fertile Journal." Here children's photographs, background information, and addresses are exchanged through computers and nationwide research efforts.

Communities are instrumental in promulgating political change. A salient case in point is the reaction of a New Jersey community following the actions of a released sexual predator. Megan Kanka was found murdered in a New Jersey park. Subsequent publicity catapulted the community safety debate back into the public spotlight. More importantly, Megan Kanka's murder brought an important 1989 Washington State statute into the public view and helped raise important questions about the protective impact of public policy initiatives.

Such criminal justice policies have raised issues including: (1) the role of the ex-convict in the community, (2) the nature of criminal offenses and acceptance of the offender as a "reformed" individual, and (3) whether legislative efforts can constitute a compromise between the needs of the released offender and the anxiety of community residents.

These are not easy issues. The community is seeking a solution for the ongoing threat of criminal victimization while accepting the sanctioning authority of the criminal justice system. The foregoing statement is relevant when considering that basic tenets of the justice system process emphasize deterrence, retribution, and incapacitation (Sagarin, 1985). Citizens grant the criminal justice system immense discretionary power, with the understanding that officials will apprehend, prosecute, and imprison the felons responsible for reprehensible deeds against society. Many defendants convicted after violent crime are granted early release after serving the legally mandated sentence and must begin a new life in the outside world. Additionally, an increasingly common reason for early release occurs when prison overcrowding dictates a constant turnover for creating jail cell vacancies.

This chapter will assess the problems related with releasing violent offenders and notifying the communities where released sexual predators might pose a threat to children or other residents. An offered analysis will discuss how sexual offender legislation incorporates these concerns along with the legal issues involved in community notification and the privacy of released sexual offenders.

Nature of Sexual Predator Legislation

Public policy issues intertwining sex offender registration, community notification, and governmental responsibility were instrumental in the creation of legislative initiatives. Contemporary sexual predator laws reflect a victims' rights perspective represented on a community-wide basis. The push toward community-based corrections emphasized the citizen as a potential victim and how the criminal justice system could protect the average person. Victims see the sexual predator legislation emphasizing registration, notification, and involuntary detention as necessary for protecting individual and family safety. Problems emerge when we must balance the constitutional rights of the offenders versus the concerns of citizens. Public policy measures often fall on one side or another depending upon the latest appellate or U.S. Supreme Court rulings. Thus, the statutes are seen as means to an end (community protection) rather than conceptualizing the practical consequences affecting sexual predators or the community.

Most consideration of sexual predator laws fails to note that sex offender registration was the last step in the process (Jerusalem, 1995). Originally, public humiliation was effected in the Colonial period with the use of the "Scarlet Letter" and continued into the modern era with the development of civil commitment statutes for sex offenders. According to a legislative appraisal in the *Harvard Law Review* (1995), the utilization of a "modern day scarlet letter" is updated in notifying community residents of ex-convicts residing in the immediate area.

However, community notification is far from a recent issue. Goldstein and Susmilch (1982) recommended that the Madison (Wisconsin) Police Department should develop new relations with ex-offenders who were living in the community and with the staff of the Division of Corrections who were responsible for supervising them. The community was not mentioned in this policy statement nor was there any mention of sex offender registration requirements.

Klein, Luxenburg, and Rogers (1990) came to the same conclusion based upon the Singleton case wherein a convicted sex offender was released. Numerous communities refused criminal justice attempts to place Singleton in a residential area. Moreover, Klein et.al. state that the criminal justice system can more directly work with the community through select notification or more extensive disclosure.

One other important problem emerges in the rush to encourage public disclosure. The utility of registration and notification requirements may be offset in isolated cases of independent community reactions against the released sexual predators (Anderson, 1994). The propensity to encourage vigilantism is an undercurrent issue in the harnessing of community reactions (Philadelphia Inquirer, 1994). Montana (1995) explains that community notification laws may encourage lawlessness because such laws heighten community fears concerning the threat of convicted sex offenders. Van Blema (1993) and the Seattle Times (1993a, 1993b) document how Joseph Gallardo was forced out of Snohomish County (Washington) after sheriffs' posters stated that Gallardo had "sadistic and deviant sexual fantasies which included torture, sexual assault, human sacrifice, bondage, and the murder of young children" (p.58, B1, B4, respectively).

The 1989 Washington Statutes

Crimes committed by sex offenders provoke public outrage. A consideration of Washington, New Jersey, and New York will provide some relevant examples. The 1989 Washington State law was a significant benchmark amid continuing public debate. The Washington statute mandates that convicted sex offenders register within twenty-four hours of their prison release with the sheriff of their residential county. According to the Washington Code, an offender moving to another county must register with the second county's sheriff within ten days of the move. Yet, commu-

nity notification is demanded by citizens convinced that registration provides safety from repeat sex offenders (Scott, 1994). Harvard's legislative
brief aptly points out that the Washington law was enacted after a seven
year old Tacoma boy was lured into a wooded area by Earl Shriner, a persistent sex offender, who committed oral and anal rape and then cut off
the victim's penis (Boerner, 1992; Hudson, 1992; Jerome, Eftimhades,
Gallo, & Sawicki, 1995; Siegel, 1990; Simon, 1990).

Notification under the Washington legislation permits police release of
information about sex offenders to the public. Community responses are
varied and diverse. Communities already impose makeshift forms of notification through "requiring a purse snatcher to wear tap shoes when he
left home, requiring drunk drivers to publish apologies in local newspapers or to place stickers proclaiming their convictions on their cars, and
requiring a child molester to post a sign at his residence stating Dangerous
Sex Offender—No Children Allowed. (*Harvard Law Review*, 1995:790).

The 1994 New Jersey "Megan's Law"

The community clearly has a genuine concern about molesters preying
on young boys. The controversy swirling Megan's Law fueled public feelings about released sex offenders living among community residents.
Megan Kanka was a seven-year-old girl living in Hamilton Township,
New Jersey. Megan was raped and murdered by Jesse Timmendequas, a
twice-convicted felon who had served six years for sexual assault
(Jerusalem, 1995). The 33 year old suspect lived across the street from the
victim. Megan was abducted and her body was found in weeds in a park
three miles away. More than 1,000 people turned out for an August 2,
1994 vigil. Fifteen hundred signatures were collected in support of a law
protecting children from sex offenders (Barrow, 1994). The community
eventually raised $100,000, bought the home that Timmendequas for-
merly lived, and tore the structure down for the establish of a memorial
park (Jerome et al., 1995).

The newly proposed law emphasized stiffer penalties for sex offenders,
registration, public notification, and involuntary civil commitment of
feared recidivists—all tenets of the original Washington State statute
(Hopper, 1994; Jerusalem, 1995; Smolowe, 1994). The bill was approved
by the state legislation and signed into law on October 31, 1994. Legislation consisted of nine bills calling for tougher punitive steps against sexual
molesters. Convicted sex offenders must register with local law enforcement officials and neighborhood residents living within 1,000 yards receive notification. The provisions included longer minimum prison terms
for sex offenders, the death penalty for murdering a child under 15, sex

offenders must report to local police or state attorneys every 90 days, possible civil confinement in a psychiatric hospital, lifetime monitoring, DNA testing, and 30 day notification before release (Sullivan, 1994).

Megan's Law underwent a significant legal challenge (Hanley, 1995a, 1995b; Jerome et al., 1995), when Diaz, a convicted sex offender, sued on the grounds that he lived in a community before the passage of Megan's law. Federal District Judge Nicholas Politan upheld the requirement that sex offenders register with police. However, Politan also ruled that community notification is unconstitutional on the grounds that individuals serving their time were denied the right to a normal life. A subsequent July 1995 Federal court decision affirmed the constitutionality of Megan's law. However, Williams (1996) informs us that the New Jersey and Connecticut laws are so wide sweeping that a Federal judge blocked legislative implementation. The New Jersey law seeks to cover anyone ever convicted of a sex crime.

New York State Sexual Predator Legislation

New York State adopted a similar law calling for registration and community notification. New York State Assembly bill 1059-C (January 18, 1995) amended the correction law with the proposed Sex Offender Registration Act. The main premise of the bill (section 1) specifies:

> The legislature finds that the danger of recidivism posed by sex offenders, especially those sexually violent offenders who commit predatory acts characterized by repetitive and compulsive behavior, and that law enforcement agencies' efforts to protect their communities, conduct investigations and quickly apprehend sex offenders are impaired by the lack of information about sex offenders who live within their jurisdiction and that the lack of information shared with the public may result in the failure of the criminal justice system to identify, investigate, apprehend and prosecute sex offenders (p. 1).

The summary further specifies that the system of registering sex offenders stands as a "proper exercise of the state's police power regulating present and ongoing conduct" (p. 1).

The mandated registration would provide law enforcement with additional information "critical to preventing sexual victimization and to resolving incidents involving sexual abuse and exploitation promptly" (p. 1). Such procedures permit law enforcement authorities the capacity of alerting the public "when necessary for the continued protection of the community" (p. 1). An interesting and overriding purpose of the legislation is worded as follows:

Persons found to have committed a sex offense have a reduced expectation of privacy because of the public's interest in safety and in the effective operation of government. In balancing offenders' due process and other rights, and the interest of public security, the legislature finds that releasing information about sex offenders to law enforcement agencies and, under certain circumstances, providing access to limited information about certain sex offenders to the general public, will further the primary government interest of protecting vulnerable populations and in some instances the public, from potential harm (p. 2).

The bill mandates ten day notification prior to the release of sex offenders from a hospital or correctional facility. The law enforcement agency having jurisdiction must give notification specifying names and aliases of the sex offender, the address at which he will reside, the address resided at time of conviction, amount of time remaining to be served, and nature of the crime. The sex offender's parole officer must provide notification of residence change to the new jurisdiction within 48 hours. There are other such provisions for circumstances covering court notification and parole or probation officer obligation.

Duty to register is another important provision of the law. The statute specifies that any sex offender who is discharged, paroled, or released from any state or local correctional facility, hospital, or institution must register within ten calendar days. Sex offenders required to register on an annual basis must conform to the following provisions: mail the verification form to the division within ten calendar days after receipt of the form and the form must be signed by the sex offender in affirming that he still resides at the last reported address. The sex offender must re-certify residential information on a quarterly basis for a minimum of ten years.

In a manner not unlike the New Jersey Sexual Predator Statute, the state must appoint a board of examiners of sex offenders. According to the New York law, the board should consist of five members appointed by the governor. Three members must be experts in the field of the behavior and treatment of sex offenders and the remaining two members must come from the criminal justice agency. The board must develop guidelines and procedures assessing the risk of a repeat offense by the sex offender and the threat posed to the public safety. Prescribed guidelines include criminal history factors indicative of high risk of repeat offense including: (1) mental abnormalities, (2) repetitive and compulsive behavior associated with drugs or alcohol, (3) whether the sex offender served the maximum term, (4) whether the sex offender committed the felony sex offense against a child, and (5) the age of the sex offender at the time of commission of the first sex offense.

Other instrumental criminal history factors include: the relationship between sex offender and the victim, whether the offense involved the use of a weapon, violence, or infliction of serious bodily harm, and the number, date, and nature of prior offenses. Other stipulations include conditions of release that minimize risk or re-offense, physical conditions that minimize risk of re-offense, whether psychological or psychiatric profiles indicate a risk of recidivism, the sex offender's response to treatment, recent behavior, recent threats or gestures against persons or expressions of intent to commit additional offenses, and review of any victim impact statement.

In addition, New York State proposed notification through telephone inquiries. Notification concerning the most dangerous sexual offenders incorporates creation of a special "900" telephone number and a sexually violent predator subdirectory (available at police stations). The "900" telephone number, which was scheduled to go into service on March 8, 1996, imposed a $5 fee per each call. The caller must tell an operator why he or she is requesting information on a particular person. Information disclosure is dependent upon how dangerous the offender is considered. Level 1 is a simple confirmation that the person is listed in the registry. Level 2 provides an approximate address, zip code, and neighborhood. Level 3 provides an exact address and the offenders modus operandi in previous crimes. Callers can also obtain information about sex offenders moving in and out of their communities (Fenner, 1996).

The New York State law specifies that the division shall decide whether the named person reasonably appears to be a person listed, based upon information from the caller providing information including an exact street address, including apartment number, driver's license number or birth date, along with additional information including social security number, hair color, eye color, height, weight, distinctive markings, and ethnicity.

The law details the nature of the "900" telephone number operation. A preamble shall be played before charges begin to accrue. The message must include the following information: notice that the caller's telephone number will be recorded, the charges for use of the "900" number, notice that the caller is required to identify himself or herself to the operator and provide a current address which shall be maintained in a written record, notice that the caller is required to be eighteen years of age or older, a warning that it is illegal to use information obtained through the "900" number to commit a crime against any person listed or to engage in illegal discrimination or harassment against such person, notice that the caller is required to have the birth date, driver's license, or identification number, address, or other identifying information regarding the person about whom information is sought in order to achieve a positive identification of that person, a statement that the number is not a crime hotline and that any suspected criminal activity should be repeated to local authorities, and anyone misusing the "900" number shall be subject to a fine of no more than $1,000.

Sexual Predator Laws and Nationwide Notification Standards

According to the National Center for Missing & Exploited Children (1995), 44 states currently have sex offender registration laws while 27 states enforce community notification laws. Sex offender registration has been newly enacted in Iowa, Maryland, New Mexico, and New York. More significantly, nine states (Arizona, Colorado, Connecticut, Iowa, Maryland, Mississippi, New York, South Dakota, and Texas) have enacted community notification laws.

Donnelly and Lieb (1993) explored the issue of law enforcement and community notification within Washington. Level 1 offenders involve notification to law enforcement personnel only. Level 2 offenders require the production and circulation of school fliers. Level 3 offenders are publicized through the distribution of home fliers.

Donnelly and Lieb (1993) also tackled the question regarding what the public should know. According to their statewide survey, Level 1 offender information is retained for use by law enforcement personnel only. Level 2 and Level 3 offenders are more publicized. The incidence of particular informational categories disseminated according to classification levels are as follows: a) approximate or exact address 74% (Level 2), 88% (Level 3), approximate address 53% (Level 2), 35% (Level 3), exact address 21% (Level 2), 53% (Level 3); b) physical description 63% (Level 2), 86% (Level 3—with photograph); c) photograph and criminal history 49% (Level 2), 74% (Level 3—criminal history), method of approaching victims 49% (Level 2), 67% (Level 3); d) vehicle model 14% (Level 2), 24% (Level 3); and e) place of employment 12% (Level 2), 47% (Level 3).

The authors also distinguish between limited information (mandated in Level 2 classifications as containing offender's name and/or address) and full information (stipulated in Level 3 cases—offender's name, address and criminal history details). The following responses were recorded in a survey response to the question—*Which individuals and organizations are granted access to sex offender information?* community corrections officers (100% full information), Child Protective Services (67% full information, 28% limited information, 5% no information), School Officials (37% full information, 58% limited information, 5% no information), individual citizens (16% full information, 72% limited information,

12% no information), community organizations (16% full information, 67% limited information, 17% no information), and media (12% full information, 77% limited information, 11% no information).

A subsequent study of adult sex offender recidivism reveals that community perceptions are reflected in research on recidivist rates (Song & Lieb, 1994). Recidivism rates for untreated sex offenders varied according to offender category. The lowest category included incest offenders (4–10%). Other categories (in ascending order) include rapists (7–35%), child molesters—girl victims (10–29%), child molesters—boy victims (13%-40%), and exhibitionists (41%-71%).

The New York, Washington, and New Jersey statutes incorporate standard notification criteria. In New York State, the sexual predator law specifies that the board shall within sixty days prior to the discharge, parole, or release of a sex offender make a confidential recommendation to the sentencing court regarding whether the sex offender warrants the designation of sexually violent predator. In addition, the board must formulate a recommendation to the sentencing court regarding three levels of notification. These three designations are Level 1 (low risk), Level 2 (moderate risk), and Level 3 (high risk).

Risk of repeat offense is low under a Level 1 designation. If the risk of a repeat offense is moderate, a Level 2 designation is assigned to the sex offender. The law enforcement agency having jurisdiction and the law enforcement agency having had jurisdiction at the time of conviction shall be notified and may disseminate relevant information including an appropriate address based on the sex offender's zip code, a photograph of the offender, background information including the offender's crime of conviction, modus operandi, type of victim targeted, and the description of special conditions imposed on the offender to any entity with vulnerable populations related to the nature of the offense committed by such sex offender.

Level 3 designation carries a high risk of repeat offense and a threat to the public safety. In this case, the law enforcement agency must freely disseminate the offender's name, address, and criminal history through posted notices in public places and the proviso of sex offender registers available for public inspection. Many states are redefining these standards to include local newspaper dissemination of the same information. One case occurred in New Jersey wherein an offender's photograph and criminal history was published in a local newspaper. Additionally, a noteworthy debate ensued regarding community notification of local sex offenders residing in the Wesleyan University (CT) vicinity (Duda, 1998).

Appeals mounted by the American Civil Liberties Union and similar groups have prevented implementation of the community notification standards. For example, police departments throughout the state of Connecticut are compelled to collect registered information supplied by the individual sex offender. However, the constitutionality of appropriate notification criteria is still unclear and remains in the jurisdiction of appellate court judges.

Public Sentiment and Privacy Issues

Community opposition to the placement of Singleton or any other sexual offender in a probationary release program is perhaps one of the more visible examples of the difficulties that our correctional system has encountered in moving from a prison-based model to a community-based transition and diversion model. Many questions still remain regarding how Washington, New Jersey, New York, and other registration/notification laws might successfully placate community residents and serve criminal justice purposes. The traditional model supported the idea that offenders should be kept apart from society in rural, institutionalized settings. Partly due to this isolation from society at large, offenders became easily stereotyped as social outcasts to be feared by all. The chief function of the correctional system is perceived to be one of protecting the public from these feared outcasts.

Since such crucial problems as overcrowding and rehabilitation have resurfaced, a different attitude toward incarceration developed within the correctional system. Realizing that there was a limit to the number of correctional facilities any state can realistically fund, and facing maintenance costs that continue to increase, correctional officials sought viable alternatives to incarceration that could alleviate overcrowding and prepare the offender for a new role in society. The trend moved toward building urban facilities, community-based half-way houses, and residential parole release programs.

In this transition, corrections officials came face to face with the reality they had not fully anticipated—public opposition. The base of this opposition is the fear of crime, much of which stems from myths concerning offenders and correctional institutions. While the courts are demanding that overcrowded conditions be eliminated, the public is demanding that the courts impose harsher sentences. Megan's Law and other legalistic efforts seem to flaunt constitutional rights. This places correctional officers in a vulnerable place—reversing public sentiment becomes problematic; however, bending the law is as much a problem as it is a cure.

Klein et al. (1990) have identified two options: either direct (officially released identification) or indirect (mediating release through a select few) notification. Holding criminal justice officials responsible for crime control creates a delicate policy balance. Several provisions seem to violate the constitutional rights enjoyed by American citizens. On one hand, the New York Civil Liberties Union believes that "grandfathering" the registration requirement for those convicted prior to the law's effective date (Jan. 21) is seemingly unconstitutional (Fenner, 1996). Several such New Jersey suits followed the imposition of the New Jersey Megan's Law. Courts ruled that sex offenders predating the law's enforcement were not affected by the new statute.

However, these debates affect the privacy of convicted sex offenders. Joseph Rossillo achieved notoriety as the first newly convicted New York State offender to register under the sexual predator law (Williams, 1996). Rossillo pleaded guilty in exchange for five years' probation. Photographers and reporters, alerted by a Westchester County District Attorney news release, covered the court proceedings. Rossillo was placed under 60 days of house arrest and was later order to leave his $800,000 house because it was about 100 yards from an elementary school. Such procedures raised questions regarding whether the new law was written so broadly that it included people who did not pose a threat to public safety, or whether the public right to know the whereabouts of sex offenders superseded any privacy rights.

A running debate between Norman Siegel, executive director of the New York Civil Liberties Union and the Westchester District Attorney's office defines the privacy debate. Siegel believes that Rossillo is not the type of recidivist sex offender that the New York law was designed to target. Siegel criticizes the DA's office for circulating the press release highlighting Rossillo's sentence. The legal position was based upon the abridgement of sex offenders' right to petition for exemption from registration (Williams, 1996).

Recent Developments in Sexual Predator Statutes

The impact of victims requesting legal protection from state and federal levels was reflected in activity surrounding Federal victims' legislation and an important U.S. Supreme Court ruling. President Bill Clinton acknowledged the concerns of community residents in their frustration toward sexual predators. A 1996 federal crime bill initiative (dubbed "the national Megan's Law") stipulated mandatory registration and notification provisions. All fifty states were required to secure notification and classify offenders according to potential recidivist behavior.

Appellate courts subsequentely sustained notification and other provisions in New York, New Jersey, Washington, and other jurisdictions throughout the country following the U.S. Supreme Court ruling on the viability of sexual predator statutes. However, as noted before, implementation of the notification process was subsequently stalled in further legal litigation.

A long-awaited ruling on voluntary civil incapacitation was released on June 23, 1997. The case of *Kansas v. Hendricks* (No. 95-1649) stemmed from the Kansas appeal of an Appellate court decision. Hendricks is a 62 year old sexual offender and self-proclaimed pedophiliac who had completed a ten year term for molesting two 13 year old boys. He cited double jeopardy and *ex post facto* criteria in challenging a 1994 Kansas law mandating notification and involuntary mental institution confinement.

The Kansas Supreme Court ruled that the law contained a vague definition of mental abnormality and the lack of medical treatment constituted a violation of the 14th Amendment guaranteeing due process. Arizona, California, Minnesota, Washington, and Wisconsin were also impacted because each of the above states contained the same provision in their sexual predator laws (Greenspan, 1997).

The high court ruled by a margin of 5–4 that states may confine violent sex offenders in mental institutions after they have served their criminal sentence. Involuntary civil confinement was deemed legitimate even if the offenders were not classified mentally ill according to a state's legal criteria. Justices Thomas, Rehnquist, O'Connor, Scalia, and Kennedy concurred that the confinement was not punishment. According to Thomas' opinion, a single finding of dangerousness was enough to warrant confinement provided that authorities establish proof of additional factors. Justices Breyer (author of the dissenting opinion), Stewart, Souter, and Ginsberg expressed the view that sexual offenders were basically punished because institutional environments restrained rather than treated the relevant psychological or behavioral problems. The minority opinion also stated that the law passed muster if it operated in a prospective manner, or provided treatment rather than incarceration.

Further, the ruling stipulated that the sexual offender was entitled to due process under the law. A trial type proceeding was necessary for official confinement. The state had the burden of proof beyond a reasonable doubt. Further, the individual had the right to an attorney, an opportunity to present his own case, and the cross-examination of any and all state witnesses. Additionally, the state must re-evaluate the case through annual reviews of the offender's progress in the mental institution.

A New York Times editorial (1997) essentially stated that the U.S. Supreme Court violated the criteria between mental abnormality versus mental illness and imposed double jeopardy and *ex post facto* problems. The statement indicated that the court condoned institutionalization based on a loose definition of mental abnormality and the assumption that the person is likely to recidivate in the future.

A separate New York Times analysis (Purdy, 1997) indicated that recidivism is not consistently predictable. The Federal Bureau of Prisons conducted a three year study in which 41 percent of the sexual predators were arrested for new felonies. Nineteen percent of the rapists during the same period were arrested for new crimes. The U.S. Supreme Court ruling in the Hendricks case cleared the way for state legislation throughout the country. Ongoing legal challenges were set aside with the nationwide implementation of sexual predator laws. New York, New Jersey, Kansas, Connecticut, and other states set October 1 as the starting date of the mandated confinement and notification provisions (Trelease, 1997). Questions regarding offender liability lawsuits claiming police infringement of civil or criminal protections stemming from good faith reporting still remain a major concern. In one case, Connecticut is faced with a December 31, 1998 deadline for drafting protective guidelines.

Another new development poses equally challenging questions. The advent of the internet permits the free flow of assorted information. According to a Microsoft Daily News website report (Seminerio, 1997), both states and individuals can post the names, addresses, photographs, and other relevant information about sexual predators obtained through Megan's Law disclosure procedures. One known web site (Pandora's Box) contains links to every state's sexual predator postings.

Another site (www.sexoffenders.net) was initiated by Ken LaCorte, a California father whose daughter was a sex offender victim. Law enforcement officials and privacy rights advocates feared vigilante justice arising from the available information. Any individuals finding their names mistakenly placed on the sex offender database could face imminent disaster. Christopher Hansen, a staff attorney with the American Civil Liberties Union points out that the practice is legal. However, the ACLU opposes community notification on the grounds that moral ambiguity surrounds the issue of drawing attention to ex-criminals who have served their time, and because of the potential legal problems. The battle over community notification is clearly far from over.

Conclusion

The various sexual predator notification laws reflect a salient concern about neighborhood safety and concerns for actual victims. We are clearly concerned about the safety of children growing up in tranquil residential neighborhoods. Sexual predators molesting young children is a heinous crime deserving criminal justice attention. But what do we do after the offenders serve their court mandated sentence? Do we affix a scarlet letter onto their personae for the rest of their natural existence?

The research regarding rehabilitation and the sexual offender is far from clear. Most literature indicates that such offenders are incorrigible. How do these laws serve the interest of crime victims? Should we formulate clinical solutions for the immediate problem? How can the panacea of a notification statute immediately serve offenders and community residents? Notably child molestation crimes in California, Washington, New Jersey, and other states carried the banner for a comprehensive notification law. But is this a viable solution or another problematic example of our criminal justice system reactively scrambling for an instant fix?

The legal system protects citizens and actual crime victims in providing comfort and often actual protection. But legal statutes are only as good as the rationale for formulation and eventual implementation. Community notification is a great concept. But who is best served through such legislative concepts? The community feels a sense of relief. But are the laws actually effective in detecting, deterring, and processing sexual predators? Therapeutic programs are clearly needed for both the victims or victimized families and the sexual predators themselves. The criminal justice system and therapeutic community either cannot effectively rehabilitate pedophiles due to offender personality resilience or lack of comprehensive treatment programs. We must pinpoint which is the likely case.

Let us ask the crucial question: can these laws help or hinder victim recovery? Placing a sexual predator or recidivist sex offender in an environment away from community contact is the desired result. But community notification and mandated state action have limited ability in assisting child victims and parents of deceased children.

Community notification is a good idea. However, are politicians and law enforcement officials threatening basic freedoms when privacy issues are disregarded in favor of monitoring and controlling released felons? Statutes in New York, New Jersey, Washington, and other state jurisdictions are under court challenge and might be unenforceable due to court challenges. The U.S. Supreme Court decision in *Kansas v. Hendricks* (1997) raised a number of interesting questions. Is involuntary civil incapacitation the necessary protection sought by sexual predator victims and law enforcement authorities throughout the United States? What happens to the constitutionally protected rights of criminal offenders?

We must face reality: the solution (cure) may be worse than the problem (disease). Everyone has a seemingly simple solution. The real answers are yet to come. We must strive to find a law that satisfies victims by facilitating treatment but one that also allows sexual predators back into the community. Both sides have clear propriety interest in the ultimate outcome. In the meantime, DO ASK, DO TELL becomes the mantra for countless community residents.

Discussion Questions

Analyze sexual predator statutes from the perspective of the victim, offender, and criminal justice system representatives? Who is best served by these policies? Why?

Discuss the issue of community notification. How much information should the criminal justice authorities reveal to community residents about sexual predators?

Analyze the U.S. Supreme Court decision on involuntary civil incapacitation. What are the moral and practical problems associated with this policy?

Part V

Sexual Harassment and Stalking

Chapter 14

Sexual Harassment: A New Look at an Old Issue

Bernadette T. Muscat

Introduction

Sexual harassment is defined in a variety of ways including, unprofessional behavior between individuals engaging in a working relationship (Childers, 1993; Hiller, 1993); unwelcome sexual advances, requests for sexual favors, and/or other verbal/physical conduct of a sexual nature (Childers, 1993); and the unwanted imposition of sexual requests, exploitation, and/or coercion in the context of a relationship of unequal power where that power is being abused (Childers, 1993; Gragg, 1992; Kulak, 1992). Some forms of harassment such as stalking, physical and sexual assault and battery, and rape amount to criminal acts in which the crime is largely a police matter and external to the employer (Echiejile, 1993).

This chapter examines sexual harassment by exploring the legal evolution of the prohibition of sexual harassment in the workplace. The information garnered herein is used to build the argument that sexual harassment mirrors the criminal aspects of domestic violence and stalking. The intent of this chapter is to highlight the criminality of sexual harassment as it relates to other forms of violence against women. As such, this chapter should not be regarded as a demand for specific policy changes, but rather as an invitation to open this topic to further discussion.

Understanding Sexual Harassment

Sexual harassment is harmful to the victim(s) because the behavior blatantly violates the person's autonomy and equality in the working relationship (Hiller, 1993). In addition, victims of sexual harassment may also, (1) be unjustly denied career advancement (e.g., loss of promotion), (2) suffer financial losses (e.g., lost wages, raises, bonuses, or court costs for filing a sexual harassment claim), and (3) suffer from mental anguish or illness (Kreps, 1993; Lee, 1995; McCann & McGinn, 1992; Wagner, 1992a, 1992b). At the same time, harassment precipitates sexual stereotypes regarding women, who are largely the targets of this type of harassment, which makes it difficult for some women to be judged in the workplace on the basis of their performance (Hiller, 1993).

The perpetrator(s) of sexual harassment may be anyone who is employed within a workplace environment. The perpetrator may be a supervisor, a co-worker, customer, supplier/vendor, or visitor. The employer is responsible for what happens on company property and in the course of conducting business at off-site locations (e.g., the owner of a delivery company is responsible for the employee when he/she delivers packages at remote locations). The employer is also responsible for after hour work-related functions such as dinners, parties, or business trips (Hiller, 1993; Wagner, 1992a, 1992b). According to Childers (1993) sexual harassment occurs under three conditions, when (1) submission to such conduct is made (overtly or covertly) a term or condition of one's employment status, (2) submission to or rejection of such conduct is used as the basis for employment decisions, and/or (3) such conduct unreasonably interferes or influences an individual's work performance by creating an intimidating, hostile, or offensive working environment. The first two conditions refer to quid pro quo sexual harassment while the latter condition parallels what is commonly regarded as *hostile environment* sexual harassment.

The Legal Evolution of Prohibiting Sexual Harassment

In 1980, the Equal Employment Opportunity Commission (EEOC) issued guidelines that treated sexual harassment as illegal sex discrimination in violation of Section 703 of Title VII of the Civil Rights Act of 1964 (Kulak, 1992; Lee, 1995). According to this Act, it is an unlawful employment practice for an employer to discriminate against any individual based upon his/her race, color, religion, sex, or national origin (Woods, 1994).

The EEOC guidelines clarify the definition of sex discrimination and harassing behavior into two categories. The first category refers to epithets, slurs, negative stereotyping, or behavior that is threatening or intimidating. The second type of harassing behavior consists of written or graphic material that denigrates or shows hostility toward an individual or group and is placed on walls or is circulated in the workplace (EEOC, 1993; Lee, 1995).

In the early 1990s, Congress enacted the Civil Rights Act of 1991 which expanded the rights of victims of sexual harassment (Piskorski,

1993). The 1991 Act made individuals who claimed sexual harassment eligible to receive compensatory and punitive damages for emotional pain, suffering, mental anguish, and the inconvenience caused by the harassment. The statute placed a graduated cap (maximum of $300,000) on the sum of compensatory and punitive damages based upon the size (in terms of number of employees) of the organization. At the same time, individuals were given the opportunity to have a jury decide the merits of the case (Payson, 1992).

The Court's Role in Defining Sexual Harassment

The courts have struggled to develop a law that determines what type of conduct is offensive or harassing and what specifically constitutes sexual harassment. Defining sexual harassment can be difficult because the genders hold different perceptions of what is appropriate sexual conduct within the workplace (Childers, 1993). At the same time, sexual harassment is primarily dealt with through civil lawsuits which diminishes the criminal aspects of this unwelcome and threatening behavior. This section focuses upon the two categories of sexual harassment—quid pro quo and hostile environment—and their respective linkages with similar criminal activities within the realm of domestic violence and stalking (Lee, 1995).

Quid Pro Quo Sexual Harassment

The first type of sexual harassment involves any unwelcome sexual advances, requests for sexual favors, or any verbal or physical conduct of a sexual nature whereby submission to such conduct is explicitly or implicitly made a term or condition of one's employment (EEOC, 1980; Lee, 1995). As such, quid pro quo, or "this for that" harassment, is defined by an exchange relationship between the perpetrator and the victim. In this relationship, job benefits (e.g., job retention, promotion, or salary increases) are denied or deliberately taken away (e.g., loss of job or a demotion) because sexual favors are not granted (Garvin, 1991; Greenlaw & Kohl, 1992; Lee, 1995; O'Leary-Kelly, Paetzold, & Griffin, 1995).

Quid pro quo harassment is also present when an employee's submission to or rejection of these unwelcome sexual advances is used as the basis for an employment decision that influences the victim (Flaxman, 1994). As such, quid pro quo harassment interferes with an individual's work performance by creating an intimidating, hostile, or offensive working environment (EEOC, 1980; Lee, 1995).

In *Barnes v. Costle* (561 F.2d 983 D.C. Circuit, 1977), the court held that an employer was unable to abolish a job in order to retaliate against an employee's resistance to the employer's sexual advances. The abolition of a position, much like the denial of job benefits, also falls under the parameters of quid pro quo harassment which is protected by Title VII of the Civil Rights Act of 1964 (Garvin, 1991).

Quid pro quo sexual harassment shares a number of commonalities with domestic violence and stalking which gives credence to the emphasis that must be placed upon the criminal aspects of sexual harassment. First, all three types of abuse (sexual harassment, domestic violence, and stalking) involve issues of power and control between the participants. In terms of sexual harassment, power and control are inherent parts of employer/manager/supervisor and employee relationships. In this circumstance, power is utilized in the exchange relationship to control the employee by forcing him/her to comply with the harassing behavior. Likewise, in violent interpersonal relationships, the batterer/stalker uses power as a means of controlling the behavior and/or actions of the other person (Walker, 1979).

A related component of power and control occurs when sexual harassment is viewed as deviant behavior between individuals, rather than as a structural problem that is an inherent part of the organizational hierarchy in which males tend to be in positions of power within the organization (Childers, 1993; Gutek & Morasch, 1982; O'Leary-Kelly et al., 1995; *Rabidue v. Osceola Refining Company*). Likewise, violence between partners tends to be viewed as deviant behavior among individuals, while society's structural contributions to the acceptance of gender inequality and violence in interpersonal relationships tend to be overlooked (Bard & Zacker, 1976; Buzawa & Buzawa, 1993; Dobash & Dobash, 1979; Ferraro, 1989).

A second point of comparison is that sexual harassment, stalking, and domestic violence each involve a quid pro quo or exchange relationship. In each circumstance, the perpetrator seeks to alter the victim's behavior through (1) exchanging a sexual activity for a job (sexual harassment), (2) compliance with the batterer's demands (e.g., preparing dinner on time and/or making sure the kids are quiet) in order to avoid violence (domestic violence), and (3) maintaining or restoring a broken relationship to avoid violence, harassment, and/or stalking tactics (stalking). In each of these situations, there is no guarantee that by giving into the demand(s), the victim will receive the intended consequence.

Finally, quid pro quo harassment can be compared to domestic violence and stalking because each are influenced by the fact that America is predominantly a patriarchal society that perpetuates gender stereotypes. As a result, the victimization of women is understood and accepted, while the reality that males are also victimized by these abuses is overlooked and/or trivialized in comparison (Micklow, 1988).

Hostile Environment Sexual Harassment

In 1986, the U.S. Supreme Court heard its first sexual harassment case, *Meritor Savings Bank v. Vinson*. In this landmark case, the Supreme Court recognized the second classification of sexual harassment—a hostile environment. The Supreme Court approved the EEOC guidelines and held that a plaintiff could establish a violation of Title VII by proving that a hostile or abusive work environment was created by sexual harassment (Karner, 1995).

The Court established that a hostile environment involves conduct that creates a hostile, intimidating, or offensive working environment for employees (O'Leary-Kelly et al., 1995; Paetzold & O'Leary-Kelly, 1994). A hostile working environment encompasses anything from verbal and psychological abuse (e.g., crude language, lewd pictures, sexual or off-color jokes, requests for sexual favors, queries about one's personal life, references to one's physical appearance or anatomy) (Altman, 1996; Kaiser, 1995; Kulak, 1992) to offensive physical acts (e.g., touching, grabbing, indecent exposure, assault and battery, and rape) that are performed in the execution of organizational tasks, duties, or functions (EEOC, 1980; Kaiser, 1995; Karner, 1995; Sherry, 1995).

The Supreme Court made three key rulings in *Meritor Savings Bank v. Vinson*. First, the Court found that workplace conduct that is sexual in nature can create a hostile or abusive environment which is unlawful under Title VII. Next, the Court disallowed a defense argument that if the victim voluntarily participated in the events in the past, he/she was disqualified from receiving relief. The Court also found that if the victim indicated via his/her actions that the conduct and/or subsequent acts were unwelcome then the individual was eligible for relief. In other words, as an extreme example, if an individual flirted with a co-worker, but communicated no interest when asked for a date, the individual was eligible for relief because he/she had indicated that the request for a date was unwelcome. In this situation, the individual's consent to the flirting did not preclude him/her from being eligible to file a claim of sexual harassment. Finally, the court rejected the notion that employers should be held strictly liable for hostile environment harassment. Instead, employer liability would be determined on a case-by-case basis (Crawford, 1994).

The 1993 U.S Supreme Court case, *Harris v. Forklift Systems*, was pivotal in further clarifying hostile environment sexual harassment for three reasons. First, the court defined the standards for establishing an abusive work environment (Silbergeld, 1993/1994). Next, the court strengthened the protection against hostile environment harassment by holding that sexual harassment is actionable even in the absence of tangible psychological suffering or injury (Brown, 1994; Crawford, 1994).

The final contribution of *Harris v. Forklift Systems* stems from the Supreme Court's decision that the plaintiff(s) in a hostile environment sexual harassment case have the burden of proof to demonstrate by a preponderance of the evidence that five elements are met:

(1) The claimant must show membership in a protected class such as gender (Garvin, 1991).

(2) The plaintiff must establish that he/she was subjected to discriminatory sexual conduct that was unwelcome and abusive in occurrence (i.e., the claimant did not invite the harassment) (Altman, 1996).

(3) The plaintiff must establish that the harassment occurred because of the plaintiff's sex (O'Leary-Kelly et al., 1995).

(4) The plaintiff must demonstrate that a reasonable person would view the conduct as sufficiently severe and pervasive so as to alter the conditions of employment and create an abusive working environment (Brown, 1994; Karner, 1995).

(5) The plaintiff must establish employer liability for the alleged harassment (O'Leary-Kelly et al., 1995).

A hostile environment claim is more difficult to determine in sexual harassment cases for a number of reasons. First, the perpetrators tend to be co-workers or other individuals who do not have any formal recognized authority over the claimant which contributes to the assumption that the claimant was never really in a position where he/she could have been harmed (Childers, 1993).

Second, a hostile environment claim requires that the offensive conduct be continuous and repetitive and part of an overall pattern, rather than a single event or an isolated incident separated by time (Wagner, 1992a, 1992b). In *Babcock v. Frank*, the court ruled that a few harassing events over a short period of time failed to constitute a hostile environment. Likewise, in a situation where a woman was slapped, that action in and of itself may not be enough to establish a hostile environment. However, a hostile environment is established once the slaps or threats to slap are repeated (Lee, 1995). As a result, hostile environment claims are actionable when the conduct has become sufficiently severe or pervasive so as to be considered an unreasonable interference with work (or the conditions of work), thereby creating an abusive working environment (Childers, 1993; Karner, 1995).

Another point of contention raised among various courts is the complainant's conduct in the harassment or his/her response to the behavior. In other words, some courts have stated that the complainant must show that the conduct was unwelcome and that he/she did nothing to invite the behavior while simultaneously doing everything possible to discourage similar harassment (Childers, 1993). In *Highlander v. K.F.C. National*

Management Co., the court ruled that even though the plaintiff promptly reported the sexual touching to her manager, she did not sufficiently demonstrate the offensiveness of the harassment because she downplayed the importance of the event that illustrated her willingness to minimize the act. As a result, the court observed that the plaintiff's behavior was not an appropriate response to unwelcome behavior (Paetzold, 1994). In the above mentioned examples, plaintiffs in hostile environment cases are potentially responsible for their own victimization or the minimization of the behavior. Paetzold (1994) notes that, in this regard, plaintiffs in sexual harassment cases are treated much like victims of rape. This analogy can be extended to include victims of stalking and domestic violence. In each of these circumstances, the victims are held responsible for the criminal act that was inflicted upon them.

In contrast, the court in *Burns v. McGregor Electronic Industries Inc.* found that it was immaterial that the plaintiff posed nude for a magazine outside of work hours. In this case, the court ruled that the plaintiff's behavior when off-duty, even if that behavior is sexual in nature, does not constitute acquiescence to unwanted sexual advances during work hours (Brown, 1994).

Finally, courts must consider several factors when deciding in favor of the plaintiff in a hostile environment claim. The court must consider the frequency of the harassment, its severity, and whether the conduct was physically threatening or merely an offensive statement. At the same time, courts must determine whether the conduct unreasonably interfered with the employee's work performance and the extent to which the plaintiff suffered psychological injury (Brown, 1994; Flaxman, 1994; Garvin, 1991). The difficulty in determining hostile environment cases rests in the fact that a societal consensus has not been reached regarding the parameters of acceptable behavior in the workplace (Kulak, 1992; Wilkinson, 1995).

Hostile environment sexual harassment can be compared to the criminal aspects of domestic violence and sexual harassment in five key ways. First, a hostile or abusive environment is created for individuals who experience domestic violence, stalking, and sexual harassment regardless of the severity of the act(s). To some extent, each of these abuses include verbal, emotional, psychological, and/or physical abuse and threats (Altman, 1996; Kaiser, 1995; Kulak, 1992; Sherry, 1995). The detrimental effects associated with being a victim of any one of these crimes are similar and include: humiliation, shame, anger, alienation, aloneness, helplessness, guilt, strained relations with others, a loss of ambition and self confidence, and tangible economic losses due to lost wages as a result of absenteeism, excessive use of sick or personal days, decreased productivity time on the job (e.g., receiving excessive phone calls from the stalker/batterer or worrying about when and to what extent an individual will be harassed again while at work) (Childers, 1993).

Second, American society tends to focus on the innocent or benign aspects of interpersonal attraction and how couples interact with one another. As a result, society is reluctant to realize the seriousness of these potentially life threatening and physically and/or psychologically damaging problems (Bell, 1985; Martin, 1976; Micklow, 1988). Likewise, the maliciousness, violence, aggression, and abuse of power which are commonplace in sexual harassment, domestic violence, and stalking are ignored, trivialized, and ultimately condoned (O'Leary-Kelly et al., 1995).

A third similarity rests in the reasonable woman or person standard that has been used in court cases in recent years. The courts established a reasonable woman or person standard in an attempt to address the inherent differences in how the genders perceive sexual harassment. This new standard has also been used in cases where a battered woman has used violence against the batterer in self defense (Gillespie, 1989). The reasonable woman or person is a controversial and contentious issue in sexual harassment, domestic violence, and stalking cases.

Fourth, blaming the victim is a common theme that runs through sexual harassment, domestic violence, and stalking (O'Leary-Kelly et al., 1995; Paetzold, 1994; Paetzold & O'Leary-Kelly, 1994). As a result, female plaintiffs in hostile environment cases tend to be treated as women of sexual assault used to be treated in the past—as potentially responsible for their own victimization (O'Leary-Kelly et al., 1995; Paetzold, 1994; Paetzold & O'Leary-Kelly, 1994).

Finally, third-party actors (e.g., police, employers, human resource departments, legal counsel, security guards, employment tribunals, courts) play a predominant role in addressing sexual harassment, domestic violence, and stalking (Micklow, 1988). As a result, a pattern of abuse must exist for documentation purposes in order to establish a case for receiving protection and/or remedies (e.g., restraining and/or harassment orders or monetary damages) from these third-party actors to alleviate sexual harassment, domestic violence, and stalking (Brown, 1994; Coleman, 1993; Collinson, 1992; *Purrington v. University of Utah*; *Waltman v. International Paper* Co).

Sexual Harassment and Aggression

American society tends to have a difficult time deciphering the difference between an individual's natural and well-intentioned attraction to another person and when that attraction becomes sexual harassment. Extreme forms of sexual harassment such as sexual touching, battery, rape, and violence tend to be universally agreed upon types of harassment (Childers, 1993). However, in focusing on the innocent or benign aspects of interpersonal attraction, the potential for maliciousness, violence, aggression, and abuse of power which tend to be commonplace in sexual harassment (regardless of severity) are ignored, trivialized, and ultimately condoned (O'Leary-Kelly et al., 1995).

Aggressive behavior is broadly defined in a way that includes a wide range of actions that can result in emotional, psychological, and/or physical harm. Sexual harassment is an aggressive action because harm is caused to the victim as a result of the sexual conduct. Furthermore, plaintiffs in sexual harassment cases must establish that they were personally harmed by the unwelcome behavior (O'Leary-Kelly et al., 1995). Despite the legal ties that bind sexual harassment and aggressive behavior, the lines among and between what is considered an innocuous comment having sexual overtones (O'Leary-Kelly et al., 1995; Quinn & Lees, 1984), legal sexual behavior among consenting co-workers (Gutek, 1992; O'Leary-Kelly et al., 1995), and unwelcome sexual conduct remain blurred (Estrich, 1991; O'Leary-Kelly et al., 1995).

Another component of aggressive behavior stems from the power dynamic that is an integral part of both employment and interpersonal relationships. In both of these relationships, women tend to be in positions of relative powerlessness which mutes how incidents of sexual behavior are perceived (Childers, 1993). As a result, sex-related conduct, statements, or acts that may not be viewed as harmful to men may be considered frightening and aggressive behavior to women (Simon, 1991; Wells, 1993).

The aggressiveness of sexual harassment has contributed to sexual harassment being addressed as a part of the overall effort to combat violence against women. Some organizations such as the United Nations and women's groups have begun to identify the struggle against sexual harassment under the penumbra of the larger movement to prevent all forms of aggression against women. Within this context, sexual harassment is regarded as just another form of violence and another crime against women much like domestic violence and stalking (Husbands, 1992).

Comparing Sexual Harassment, Domestic Violence, and Stalking

Sexual harassment, domestic violence, and stalking can be compared according to three overarching themes—abuse factors, societal factors, and legal factors. Each of these factors have been addressed in the previous sections. However, for the sake of clarity and to highlight the similarities, each of these factors are placed in the following comprehensive listing.

Abuse Factors

(1) Sexual harassment, stalking, and domestic violence each include varying degrees of verbal (emotional/psychological) and/or physical abuse and threats (Altman, 1996; Kaiser, 1995; Sherry, 1995).

(2) Issues of power and control are in place for relationships involving sexual harassment, domestic violence and/or stalking (Walker, 1979).

(3) A hostile or abusive environment is created for individuals who experience domestic violence, stalking, and sexual harassment regardless of the severity of the act(s).

(4) Sexual harassment, stalking, and domestic violence each involve a quid pro quo or exchange relationship. These include (1) exchanging a sexual activity for a job benefit (sexual harassment), (2) complying with the batterer's demands (e.g., cooking dinner on time and/or making sure that the kids are quiet, etc.) in order to avoid violence (domestic violence), and (3) maintaining or restoring a broken relationship to avoid violence, harassment, and stalking tactics (stalking). In each of these situations, there is no guarantee that by giving into the demand(s) the victim will receive the intended consequences.

(5) The detrimental effects associated with being a victim of sexual harassment, domestic violence, and/or stalking, are similar and include: humiliation, shame, anger, alienation, aloneness, helplessness, guilt, strained relations with others, and a loss of ambition and self confidence (Childers, 1993).

(6) To some extent, sexual harassment, stalking, and domestic violence each include a tangible economic loss due to altering one's work behavior in an attempt to cope with the abuse (Childers, 1993).

Societal Factors

(1) Credibility issues exist when society is reluctant to see the serious and potentially life threatening or physically and/or psychologically damaging aspects of the abuses caused by sexual harassment, domestic violence, and stalking (Bell, 1985; Martin, 1976; Micklow, 1988).

(2) Blaming the victim is a common theme that runs through sexual harassment, domestic violence, stalking (O'Leary-Kelly et al., 1995; Paetzold, 1994; Paetzold & O'Leary-Kelly, 1994;).

(3) Female plaintiffs in hostile environment cases are treated as women of sexual assault used to be treated—as potentially responsible for their own victimization (O'Leary-Kelly et al.,1995; Paetzold, 1994; Paetzold & O'Leary-Kelly, 1994).

(4) America is predominantly a patriarchal society that perpetuates gender stereotypes in which women are largely viewed as the victim in sexual harassment, domestic violence, and stalking. As a result, the reality that males are also victimized by sexual harassment, domestic violence, and stalking is overlooked and trivialized (Micklow, 1988).

(5) Sexual harassment can be viewed as deviant behavior between individuals, rather than as a structural problem that is an inherent part of the organizational hierarchy in which males tend to be in positions of power within organizations (Childers, 1993; Gutek & Morasch, 1982; O'Leary-Kelly et al., 1995; *Rabidue v. Osceola Refining Company*). Likewise, violence between partners (domestic violence and/or stalking) tends to be viewed as deviant behavior among individuals, while society's structural contributions to this problem tend to be overlooked (Bard & Zacker, 1976; Buzawa & Buzawa, 1993; Dobash & Dobash, 1979; Ferraro, 1989).

(6) American society focuses on the innocent or benign aspects of interpersonal attraction and how couples interact with one another. As a result, the maliciousness, violence, aggression, and abuse of power which are commonplace in sexual harassment, domestic violence, and stalking are ignored, trivialized, and ultimately condoned (O'Leary-Kelly et al., 1995).

(7) Third party actors (e.g., police, employer, human resource departments, legal counsel, secuity guards, employment tribunals, courts) play a predominant role in addressing domestic violence, stalking, and sexual harassment (Micklow, 1988).

Legal Factors

(1) In order to receive a restraining or harassment order for domestic violence or stalking, a pattern of abuse must be established. Likewise, a pattern of sexual harassment must exist for
sexual harassment cases (Brown, 1994; *Waltman v. International Paper Co.*; *Purrington v. University of Utah*).

(2) Documentation procedures are important to establish a case
for sexual harassment, domestic violence, and stalking
(Collinson, 1992; Coleman, 1993).

(3) The punishment for sexual harassment, domestic violence, and
stalking tends to be more lenient as compared to punishment
for the same incident committed by a stranger (Berk & Loseke,
1980–1981; Goolkasian, 1986).

(4) A reasonable woman or person standard is also relevant in cases
where battered women have used violence against the batterer
in self defense (Gillespie, 1989). The reasonable woman or person standard is a controversial and contentious issue in sexual
harassment, domestic violence, and stalking cases.

(5) Third party actions (e.g., verbal and/or written complaints, restraining orders, and harassment orders) are utilized by the victims in an attempt to stop the unwelcome behavior (Collinson,
1992; Coleman, 1993).

Conclusions

The most extreme forms of sexual harassment are acts of aggression in
which power and control are utilized to dominate another person. These
acts of aggression are threatening and unwelcome and can range from verbal to psychological to sexual and physical abuse. Within this context,
sexual harassment has a great deal in common with other acts of aggression perpetrated predominantly against women such as domestic violence
and stalking. The latter types of abuse are largely viewed as illegal criminal acts whereas the emphasis in sexual harassment remains in the realm
of civil law. As a result, the violent and criminal aspects of sexual harassment continue to be overlooked.

The intent herein was to highlight the criminal aspects of sexual harassment in a comparative context with domestic violence and stalking.
The focus on the criminality of sexual harassment set forth throughout
should not be regarded as a demand for specific policy changes, but rather
as an invitation to open this topic for further discussion.

Discussion Questions

It has been argued that the severity of sexual harassment is trivialized by legal complaints that are made regarding a single comment and/or joke with sexual overtones. At the other extreme, this chapter focuses on the criminal aspects of sexual harassment as it parallels domestic violence and stalking. In making the latter argument, are lesser acts of sexual harassment being trivialized? If not, why not? And, if yes, how can a balance be achieved so that both extremes of the sexual harassment continuum can avoid being trivialized?

Sexual harassment, domestic violence, and stalking are deviant acts in which women are the primary targets of the victimization. If the victim of sexual harassment is a male, can the argument still be made that the sexual harassment mirrors the criminal aspects of domestic violence and/or stalking? Regardless of the answer given, what does this say about gender role stereotypes? How do these stereotypes influence what is considered criminal behavior?

Chapter 15

A Comparative Examination of Stalking Laws and Related Methods of Victim Protection

Lisa Bozenhard

Introduction

In July 1989, a young actress named Rebecca Schaefer was murdered by an obsessed fan after he pursued her for two years. One year later, California passed the nation's first stalking law which defined the act as the "willful, malicious, and repeated following and harassing of another person" (California Penal Code, 1990). It is estimated that approximately 200,000 people, mostly women, are stalked annually in the United States (Bernstein, 1993; Ward, 1994), and that "as many as 90 percent of women killed by their husbands or boyfriends were stalked prior to the attack" (Sohn, 1994, p. 205). Since enactment of the California law and the reporting of victim statistics, the trend to establish such legislation has continued nationwide.

Although public awareness of stalking has increased, we still do not know a lot about the crime. However, criminalizing the behavior suggests previous methods of victim protection are not effective (Walker, 1993). Such legal strategies are in response to treating stalking behavior as an antecedent to other crimes, not as a crime itself (McAnaney, Corliss, & Abetyta-Price, 1993).

Has the passage of new laws been instrumental in protecting victims and deterring stalking behavior? This is a debatable issue, and the focus of this chapter. Herein the chapter focuses on the criminalization of stalking behavior and its impact on the deterrence of potential stalkers and the protection of stalking victims.

Definition

The term stalking covers a broad sphere of actions, contexts, and criminal culpability (Holden, 1993). Essentially, no single definition exists which encompasses the behavior and its components (Lingg, 1993; Sohn, 1994).

Relevant terminology focuses on the pursuant behavior of a victim, rather than the attack. Usually, this behavior includes threats, harassment, and/or other types of actions which cause fear in the victim (Sohn, 1994).

Characteristics of Stalkers

Stalking cases vary considerably relative to the motives and goals of the perpetrator. Primarily, stalkers are those "who engage in an abnormal or long term pattern of threat or harassment directed toward a specific individual" (Meloy, 1995, p. 2).

Stalkers are likely to suffer from mental disorders (Hammell, 1995; Meloy & Gothard, 1995), and have a much higher rate of affliction than the general criminal population (Hammell, 1995; Meloy & Gothard, 1995). Stalkers have character disorders and are much more pathological than their counterparts (Hammell, 1995).

Based on cases known to police and the public, three classifications have emerged, which give consideration to the victim's knowledge of the stalker. These groupings are former intimate, acquaintance, and stranger. Frequently, these categories determine the methods of case management employed by law enforcement officials, as well as provide insight into the mental stability of the perpetrator.

Narcissistic Characteristics and Abandonment/Rage Stalking

Narcissistic characteristics are exhibited among stalkers, primarily those stalking incidents that occur as a result of broken relationships (Hammell, 1995; Meloy & Gothard, 1995). In practice, cases of domestic violence are the most common examples of narcissistic abandonment/rage.

The behavior, which begins after the victim has left the relationship, may be a desperate attempt to salvage the relationship or seek revenge for the break up (McAnaney et al., 1993; Schaum & Parrish, 1995). Ultimately, the stalker may feel that this "relationship" with the victim is better than no relationship at all (Bernstein, 1993). Stalkers in this category also frequently believe that the victim "belongs to them, and are theirs to control or punish for trying to escape" (Schaum & Parrish, 1995, p. 56).

Those who engage in stalking behavior out of narcissistic rage are also likely to feel shame or humiliation related to the damage of their pride (Meloy, 1995). The resulting rage is ultimately a defense against these feelings (Meloy, 1995).

Schizophrenia and Erotomania

Cases involving the stalking of victims with whom no prior relationship exists are frequently found within delusional disorders, such as schizophrenia and erotomania (Anderson, 1993; Harmon, Rosner, & Owens, 1995; Meloy & Gothard, 1995). A brief examination of these disorders and their association with stalking behavior follows.

Erotomania. The delusional belief that one is deeply loved by another person who is usually of a higher social status is called erotomania (Anderson, 1993; Harmon et al., 1995; Meloy, 1989; Schaum & Parrish, 1995; Zona, Sharma, & Lane, 1993). Those who suffer from the disorder are usually women who are lonely, unwed and employed in menial jobs; however, the disorder is not limited to women (Anderson, 1993). Men account for a growing number of cases, and are more likely to become violent in their pursuits (Meloy, 1989).

Erotomanics also believe that the object of their pursuit initiated the "relationship" (Leong, 1993) and "communicates" with them secretly through signals, messages, or by telepathic means (Leong, 1993). In reality, however, the "relationship" between the object and the erotomanic ranges from having never met to a casual contact (Harmon et al., 1995; Meloy, 1989). Ultimately, when the object fails to reciprocate the erotomanic's affections the rejection frequently creates a more dynamic situation as the erotomanic perceives these attempts as a "test of love" (Anderson, 1993; Harmon et al., 1995; Leong, 1995).

Schizophrenia. There is little research examining the relationship between schizophrenia and other delusional disorders with stalking behavior. The only available evidence concerns cases of schizophrenics with erotomania as a secondary diagnosis. Some findings, however, have been disseminated from related research to shed light on this relationship to stalking behavior.

Those who stalk out of non-erotomanic psychoses are known to have a range of beliefs relative to their pursuant behavior (Zona et al., 1993). These include the perception that the victim might love them if given the chance, to any number of obscure ideas (Zona et al., 1993). Regardless of the specifics of the belief, the individual begins his attempts to become known to the victim (Zona et al., 1993). It is this behavior that differentiates this individual from an erotomanic, as the person is pursuing his object in order to begin a relationship. In contrast, an erotomanic believes the relationship already exists.

Previous Remedies to Stalking Behavior

Prior to the passage of the country's first stalking statutes in 1990, states applied anti-harassment laws to stalking cases and encouraged victims to obtain court orders as their sole means of protection. Although many law enforcement officials still advise victims to obtain such orders, the applied laws have been replaced with stalking legislation. However, since many of these previously applied laws are still utilized, a discussion is warranted in order to review their components and breadth. The anti-harassment laws consist of harassment, menacing, loitering, trespassing, intimidation, and terroristic threats—all described below. Civil order consist of restraining and protective orders. Each is also described below.

Anti-Harassment Laws. Harassment is commonly defined as "the persistent and unwelcome communication of demands or feelings" (Robinson, 1984, p. 507). The statutes pursuant to this act are varied (Robinson, 1984), however, all states have legislation criminalizing both inappropriate telephone use and non-telephonic forms of harassment (Attinello, 1993; Robinson, 1984).

Menacing is commonly referred to as intentionally placing or attempting to place another person in fear of imminent serious physical injury (Kentucky Revised Statutes Annotated, 1984; Ohio Revised Code Annotated, 1993). Elements of state laws extend to property and members of one's immediate family (Robinson, 1984).

Loitering, as used in the Colorado statute, means "to be dilatory, to stand idly around, to linger, delay, to wander about, or to remain, abide, or tarry in a public place" (Colorado Revised Statutes Annotated, 1990). In their variations, state statutes are reflective of the acts proscribed in the Colorado statute (Arizona Revised Statutes Annotated, 1989; Kentucky Revised Statutes Annotated, 1984).

Trespassing is commonly referred to as knowingly entering or remaining unlawfully in or upon a premises (Florida Statute Annotated, 1993; Kentucky Revised Statutes Annotated, 1984). The specifics of these statutes also consider those instances in which an offender "enters or remains with the intent to commit an offense thereon, other than the offense of trespass" (Florida Revised Statutes Annotated, 1993).

Intimidation, as defined in the Montana statute, occurs when a person is caused to perform or omit the performance of an act, upon the communication of another's intention to inflict physical harm on them, subject them to physical restraint, or to commit a felony (Montana Code Annotated, 1991). The communication must occur under circumstances that reasonably tend to produce fear that it will be carried out (Montana Code Annotated, 1991).

Terrorists threats or communications are best described in the New Jersey statute. The law defines the acts as "a threat to kill another with purpose to put him in imminent fear of death under circumstances reasonably causing the victim to believe the immediacy of the threat and the likelihood it will be carried out" (New Jersey Statutes Annotated, 1982).

Civil Orders

Stalking victims have frequently attempted to deter their pursuers through restraining orders or protective orders (Bernstein, 1993; Buckley, 1994; Sohn, 1994; Wood, 1993). A restraining order is defined as "a temporary injunctive order forbidding the defendant from performing a threatened act until a hearing on the application for a permanent order" (Sohn, 1994, p. 207). Relative to this is the protective order, which is a "court order or decree protecting a person from enumerated behaviors by a specific individual" (Sohn, 1994, p. 207).

Assessing the Effectiveness of Victim Protection Legislation

Early Legislative Efforts. One of the main obstacles to the effectiveness of related laws is the unlikely success of such charges (Buckley, 1994). In stalking cases the benefit of these laws is typically only available when the perpetrator's actions are specific enough to fit within the narrow definition of such statutes (Buckley, 1994).

Such legal avoidance is exemplified by statutes pertaining to threats of immediate harm. While many related statutes require a threat of immediate physical harm, many stalkers were able to successfully avoid prosecution by maintaining a distance which would not make the victim feel immediately threatened (Attinello, 1993; Walker, 1993).

Trespass laws are also deemed ineffective as they only apply if the stalker enters private property (Buckley, 1994). Therefore, if the pursuer maintains his presence on public property or limits his contact to the phone or mail, he may not be in violation of trespassing statutes (Buckley, 1994).

The weaknesses inherent in previously applied laws also include their limitation to addressing single incidents (McAnaney et al., 1993). Although perpetrators are more likely to violate anti-harassment laws due to the absence of a requirement to repeatedly engage in the stalking behavior, the scope of these laws is also narrower (Buckley, 1994; McAnaney et al., 1993).

Limited Effectiveness of Court Orders

Before the enactment of stalking laws, court orders were not always available to protect victims of stalking behavior (McAnaney et al., 1993; Wood, 1993). The main reason was that the stalker had usually not done anything more than verbally threaten the victim (Perez, 1993). In these cases, no criminal laws had been violated, as physical actions had not occurred (Buckley, 1994; Wood, 1993).

If a victim has been successful in obtaining a restraining order or a protective order, the enforcement of that order and punishment for its violation frequently do not have a deterrent effect on future abuse (Bernstein, 1993; Buckley, 1994; Wood, 1993). One limitation of these orders involves legislative restrictions which may limit the scope of the order (Wood, 1993).

The effect of these limitations is that they may simply be little more than a hurdle for many stalkers (Attinello, 1993; Sohn, 1994). Many offenders merely have to alter their behavior slightly to circumvent the restrictions imposed by the terminology of the specific order (Attinello, 1993; Sohn, 1994). This enables many to avoid prosecution on the grounds of technicalities, and leaves victims unprotected and in fear, knowing there is a strong likelihood that they have further antagonized the perpetrator (Schaum & Parrish, 1995; Sohn, 1994).

Along with the fear of further aggravating the stalker comes the frightening thought of the actual harm or harassment that is required before police can arrest the offender for violating the order. Essentially, the stalker may not be performing acts that are considered criminal and police powers are limited unless the offender's actions escalate into a serious violent crime (Buckley, 1994; Wood, 1993).

Overall, the motivation of a stalker to pursue a victim over a continuous period of time "suggests that even the maximum sanctions available for violation of a protective order may be an insufficient deterrent" (Wood, 1993, p. 459). The enactment of stalking laws have been the legislative response to the perceived inadequacies of court orders (Wood, 1993).

Rationale for the Enactment
of Stalking Legislation

Prior to the enactment of stalking laws, victims had only a few legal recourses available for protection. When these remedies failed, victims often found themselves increasingly terrorized, as their actions against the stalker fueled his rage (Schaum & Parrish, 1995).

The enactment of stalking legislation is aimed at responding to the need for more effective methods of deterrence and intervention. With the passage of stalking legislation, the act of stalking escalated from a civil violation to a criminal act (Bernstein, 1993; Holden, 1993; McAnaney et al., 1993).

Legislative Components. Essentially, these laws have three main components: threat, intent, and course of conduct (Bernstein, 1993; Holden, 1993; Sohn, 1994). This section presents the basic elements of the laws and the variances found in legislation throughout the country.

Threat. The majority of states require that a stalker's actions make a reasonable person feel threatened, even if the accused stalker did not verbally threaten the victim (Bernstein, 1993; Holden, 1993; Lingg, 1993). Others stipulate an overtly communicated threat to kill (Bernstein, 1993; Holden, 1993).

Intent. Nearly every state requires that the stalker "intend to cause fear in the victim, with the conduct being *willful, purposeful, intentional,* or *knowing*" (Holden, 1993, p. 13). The standards of intent vary considerably, ranging from the intent to cause alarm or annoyance, to the need for acts to be performed in furtherance of a threat (Holden, 1993; Sohn, 1994).

Course of Conduct. Nearly every state's legislation requires a course of conduct, thus requiring that the criminal actions are not isolated, but a series of actions (Bernstein, 1993; Holden, 1993; McAnaney et al., 1993; Perez, 1993; Sohn, 1994). The acts, however, can occur within a short time frame, as state statutes do not stipulate a period of inactivity (Perez, 1993).

Related Statutory Provisions. Some statutes have aspects of their laws focused on specific behaviors of the stalker. Actions addressed in this legislation include surveillance and stalking with a weapon (Lingg, 1993; Patton, 1994; Sohn, 1994).

Critique of Stalking Laws

Stalking statutes are supported by victims' rights groups, who believe the laws fill voids not covered by previously existing statutes and court orders (Morville, 1993). On the other hand, critics of the laws consider them to be poorly defined, difficult to enforce, potentially unconstitutional, and easily abused by law enforcement personnel (Lingg, 1993; Morville, 1993).

This section focuses on whether criminalizing stalking behavior is truly an effective means of protecting victims of stalking. A number of issues will be presented along with the positions of both supporters and critics of stalking laws.

Stalking Laws vs. Related Laws. For those states which have existing statutes addressing harassment and threats of violence, critics contend that the enactment of stalking legislation is repetitive (Sohn, 1994). Their critique is based on the fact that stalking laws in most jurisdictions are no more severe as they do not increase the classification from misdemeanor to felony (Sohn, 1994).

Opponents also state that narrow laws impose a greater burden on the victim who wishes to file criminal charges against a stalker (Wood, 1993). In some instances, the victim may be completely beyond the realm of protection afforded by the law (Wood, 1993). This is especially true when the offender's method involves low levels of intimidation (Wood, 1993).

The effectiveness of stalking laws relative to threats, course of conduct, and intent has also been criticized. Opponents argue that unless a threat is openly communicated to the victim, the new laws are frequently ineffective (Bernstein, 1993).

The opponents of the mandated course of conduct in stalking laws note that this requirement does not guarantee that authorities will pursue violations of court orders any more efficiently (Sohn, 1994). Therefore, victims are not afforded any more security, and the risk of retaliation often feared by victims is not alleviated (Sohn, 1994).

The component of intent is also a source of debate. In order for the stalking law to be effective, the perpetrator must intend to pursue or harass the target (Buckley, 1994). Ideally, a stalker who truly intends to harass and/or harm his victim may successfully circumvent the scope of statutes by merely claiming his desires otherwise (Buckley, 1994).

Refuting these arguments, proponents (McAnney et al., 1993) cite the ability of stalking laws to address the perpetrator's actions as more than single incidents (i.e., individual misdemeanor, harassment, and trespassing charges). They further contend that the legislation makes it possible to pursue the "series" of acts as a more serious crime, instead of multiple unrelated minor offenses (McAnaney et al., 1993).

The laws are also endorsed because they differentiate between stalking and harassment (McAnaney et al., 1993). Related anti-harassment statutes address actions that could be a component of stalking, and are not appropriately applicable to stalking situations, as the more severe penalties for repeat offenses are a necessary component (McAnaney et al., 1993).

Supporters of stalking laws have also cited the ability of statutes to protect victims before overt acts of violence occur (Buckley, 1994). Stalking laws authorizing arrest based on a subjective reasonable fear standard can fill the void created by those statutes which require physical violence before arrest (Buckley, 1994).

Proponents of stalking legislation also believe that additional deterrence has been provided in jurisdictions that did not increase the level of criminality (Bernstein, 1993). These individuals stress the enacted increase in penalties (Bernstein, 1993). They argue that

> "general deterrence is increased because a message will be sent to society that this conduct will not be tolerated; and the specific deterrence is increased because when the law fails to deter the conduct, at least the offenders will be restrained in jail for longer periods of time" (Bernstein, 1993, p. 566).

Stalking Legislation vs. Court Orders. One element of the rationale for stalking legislation concerns the ineffectiveness of court orders in deterring stalking behavior. Many supporters praise the intent of the law to stop abusive and violent behavior that was previously not classified as criminal and, consequently, inadequately deterred by court orders (Bernstein, 1993; Lingg, 1993; Wood, 1993). In addition, they cite the power it gives police to act on a victim's behalf before violence occurs (Bernstein, 1993; Buckley, 1993). Stalking legislation is also praised for its ability to complement civil orders by working with existing orders and providing other options for stalking victims. This is especially true when the identity of the stalker is unknown to the victim (Bernstein, 1993). "Civil remedies totally fail in this regard since the name of the offender is a prerequisite to obtaining a protective order" (Lingg, 1993, p. 361).

In contrast, opponents fail to find much evidence to support the greater effectiveness of stalking laws (Sohn, 1994). They contend that the new laws do not prevent the victim from suffering the acts necessary to constitute violation of a court order (Sohn, 1994). Central to this position is the victim's ability to obtain a civil order before criminal actions occur (Sohn, 1994).

Advantages of court orders also include their provision for temporary relief which is often made immediately available by state statutes (Wood, 1993). Stalking laws do not have the capacity for such immediacy (Wood, 1993).

Additionally, civil orders also include a lesser burden of proof than is necessary in a criminal proceeding (Wood, 1993). Therefore, even if the evidence is not sufficient to secure a conviction, protection may still be secured through a court order (Wood, 1993).

Legal scholars point out that stalking legislation does not compensate for the fact that civil orders are easy to avoid on technicalities (Sohn, 1994). Moreover, they state that court orders may still be more effective, as behaviors specific to the situation can be incorporated into the prohibited actions of the court order (Sohn, 1994; Wood, 1993).

Researchers also note that doubt exists relative to the effectiveness of any measures when they are applied to stalkers with mental illnesses (Attinello, 1993; Ward, 1994). Essentially, these stalkers may not have the capacity to comprehend the illegal nature of their actions, and may not understand the injunctions being pursued against them (Attinello, 1993).

Future Issues

Although issues are unresolved, stalking laws have the potential to address victims' needs: they attempt to protect victims before serious physical harm occurs. However, there are limitations as many statutes rely on previously enacted related laws. Such reliance on past remedies, which were independently inadequate in victim protection and criminal prosecution is a major weakness of stalking laws. Theoretically, the existence of laws does provide a greater opportunity for victim protection and successful prosecution by giving the victim and police some leverage in the handling of cases. However, their long-term effectiveness is as yet undetermined.

One of the greatest benefits of the laws is the focus attributed to repeated behaviors. Frequently, it is the repetitive nature of the stalkers' actions which creates the most fear in the victim. Previous intervention strategies did not fully address this characteristic of stalking behavior and left the victim vulnerable and in fear. This element is a necessary component, especially considering the likelihood of repeated actions being initiated by the perpetrator.

Perhaps the elements of the laws that are most likely to leave victims vulnerable are those of intent and threat. Although intent is an element that can protect a suspect from false accusations, it can hinder the victim's ability to file charges and obtain protection under the law. There is a great potential for this in cases rooted in "love," in which a stalker may pursue the victim seeking a relationship with no harmful intentions.

This scenario is also applicable when considering the threat component of the legislation. A perpetrator seeking a relationship is unlikely to threaten the victim with harm. However, the limitations go even further. A stalker who is pursuing his victim with harmful intentions may easily circumvent the law by not threatening the victim. It is this avoidance potential which has prompted some states to reevaluate the inclusion of threat in their respective statutes.

Recommendations

There are a number of recommendations that can be made aimed at providing victims with sufficient protection from their pursuers. First, it is essential that the threat requirement in statutes be modified or eliminated. While the California model mandates the communication of a credible threat of bodily injury or death, some states require a communication of a threat to kill. Under the California model, if the victim has a reasonable means to believe that the perpetrator will cause harm or death, then she can pursue protection under the stalking law. In some states, however, the courts mandate an overt threat to kill, leaving victims vulnerable to physical violence which may ultimately result in death. Therefore, modifications are suggested as a means of protecting victims and increasing their ability to remain in control of their case.

Other suggestions concern the actions taken against a perpetrator once he is captured. Primarily, bail should not even be a consideration. The risk of repeated and escalated behavior against a victim is too great.

Furthermore, the system should recognize that counseling and related programs are rarely a cure. The stalker is unlikely to complete counseling, reflect on his actions, and stop engaging in the behavior. Therefore, mandatory placement in a secured facility must be considered for those inflicted with serious mental illness, and incarceration followed by mandatory relocation in conjunction with probation should be considered for cases involving felons and actions associated with rage. Relocation should be at a safe distance from the victim to prevent the stalker from achieving contact. Probation enables the system to monitor the stalker's actions. It also provides a contact within the system, should the stalker locate the victim, or if the perpetrator should escape from the system.

Other measures aimed at victim security include strategies to relocate the victim and the notification of both the victim and police that the stalker is no longer under the control of the system. Relocation enables victims to participate in a victim protection program, providing them with a new identity and making future contact by the stalker nearly impossible. Notification assists police in providing protection to the victim, primarily by trying to engage in follow up after the original stalking activities. Previous failures of the system to communicate such information have hindered the ability of police to protect victims. Better notification systems may improve the procedures currently in existence.

Changes relative to the way stalking cases are handled by law enforcement agencies should be instituted. Primarily, officer education and training is a necessity. One of the most frequent complaints of victims concerns the response of officers. Many victims feel that officers treat victims as the perpetrators while others comment that officers make victims feel as if they are exaggerating their complaints and are accused of being "paranoid" (Personal Communications, May and June, 1996). In these scenarios victims in need of protection may be hesitant or even fail to approach the police for help.

The way stalking cases are managed must change. While the majority of stalking cases are domestic violence-related and are appropriately handled by domestic violence units, a substantial number of cases are not domestic violence cases. This fact may make some victims feel alienated as they are hesitant to approach a domestic violence detective or are inappropriately referred elsewhere. While most departments are unable to justify the institution of a threat management unit like the one in the Los Angeles Police Department, it seems appropriate to appoint detectives specially trained to handle stalking. This measure would provide maximum protection for victims regardless of the nature of their case by placing it in the hands of experienced and knowledgeable detectives.

The victim must realize that while the police are there to assist, they cannot always be at his/her side. Therefore, he/she must take cooperative efforts that will enhance his/her relationship with the system and provide maximum assistance to police agencies. Regardless of how proactive the police are in stalking cases, an uncooperative victim can hinder the likelihood of effective case management.

Proactive approaches to preventing stalking behavior must also be considered. These include educational models in elementary schools that focus on enhancing male/female communication skills and the empowerment of females through educational objectives aimed at improving self-image. Curriculum focused on these objectives will also assist in changing societal attitudes regarding interpersonal violence.

New treatment strategies for offenders must also be implemented. These include the development of educational programs that focus on approaches to victim confrontation and the development of mediation skills for offenders.

Central to the debate surrounding the effectiveness of stalking laws is the non-existence of empirical data. Regrettably, such research is lacking. Examinations must be made into arrest and recidivism records to better evaluate the strengths and weaknesses of stalking statutes.

Overall, when dealing with stalking cases it appears that the most effective methods of protection and prevention are achieved through a multi-faceted approach that includes victim education. Those involved must be mindful that the perpetrators they are dealing with are obsessive, enraged, and dangerous and should be handled as "violent," not merely as "harassing." Hopefully, state legislatures will continue to broaden the scope of stalking legislation which will expand the protection available to victims and provide a means for successfully ending the torment and fear of impending harm which victims must endure. Ultimately, it is the breadth of protection provided by the law that empowers police and victims. Otherwise, they remain powerless, remanding all power and control to the stalker.

Discussion Questions

Considering the legal definitions and acts required to constitute arrest for stalking, what are some of the advantages of anti-harassment laws? Are stalking laws more beneficial? Why?

What are some limitations of existing laws? What can be done to provide more protection to victims and prevent stalking behavior?

How should society respond to stalking? Law enforcement agencies? Social service agencies?

What are some proactive measures that can be initiated that will enhance awareness of stalking behavior and stalking laws?

Chapter 16

The Female Stalker

M.A. Dupont-Morales

Introduction

This research presents information about female stalkers and addresses structural obstacles within the criminal justice system that impair the investigation and prosecution of these stalkers. This chapter adds to the knowledge about crimes of interpersonal violence because statutes and enforcement of statutes are not always gender neutral. Further, the boundaries between gender and the character of the victim and offender are often socially constructed. Victims' personal journals and interviews will contribute insight into the policies of the criminal justice system, contribute information that yields subjective evaluations of the impact of stalking as related by the victims, and provide data describing the overt acts that form the victim-offender relationship of stalking activity. Additionally, these cases will be used to consider a theoretical inquiry into the development of criminality in women that is well outside the accepted age-related theories. These cases illustrate stalking resulting from acquaintance, intimate, and familial relationships with discordant termination. This chapter does not address erotomania, the stalking of individuals (usually celebrities) by strangers (Meloy & Gothard, 1995).

Stalking is an abnormal or long term pattern of threat or harassment directed at a specific individual; the willful, malicious, and repeated following, or credible threatening of another individual in an attempt to frighten, cause harm, and/or control (Hunzeker 1992; Kolarick 1992; Kruttschnitt 1994; Sohn 1994). Meloy (1992, 1996) describes stalking as a violent and obsessional attachment which reflects the result of a psychological assault on the narcissistic well-being of the stalker when the victim rejects him/her or threatens his/her well being.

Zona, Sharma, and Lane (1993) reported that males accounted for 70 to 75 percent of stalkers reported to the police and that this behavior usually followed the termination of an intimate relationship. Further, stalkers are older than most violent offenders, are educated, employed or somewhat underemployed, may have some history of substance abuse, and tend to demonstrate difficulties with socialization (Zona et al., 1993).

The most prevalent form of stalking is associated with domestic violence. However, as anti-stalking legislation has survived constitutional challenges and revisions, the termination of an intimate relationship is no longer the basis by which to define stalking. While this continues as the most documented pattern of stalking, law enforcement now investigates and prosecutes stalking of secondary victims, victims who have solely been acquaintances of the stalker, and male victims.

Stalking is an old behavior but a new crime (Lowney & Best, 1995; Perez, 1993; Saldana, 1986; Winter, 1982). It is the systematic and deliberate infliction of emotional and/or physical trauma. The stalker engages in methodical activity as a means of exerting control, as a form of intimidation to regain a previous status or relationship, and as retaliation for perceived emotional and/or physical injury sustained by the loss of a previous status or relationship. Stalkers rehearse the motions, plan the activities, and repeatedly carry out this victimization in their fantasies. Their repetitive rehearsals are rewarded when the enactment of the fantasies result in trauma for the victim and the stalker views or hears about the degrees of trauma experienced by the victim. This last factor is pivotal for the deviant well-being of the stalker.

Beginning in 1990, states passed legislation directed at curbing this criminal activity (Perez, 1993). This legislation has survived state and federal constitutional challenges. Misdemeanor and felony penalties reflect the seriousness of the crime (U.S. Department of Justice, 1993). Further, as research continues to add to the knowledge about stalkers, legislation has extended to the loss of child visitation for stalkers, loss of gun ownership and permission to carry a concealed weapon, corporate restraining orders to enhance workplace security, extended and permanent restraining and Protection From Abuse orders, increased civil penalties, and enhanced victim services (Bensimon, 1993; de Becker, 1988; U.S. Department of Justice, 1996).

Because little is documented about the personal impact such criminal behavior has on the victim when coupled with the criminal justice system's response to stalking, research directed toward the impact of stalking on victims has been called for by threat management professionals, investigating stalking behaviors for the criminal justice system, and forensic behavioralists, researching definitional issues affecting stalking. Stalking behavior includes harassing telephone calls, surveillance, unsolicited e-mail, faxes and use of message systems, unwanted notes and mail, uninvited work and home visits, threats, assault, and death. The stalking behavior may extend to secondary victims (family or friends) or tertiary victims (police officers, therapists, victim-witness workers). The stalker employs a "signature" or a distinguishing factor enabling the victim to identify the behavior as coming from the stalker. Stalking victims may experience internal trauma resulting from the long term victimization caused by the external behaviors committed by the perpetrator that escalate in intensity, duration, frequency, significance, and intimidation.

While cases may not evidence the full extent of escalating activity, the long term course of activity is reported to have psychological impact. It is possible that early intervention through education about Posttraumatic Stress Disorder (PTSD) for these crime victims may enhance the detection of stress related to the trauma and increase the benefits of any treatment provided to stalking victims. Such has occurred for victims of sexual assault (Kaniasty & Norris, 1992) and other violent crimes (Hanson, Kilpatrick, Falsetti, & Resnick, 1995). These illustrative cases are important because they report exacerbating stressors associated with a crime that is cyclical in nature, has escalating behaviors, is of a long duration and reflects predatory criminal behavior by women. Additionally, these cases provide concepts that invite further research on female and adult-age onset criminality.

Studies associated with trauma resulting from criminal activity usually reflect an end to the trauma through arrest or adjudication. However, the posttraumatic stress experienced by stalking victims may be more complex than that usually seen in crime victims as stalking may include escalating activities, periods of respite followed by the introduction of new forms of victimization. What does this mean to the victim in terms of social and professional support from treatment agents, colleagues, friends, and family, and from repeated interaction with the criminal justice system? What does this mean to a male victim when investigators describe the stalker as "just a little thing" in terms of confidence in the system to apprehend the stalker and terminate the victimization? What does this mean to a couple when statutory design does not and law enforcement is unable to address their stalking victimization engaged in by their sister/sister-in-law? The objective of this study is to address these dilemmas.

Methodology

This analysis is part of a larger study of stalkers. These specific female stalkers were selected because of their predatory behavior, the documentation provided by the victims, and the focus of this chapter.

As with other research trends in violent victimizations, the victims and offenders mirror one another in several characteristics (Reiss & Roth, 1993; U.S. Bureau of Justice Statistics, 1996). The offenders are above the generally reported age for violent offenders; however, this fact appears to reflect the data reported on stalkers (see Zona et al., 1993). The diagnosis of PTSD in crime victims is used to analyze the consequences of violent crimes such as sexual assault, physical assault, robbery, workplace violence, and civilian unrest (Cassidy, McNally, & Zeitlin, 1992; Davis & Breslau, 1994; Hanson, Saunders, & Lipovsky, 1992; Kaniasty & Norris, 1992; Moscarello, 1991; Nadelson & Notman, 1979; Resnick, Kilpatrick, Dansky, Saunders, & Best, 1993; Winkel, Denkers, & Vrij, 1994).

This chapter reflects research that chronicles the victim-offender relationship in the interpersonal crime of stalking. Victims' journals, police and court documents, notes and audiotapes from the stalkers to the victims, telephone records, interviews with therapists and families (when possible) were used to validate the crime of stalking.

Summaries and observations have been discussed with the victims. The impact of stalking victimization will be reported using the DSM-IV diagnosis of Posttraumatic Stress Disorder (DSM-IV, 1994, p. 309.81) as the model. The illustrative cases fulfill the following criteria.

The victims have been exposed to a traumatic event in which both of the following were present:

> (1) the person experienced, witnessed, or was confronted with an event or events that involved actual or threatened death or serious injury, or a threat to the physical integrity of self or others.
> (2) the person's response involved intense fear, helplessness, or horror (DSM-IV, 1994, pp. 427–428).

The victims' responses to the initial trauma and the escalating stalking activities include behaviors not present prior to the trauma and the results of the trauma cause "...clinically significant distress or impairment in social, occupational, or other important areas of functioning" (DSM-IV, p. 429). The victims have been diagnosed as having chronic PTSD with acute symptoms occurring with each escalating activity by the stalker.

Stalking differs from interpersonal crimes such as sexual and physical assault because it involves long term methodical activities that may not terminate for a significant period of time so that a healing process can occur. Further, not all of the victims' treatment agents diagnosed them with Posttraumatic Stress Disorder (PTSD). The couple was sent for psychiatric treatment based on their symptoms and reported being further traumatized by the experience.

The fact that one of the stalkers is a female and involved in the criminal justice system, while not typical, is not a rarity. Research indicates that 25 percent of simple obsessional stalkers, stalkers who had a previous relationship with the victim, are females and that the educational and intelligence level of stalkers is above average (Meloy, 1995; Zona et al., 1993). Also, sometimes members of the criminal justice system have been reported as engaging in stalking behavior. The most notorious case being the 1992 stalking of Joy Silverman by Chief Judge Sol Wachtler in New York (Franks, 1994). Lott, a criminal justice professional, wrote about physical and emotional aggression reported by spouses or companions of police officers. He related the difficulty associated with the code of silence, the police culture, and the enforcement of acceptable performance policies (Lott, 1995).

The policies of the system have not always followed the statutes passed to address stalking. In particular, the victims in these three cases have reported decisions by the police not to take the initial criminal reports seriously because of the gender of the offenders and the victims. The victims were ordinary individuals and the police related to each of the victims that the caliber of the threatening and escalating behavior was attenuated because of the stalker's gender. The socio-economic status of the victims and the offenders may have enticed the criminal justice system to decline investigation and prosecution of the stalkers or mitigate the seriousness of the stalking. This will be discussed later.

Case Summaries

Case 1. The victim and offender are both in their forties, are Caucasian, and have a middle class existence reflective of economic stability. They live in two different towns and have each been married once. During the positive time of the relationship, both lived in separate homes, were socially active, traveled, and had supportive networks that came from work and leisure activities.

The victim is a male attorney. The stalker is a female attorney employed by the criminal justice system and is a member of a military reserve. She is proficient with handguns, semi-automatic and automatic weapons as part of her continued military service and her career in the criminal justice system. When the victim turned to the criminal justice system for assistance in addressing the stalker's behavior her agency engaged in obsequious behavior for the benefit of the victim while facilitating the transfer of the stalker to active military duty. The stalking behavior, however, continued.

The stalker's periodic explosive anger noted by the victim and his friends and the stalker's taped messages on the victim's answering machine are indicative of a troubled individual. Clinical psychologists and a psychiatrist also listened to the stalker's taped messages and warned the victim concerning the stalker's potential for violence. The obsession with the victim is related to the discordant termination of the previous intimate relationship. Initially, the stalker persisted in a fantasy of regaining the love of the victim. When her behavior failed to regain this love, she retaliated for perceived emotional and/or physical injury sustained by the loss of the relationship.

The victim reported that he kept a journal for the following reasons. First, every lawyer and counselor he consulted concerning the activities by the stalker highly encouraged him to provide documentation of his attempts to stop the criminal behavior. Second, as he began to investigate if his victimization was an isolated activity by the stalker, he began to acquire notes and information that were best organized through the use of a journal. Finally, he found the journal to be therapeutic and reflective as it documented what he had endured, his reactions, and the changes he had experienced. The victim's journal, including supporting documents, is the primary source of data followed by personal interviews. It is the victim's hope that this case study might enhance the comprehension of a stalking victimization and information concerning female stalkers.

The stalking activity began with signature pattern hang-up phone calls, unauthorized accessing of the victim's answering machine at work and home, nonconsensual notes and cards, and drive-bys of the victim's residence. When the victim did not respond by resuming the relationship, the stalker's activities escalated to surveillance of the victim from an alley in an unmarked police car, jogging in front of the victim's home, and through the victim's alley, poisoning of the victim's pet, and stealing his mail.

The mail stolen by the stalker occurred over a three day period and was methodically planned. The stalker stole the victim's birthday cards, including those from his family. When the victim did not receive any cards he reported that it was devastating given the previous activities of the stalker. When he saw his mailperson at his house, he asked if she recalled "any birthday cards from family." She responded that over a three day period, "near your birthday," she recalled delivering "twenty to thirty birthday cards."

The victim comprehended that the stalker had taken his birthday mail. When he asked neighbors if they had seen the stalker, they responded that she had recently been on his property and inside his home. He informed them that their relationship had been terminated and requested they call him if she should return. The victim changed his locks and began locking his doors.

The victim reported the mail theft to the Postal Inspector who requested mail that the stalker may have handled. The victim complied and waited for the completion of an investigation. The postal inspectors declined to complete an investigation labeling the incident a "simple domestic problem."

The stalker's behavior escalated to the destruction of the victim's boat. Sand was found in the gas tank of the engine and caused substantial damage. The stalker began making workplace visits that were witnessed by other building tenants. The accessing of the victim's answering machine provided the stalker with phone numbers of the victim's friends, family, therapist, clients, and investigative agencies that attempted to assist the victim with terminating the stalking. This resulted in pattern phone calls to forty-six second and third party victims. The victim had not removed the remote accessing numbers from underneath the phone and he concluded that this provided the stalker with his code.

The pattern phone calls are the stalker's signature and a direct taunt to the victim. These signatures or taunts are reflective of the interpersonal nature of the crime. She made two phone calls with a minute interval to the victim and then moved on to a series of calls to friends, clients, or family with the same pattern. One example was a series of nine second- and third-party victims in approximately thirty minutes who reported the calls to the phone company and the victim. Those most likely to receive the calls were those who left recent messages on the answering machine. In the face of this continuing pattern of stalking behavior, extreme psychological distress and physiological reactivity became a consistent part of the day to day life of the victim. The victim entered a state of chronic PTSD after his initial efforts to control her stalking failed during the first six months of the victimization.

Case 2. The victim and offender are in their late forties and are Caucasian. The victim and offender live in adjoining towns and have similar business interests and acquaintances. He owns a substantial business concern and she has a position in an organization that assists in community economic development. Both have considerable economic security and neither have a history of documented criminality. They both have graduate degrees in business with the stalker's degree being an executive Masters of Business Administration from an excellent school. He is still married to his first wife and the stalker has been divorced and is currently single.

Because of the stalker's role in economic development, she regularly encountered the victim for business and social activities. Thus, the stalking activity began shortly after the victim responded to the personal approaches made by the stalker by reminding her of his happily married status. He made it clear that he had no intention of developing a relationship other than continuing their professional relationship. Hang-up phone calls, nonconsensual notes and gifts, and opportunistic meetings became the method chosen by the stalker to bring the victim into her control and environment.

The victim finally informed his wife and later the police because the stalker escalated to destroying property. Broken lawn pottery, vandalism of his auto, notes on his windshield, and harassing telephone calls resulted in the victim contacting the police. The victim was reticent to report the behavior of the stalker to his colleagues. He feared being charged with over reacting and misunderstanding the business relationship that was necessary to the success of the project. When he finally began to discuss the stalking, he found that his reticent attitude was well deserved. Friends and business colleagues doubted his view of the stalker's behavior and encouraged him to discuss the "irritating behavior" with her.

The police were first amused at the report and the victim's attempts to file charges. They had not considered stalking by a female as a crime but rather a nuisance. However, they became more annoyed at the persistence of the victim when the victim's colleagues noted no impropriety in the stalker's behavior. After escalation of the stalker's activity that included the mysterious shooting at his son while walking on his college campus, the victim hired a private investigator and had his son transfer to another college.

The victim requested the private investigator to conduct a full investigation into the stalker's background. As the private investigator began to acquire information about the stalker from prior places of employment, documentation of prior unprosecuted aberrant activity began to unfold. This increased anxiety for the victim and was thought to have been the primary cause for a heart attack.

This victim did not keep a journal but did keep the unsigned notes and memorandums that the stalker sent as a rouse. The notes and the placement of the notes by the stalker were her signature. The victim reported that she always knew where he would be and that he would find the notes. Memos would call for a meeting to discuss business strategies. Later, the victim would find that he was the only person receiving the memo. Once at the meeting, the stalker would become aggressively sexual and harassing.

Case 3. The victims are a Caucasian married couple who were stalked by his sister, her sister-in-law, for two years. The victims and stalker are both in their early thirties and lived in the same town until the stalking escalated and resulted in court intervention. The family has lived in this same location for several generations. The stalker is a licensed counselor who is pursuing graduate work for a terminal degree. The female victim is a graduate in the humanities and the male victim is employed by a research institution. Both victims report that the stalker comes from a dysfunctional family where abuse occurred.

The victims became victims only after their marriage. They reported that the stalker's realization that she was no longer the favored or sole educated female in the family may have generated the criminal activity. The victims related that the stalker's promiscuity and inability to establish a traditional role as defined by the family led to conflict. The conflict increased as the couple reflected the traditional role of a married couple as well as the role of a married couple successfully employed and respected.

The stalking began with public altercations engineered by the stalker to cause the victims embarrassment. The stalker then moved onto threatening the victims and finally, escalated to the victims being charged with stalking the stalker. Where all three routinely were at the same location, the stalker would report the presence of the couple (individually or together) to the police and accuse them of stalking her. When the police would determine that all three had a reason for their presence, the stalker would retreat only to make similar charges elsewhere in the community.

The victims later learned that she engaged in surveillance of their activities. As the victims were embarrassed by the incident, they had not informed neighbors about the stalking. Instead, they attempted to conduct routine activities outside of their community and together whenever possible. Neighbors later informed the victims that the stalker was often parked near their home watching them. Because of this information, the victims varied their activities by changing churches, shopping areas, and physicians. Both became concerned for their safety and their freedom given the stalker's behavior.

These methodical activities continued until the entire family was called into court because of charges and counter-charges. Numerous statements were made by law enforcement and the court to the couple that the criminal justice system should not have a role in addressing private familial matters. However, because of the nature of the stalking, the court issued a Protection From Abuse Order (PFA) for both parties for the period of one year. The judge informed everyone that he felt that the intent of the PFA legislation did not address this type of relationship. A PFA was requested because a violation of a PFA resulted in incarceration rather than a fine as found in the violation of a restraining order.

The couple would make attempts to visit their in-laws only to have the stalker visit as well and report their presence to the court. This cyclical behavior continued until the couple left their home and terminated their relationship with the family. The couple moved a substantial distance to escape the stalking behavior. The court order remains in effect and the family has elected to cease contact with the couple.

The stalker has now escalated into abusing the mother/mother-in-law, a secondary stalking victim, as a taunt to the victims. The mother has no contact with the victims but the victims were informed of the abuse through friends. They have now terminated those friendships as a means of complying fully with the court order. They have been informed by their attorney that any attempt to contact the mother will provide the stalker with a reason to call the police.

Analysis

What is the impact of such victimizations and what causes the stalker to select this type of predatory behavior? Inherent in the crime of stalking is the fact that the initial traumatic event is reexperienced by the victim with each new escalating activity. Likewise, victims recollected previous stalking behaviors while experiencing new escalating stalking behavior. The victims reported that the period of respite between the stalking behaviors are filled with dread and heightened arousal awaiting the next event. The victims do not report their fear of a female stalker as exaggerated.

While the victims would like to avoid any and all aspects of the victimization, the nature of the crime of stalking assures the continuing presence of the trauma. The victims reported that this persistent presence of the trauma as well as the anxiety towards the next event led to diminished participation in day to day personal and occupational activities, leisure activities, and social activities. With the loss of such socialization, friendships, and intimacy, the victims reported a feeling that what was once going to be personally and professionally possible may no longer be probable.

With each new escalation of stalking activity, the victims experienced acute PTSD. These two aspects of PTSD cause victims to believe the stalker to be more powerful and adept than any attempts to terminate the victimization. Because of the stalker's position within the system, the victim in Case 1 began to question the stalker's adeptness at mitigating her behavior to elected criminal justice officials as alarming. Matters were made even more difficult when family and friends repeatedly informed the victim that he should be capable of "outsmarting" the stalker. When he failed in stopping her, he reported feeling incompetent and ashamed.

The victim in Case 2 found that his heart attack left him with diminished physical stamina to run a business and address the stalking. As the investigator acquired more information, the victim became convinced that the stalker must be stopped or that he leave the area for his personal safety, the safety of his family, and the integrity of his business. This realization added to the stress he experienced.

The victims in Case 3 left their home, family, and community in an attempt to comply with the court directive. The ongoing stress of the stalking resulted in a miscarriage and other stress related problems. When the wife sought medical attention she attempted to explain the stalking activity to her primary care physician. He responded by placing her on five different medications for the symptoms she described and recommended psychiatric counseling for "her problems." A further recommendation was made that her husband accompany her to the psychiatric counseling as a means of learning how "to help her."

Since that time the victims have found a new physician—someone who is knowledgeable about the crime of stalking. She has discontinued three of her medications and is undergoing victim support intervention with a knowledgeable therapist. Both are working and making attempts to become part of their new community.

What causes such aberrant behavior? Einstedter and Henry (1996, p. 12) define "cause" as "the forces or conditions that shape and influence humans to commit criminal acts." Henry (1990, pp. 145–146) delineated the basic rewards produced by criminal behavior as intrinsic, personal and psychological, economic, monetary or material rewards, interpersonal or social rewards, political rewards, and religious or moral rewards. Sampson and Laub (1993, p. 140) offer that "strong attachment to a spouse (or cohabitant) combined with close emotional ties creates a social bond or interdependence between two individuals that, all else being equal, should lead to a reduction in deviant behavior." Aspects of these factors are operating in the female stalkers' behavior.

What caused these women to engage in stalking, a crime of interpersonal violence? It was the cessation of Sampson and Laub's "strong attachment" by the victim that activated the deviant behavior in the stalker. Similarities in the cases indicate that two of the stalkers related information about familial abuse in their childhood to their victims when the relationships were still affable. Dependence evolved into obsessive stalking of the victims.

The stalkers and victims report no criminal behavior or other prior criminal victimizations. This was verified by one stalker's position as a prosecutor, one stalker's position as an economic developer who was trusted with large sums of money, and one stalker's state licensing as a counselor.

Causation for this criminality reflects a series of reconstructive activities. First, the routine role of a male victimizing a female is reversed. Secondly, the established concept of viewing past victimization and/or offending as facilitating the current victimization does not appear applicable. The presence of dysfunctional families may have contributed to the deviant socialization patterns. As the deviance process develops, the escalating activities become resonators of the crime.

The female stalker interprets the victim's renouncement of her attention as a process of marginalization. Her personal and psychological well-being are threatened. Marginalization as viewed by the stalker is the acknowledgement that the object of her obsession has diminished her status within the relationship and within their immediate social circle. She recognizes that she has been marginalized but refuses to comprehend that the relationship has terminated. She also fears that others will learn that she has been marginalized by the object of her obsession. As the stalker is obsessed with her victim and the power over the relationship, she engages in the reconstruction of the power differential. This reconstruction allows her to believe that she can regain control.

She may begin by fantasizing about what she would like to do to this person and how he will eventually respond to her activities. At this point, the potential stalker is engaging in behavior that may be considered routine after the termination of any relationship. If her fantasies are not enough to sustain her, she then chooses to fulfill those fantasies. She can engage in activities that are threatening and emotionally and physically harmful to the object of her obsession. The ultimate goal appears to be the resumption of the previous status of the relationship or punishment for what the stalker perceives the victim has done to her.

The stalker now must reconstruct the significance of the object of her obsession so that she can now initiate the stalking activity. The stalking activity escalates as the impact of the activities result in increased traumatization for the victims. Thus, the inability for the victims to function at work, their decreased social activity, the incredulous attitudes by some of their friends toward the stalking activities, the minimal intervention by the criminal justice system, and the physical ailments are sectors of power that are added to the stalker's power differential.

The role of economics in crime is primarily associated with rational choice theory and the lack of economic autonomy. In stalking, the predatory behavior is often facilitated by the financial independence and employment of the stalker. These case studies illustrate that the stalkers' economic autonomy was critical to their ability to engage in stalking and escalating activities. The socio-economic status of the stalkers became an obstacle for the victims in terms of statutory compliance.

The intrinsic and interpersonal rewards are the thrills associated with the victim impact and the knowledge that the victim comprehends that the behavior is in response to the termination of the previous status quo. The stalker enters into a long term course of behaviors that generate and sustain criminality. The accepted context of where stalking takes place, how it takes place, and who engages in stalking is reconstructed.

Discussion

The criminal justice system appeared to reconstruct the criminality of these stalkers as well as the impact of the victimization. Possibly because of the status of the offenders and the victims, the system determined that it had the authority to reconstruct the criminal activity into an issue of conflict. However, the stalking described in these case studies was more than conflict. Of greater concern is the independent determination by the criminal justice system to find some alternative resolution to felonious behaviors. It is difficult to determine if the decision was made for the benefit of the stalker, the victims, or the system.

Further, the stalkers' failure to fulfill traditional or missing role expectations coupled with their ability to manipulate their power over others formed a symbiotic relationship with their socio-economic status. A new role emerged that thrived on this resulting mutualism of deviant behavior with financial independence. The result was stalking as a means of reprisal for perceived injury. "Injury" reflects the stalker's initial belief that her predatory behavior will result in a return to the previous acceptable status much like reconstructive surgery does for an accident patient.

The context of these case studies reveals information about stalking victimization as it relates to Posttraumatic Stress Disorder (PTSD). The stalkers engaged in behaviors that were of some concern to the victims prior to the termination of the relationship. In retrospect, the victim in Case 1 reported that the jealousy, the demanding behavior, and the acting out he initially found acceptable were pre-stalking behaviors. Further, it is probable that the stalker secretly accessed the victim's answering machine while they were dating. When training about the crime of stalking, such warning signals should be identified and stressed as issues for investigation and prevention.

The victim's initial attitude about this being a case for law enforcement appeared to prevail; however, as the stalking continued he reluctantly identified the political issues that had overtly controlled the case. The stalking became and remains an act of personal terrorism for the victim. The stalker however, managed to remain just outside the reach of law enforcement because she was assisted by the politics of the code of silence and conventional investigative tactics that often ignore the victim's role in the apprehension of the criminal.

The cyclical nature of the victimization and the long term course of the behavior has resulted in serious consequences to the victims. The victims describe a series of "yo-yo" emotional experiences. The victim in Case 1 goes from believing that a criminal justice agency will arrest the stalker to understanding that nothing is going to be done. Secondly, the victim goes from extreme agitation during the stalking activity to serious anxiety when the activity ceases as he has been programmed by the stalker to comprehend that the behavior will eventually resume. The stalking activity has occurred over a four year period. The victim is blamed for the stalking because he failed to outsmart the stalker, because he did not purchase a new answering machine, and because he could not ignore her activity. This stalking case results from previous intimacy. The criminal justice system often engages in victim blaming when the victim and perpetrator were previously intimate.

The victims in Case 1 and in Case 3 also evidenced a common behavior found in many stalking victims. They repeatedly cycle through the stalking experience and all of the attempts to have the stalker arrested. They do this in their journals, during discussions and social conversations. The process of this recycling is evidence of trauma and is an example of the rituals reported by stalking victims that are often termed "obsessive behaviors." For instance, a female victim of a male stalker reports checking her front door, her windows, her basement door, and her sliding glass door with rod iron barricades throughout the evening. She reports that she engages in this behavior, in this precise order, from dusk until she takes her sleeping pill at 10:00 P.M. It is ironic that the victims and the stalker engage in obsessive behaviors as a response to their trauma.

The victim in Case 2 had his stalking come to a resolution, albeit outside of the criminal justice system. His private investigator substantiated a history of stalking and harassing behavior by the executive MBA. Using her personal resume, the investigator traveled to places of prior employment and related his client's story. Previous victims mirrored the client's story and their embarrassment and humiliation at not being able to activate the criminal justice system because of the stalker's gender and status in the community. They added that they were also concerned about the impact of being identified as a victim of a woman.

When the investigator and the victim informed the police chief about the documented previous behavior, the stalker was confronted with the information. The stalker, with the agreement of the victim, left the state for a similar position elsewhere. The victim felt vindicated and went into semi-retirement because of his health. In this case, the financial independence of the victim facilitated the termination of his victimization. After his investigator found the evidence, law enforcement initiated action.

Conclusion

These case studies taken from journals and interviews reflect the reality of stalking. While the criminal profiling of the stalker can be clinical, the experiences of the victims have become a substantial part of their lives. The victim in Case 1 wrote in his journal that anticipation of the next event was as stressful as the actual stalking. Further, even the treatment agent was surprised at the periods of respite followed by escalation of the stalker's activity which only served to increase the victim's trauma. Treatment agents should be aware that one aspect to working with crime victims is an educational process about the legal system and the forensics of particular crimes.

Of continuing concern to the victim is the conflicting information he has received from psychologists and law enforcement agencies about the retention of the answering machines. Both disciplines offer sound evidence as to why the machines should be replaced or maintained. This conflict exacerbates the victim's trauma as he now relates that "No one knows what they are doing." The victim, the victim advocate, and the treatment agent believe that after the stalker's military service is terminated with the JAG, she will attempt to return to her senior position with state law enforcement. It is the complexities of such trauma and the potential for re-initiation of stalking activity that may hold a key to providing victim services to stalking victims.

Stalking victimization by partners and acquaintances are two different types of violent assaults. The victims in Case 3 should have full expectation that legislation and compliance with the legislation is the responsibility of the criminal justice system. Familial violence, be it child abuse, domestic violence, or elder abuse, is not a private matter. It is a criminal matter when such abuse is facilitated and tolerated.

A joint investigation by a knowledgeable victim advocate and a police investigator may offer victims a level of maintenance over their trauma. The victims were advised that their wisdom at not negotiating with the stalkers was correct. Each time the victims are forced to confront or meet with the stalker is viewed as a positive result of the escalating activities by the stalker. It is the duty of law enforcement to terminate the behavior. The victim advocate should continue contact with the victim during periods of respite for a number of reasons. First, continued contact with law enforcement is particularly vital in cases where obsessional following has been documented because obsessional stalking is measured in months and years. Secondly, establishing an ongoing relationship based upon managing the victim's stalking case provides the victim advocate with information about pre-stalking behavior. This information may lead to establishing a protocol for early intervention by authorities, may prevent the full onset of stalking, and offer information about victim-offender dynamics.

Interaction with the criminal justice system has been documented as terminating stress, causing stress, and exacerbating the victimization. Some suggestions might be made for the processing of stalking cases. First, a victim must keep an accurate and timely journal about the stalking activity, their attempt to report it, and the response to their report. The journal must include the time, date, stalking activity, list of witnesses, when reported, who reported to (officer, badge number, shift), and the resulting activity or directives given by law enforcement. The victims must then request a full copy of the police report as indication of "long term, on-going stalking activity."

Secondly, the victim must report the stalking activity to their phone service (local and long distance) and follow their suggested protocol. The victim must also inform close friends, neighbors, family, co-workers, and employers about the stalking. This fosters a vigilant attitude by family and friends and encourages employers to activate workplace anti-violence policies. As these individuals may be secondary victims, there is a responsibility to prevent any potential violence directed toward them.

Lastly, victims must be encouraged by law enforcement to take an active role in controlling the informational aspect of the case. There is one exception to this—the victim should not be required to meet with the stalker. Victim-witness workers may be the only intervention necessary for the victims. However, if a referral for formalized treatment should be necessary, it should be with an advocate who is knowledgeable about this predatory type of behavior. Police, victim-witness workers, prosecutors, and judges should feel compelled to uphold the stalking statutes as written. If revisions are necessary, they should be the result of astute observation and documentation and not the death of a stalking victim.

Further research is needed to determine which types of stalkers, stalking victims, and stalking relationships require differential investigation, prosecution, treatment, and what those interventions should be. Any intervention should support the victim, prevent violent escalation of activity, comply with the criminal codes, and assist in apprehension and prosecution.

Note: The author wishes to thank Dr. Eric Hickey for his assistance and the victims for their courage.

Discussion Questions

Stalking is an old behavior and a new crime. What has changed in society that has resulted in the increased documentation of stalking activity?

What makes stalking a predatory crime?

If addressed early the escalation of predatory violence can be prevented. Discuss how this might be done in an educational setting, the workplace, and the community.

Discretion, the ability to make decisions without consideration for rules and facts, continues to be an important factor in the processing of stalking cases. Why is it permissible to use discretion when addressing familial or non-stranger victimization?

References

Chapter 1

Alderson, J. (1977). *Communal policing*. London: Devon and Cornwall Constabulary.

Baumer, T. (1985). Testing a general model of fear of crime: Data from a national sample. *Journal of Research in Crime and Delinquency, 22,* 239–255.

Bayley, D. (1988). Community policing: A report from the devil-advocate. In J. Greene & S. Mastrofski (Eds.), *Community policing: Rhetoric or reality?* (pp. 225–237). New York: Praeger.

Brady, T. (1996). Measuring what matters: Part one: Measures of crime, fear and disorder. Washington, DC: National Institute of Justice.

Brown, L. (1985). Police-community power sharing. In Geller, W. (Ed.), *Police leadership in America* (pp. 70–83). New York: Praeger.

Davis, R. (1985). Organizing the community for improved policing. In William Geller (Ed.), *Police leadership in America* (pp. 84–95). New York: Praeger.

Garofalo, J. & Laub, J. (1978). The fear of crime: Broadening the perspective, *Victimology: An International Journal, 3,* 242–253.

Goldstein, H. (1990). Problem-oriented policing. Philadelphia: Temple University Press.

Goldstein, H. (1987). Toward community-oriented policing: Potential, basic requirements and threshold questions. *Crime and Delinquency, 24,* 6–30.

Greene, J. & Taylor, R. (1988). Community based policing and foot patrol: Issues of theory and evaluation. In J. Greene & S. Mastrofski (Eds.), *Community policing: Rhetoric or reality?* (pp. 185–224). New York: Praeger.

Hindelang, M., Gottfredson, M., & Garofalo, J. (1978). *Victims of personal crime: An empirical foundation for a theory of personal violence*. Cambridge: Ballinger.

Hunter, A. (1978). *Symbolic communities: The persistence and change of Chicago-local communities*. Chicago: University of Chicago Press.

Kelling, G., & Coles, C. (1996). *Fixing Broken Windows*. New York: Free Press.

239

Kelling, G., & Moore, M. (1988). The evolving strategy of policing. *Perspective on Policing*. Washington DC: National Institute of Justice.

Skogan, W. (1977). Public policy and fear of crime in large American cities. In J. Gardiner, (Ed.), *Public law and public policy* (pp. 1–18). New York: Praeger.

Skogan, W. (1986). Fear of crime and neighborhood change. In A. Reiss & M. Tonry (Eds.), *Communities and Crime* (pp. 203–229). Chicago: University of Chicago.

Skogan, W. (1990). *Disorder and decline: Crime and the spiral of Urban Decay in American Neighborhoods*. New York: Free Press.

Skogan, W., & Klecka, W. (1977). *The Fear of Crime*. Washington, DC: The American Political Science Association.

Skogan, W., & Maxfield, M. (1981). *Coping with crime: Individual and neighborhood reactions*. Beverly Hills: Sage.

Sparrow, M., Moore, M., & Kennedy, D. (1990). *Beyond 911: A new era for policing*. New York: Basic Books.

Stinchcombe, A., Heimer, C., Dliff, R., Schepple, K., Smith, T., & Garth, T. (1978). *Crime and punishment in public opinion: 1948–1974*. National Opinion Research Center, Chicago.

Toseland, R. (1982). Fear of crime: Who is most vulnerable? *Journal of Criminal Justice*, 199–209.

Wilson, J., & Kelling, G. (1982). The police and neighborhood safety. *The Atlantic*, 29–38.

U.S. Bureau of the Census (1990). *Census of population and housing*, Population and Housing Counts, Massachusetts.

U.S. Census of Manufactures (1987). *General statistics for principal industrial counties*, Massachusetts.

Chapter 2

Akers, R.L., LaGreca, A.J., Sellers, C., & Cochran, J. (1987). Fear of crime and victimization among the elderly in different types of communities. *Criminology, 25*, 487–505.

Bankston, W.B., & Thompson, C.Y. (1989). Carrying firearms for protection: A causal model. *Sociological Inquiry, 59*, 75–87.

Bartol, C.R., & Bartol, A.M. (1994). *Psychology and law: Research and application*. Pacific Grove, CA: Brooks/Cole.

Baumer, T.L. (1985). Testing a general model of fear of crime: Data from a national sample. *Journal of Research in Crime and Delinquency, 22*, 239–255.

Brantingham, P.J., & Brantingham, P.L. (1982). Mobility, notoriety and crime: A study in crime patterns of urban nodal points. *Journal of Environmental Systems, 11*, 89–99.

Clark, A.H., & Lewis, M.J. (1982). Fear of crime among the elderly. *British Journal of Criminology, 22*, 49–62.

Clemente, F., & Kleiman, M. (1976). Fear of crime among the aged. *The Gerontologist, 16*, 207–210.

Federal Bureau of Investigation. (1983). *Uniform crime reports for the United States, 1982*. Washington, DC: Government Printing Office.

Federal Bureau of Investigation. (1993). *Uniform crime reports for the United States, 1992*. Washington, DC: Government Printing Office.

Felson, M. (1986). Crime at any point on the city map. In R.M. Figlio, S. Hakim, & G.F. Rengert (Eds.) *Metropolitan Crime Patterns* (pp. 127–136). Monsey, NY: Criminal Justice Press.

Felson, M. (1987). Routine activities and crime prevention in the developing metropolis. *Criminology, 25*, 911–932.

Ferraro, K.F. (1995). *Fear of crime: Interpreting victimization risk*. Albany: State University of New York Press.

Ferraro, K.F., & LaGrange, R. (1988). Are older people afraid of crime? *Journal of Aging Studies, 2*, 277–287.

Garofalo, J., & Laub, J. (1978). The fear of crime: Broadening our perspective. *Victimology, 3*, 242–253.

Gallup, G. (1992). *The Gallup Poll Monthly*, No. 318. Princeton: The Gallup Poll.

Gibbs, J. (1987). The state of criminological theory. *Criminology, 25*, 821–841.

Goldsmith, J., & Goldsmith, S.S. (1976). *Crime and the elderly*. Lexington, MA: DC Heath and Company.

Gomme, I.M. (1988). The role of experience in the production of fear of crime: A test of a causal model. *Canadian Journal of Criminology, 30*, 67–76.

Hahn, P.H. (1976). *Crimes against the elderly: A study in victimology*. Santa Cruz: Davis Publishing Company, Inc.

Inciardi, J. (1980). *Radical criminology: The coming crisis*. Beverly Hills, CA: Sage.

Kennedy, L.W., & Silverman, R.A. (1985a). Perception of social diversity and fear of crime. *Environment and Behavior, 17*, 275–295.

Kennedy, L.W., & Silverman, R.A. (1985b). Significant others and fear of crime among the elderly. *International Journal Aging and Human Development, 20*, 241–256.

Kiess, H.O. (1996). *Statistical concepts for the social sciences* (2nd ed.). Boston: Allyn and Bacon.

LaGrange, R.L., & Ferraro, K.F. (1987). The elderly's fear of crime: A critical examination of the research. *Research on Aging*, 9, 372–391.

LaGrange, R.L., & Ferraro, K.F. (1989). Assessing age and gender differences in perceived risk and fear of crime. *Criminology*, 27, 697–719.

Lee, G.R. (1982). Residential location and fear of crime among the elderly. *Rural Sociology*, 17, 655–669.

Lee, G.R. (1983). Social integration and fear of crime among older persons. *Journal of Gerontology*, 38, 745–750.

Liska, A.E., Sanchirico, A., & Reed, M.D. (1988). Fear of crime and constrained behavior: Specifying and estimating a reciprocal effects model. *Social Forces*, 66, 827–837.

Mawby, R.I. (1982). Crime and the elderly: A review of British and American research. *Current Psychological Reviews*, 2, 301–310.

Maxfield, M.G., & Babbie, E. (1995). *Research methods for criminal justice and criminology*. Belmont: Wadsworth.

Mullen, R.E, & Donnermeyer, J.F. (1985). Age, trust and perceived safety from crime in rural areas. *The Gerontologist*, 25, 237–242.

National Advisory Commission. (1973). *Criminal justice standards and goals*. Washington, DC: Government Printing Office.

Neuman, W.L. (1997). *Social research methods* (3rd ed.). Boston: Allyn and Bacon.

Norris, F.H., & Kaniasty, K. (1994). Psychological distress following criminal victimization in the general population: Cross-sectional, longitudinal, and prospective analyses. *Journal of Consulting and Clinical Psychology*, 62, 111–123.

Norton, L. (1982). Crime prevention education for elderly citizens: Fear of crime, and security conscious behavior. *Criminal Justice Review*, 7, 9–15.

Ollenburger, J.C. (1981). Criminal victimization and fear of crime. *Research on Aging*, 3, 101–118.

Ortega, S.T., & Myles, J.L. (1987). Race and gender effects on fear of crime: An interactive model with age. *Criminology*, 25, 133–152.

Parker, K.D., & Ray, M.C. (1990). Fear of crime: An assessment of related factors. *Sociological Spectrum*, 10, 29–40.

Parker, K.D., McMorris, B.J., Smith, E., & Murty, K.S. (1993). Fear of crime and the likelihood of victimization: A bi-ethnic comparison. *Journal of Social Psychology*, 133, 723–732.

Pelfrey, W.V., & Dull, R.T. (1982). *Survey of crime and justice in Tennessee*. Memphis: Memphis State University.

Pelfrey, W.V., Bohm, R.M., Dean, C.W., Humphrey, J.A., Moriarty, L.J., Vasu, M.L., Willis, G.W., & Zahn, M.A. (1992). *Final report of the North Carolina violent crime assessment project*. Raleigh: Governor's Crime Commission.

Ross, C.E. (1993). Fear of victimization and health. *Journal of Quantitative Criminology, 9*, 159–175.

Sampson, R.J. (1987). Does an intact family reduce burglary risk for its neighbors? *Sociology and Social Research, 71*, 204–207.

Schwendinger, H., & Schwendinger, J. (1982). The paradigmatic crisis in delinquency theory. *Crime and Social Justice, 18*, 70–79.

Skogan W., & Maxfield, M.G. (1981). *Coping with crime: Individual and neighborhood reactions.* Beverly Hills: Sage.

Smith, L.N., & Hill, G.D. (1991). Victimization and fear of crime. *Criminal Justice and Behavior, 18*, 217–239

Stanko, E.A. (1992). The case of fearful women: Gender, personal safety and fear of crime. *Women and Criminal Justice, 4*, 117–135.

Taylor, D.G., Taub, R.P., & Peterson, B. (1986). Crime, community organization, and causes of neighborhood decline. In R. Figleo, S. Hakim. & G. Rengert (Eds), *Metropolitan crime patterns* (pp. 161–177). Monsey, NY: Criminal Justice Press.

Thompson, M.P., & Norris, F.H. (1992). Crime, social status, and alienation. *American Journal of Community Psychology, 20*, 97–119.

Trojanowicz, R., & Bucqueroux, B. (1990). *Community policing: A contemporary perspective.* Cincinnati: Anderson.

Vasu, M.L., Moriarty, L.J., & Pelfrey, W.V. (1995). Measuring violent crime in North Carolina utilizing mail and telephone surveys simultaneously: Does method matter? *Criminal Justice Review, 20*, 34–43.

Voigt, L., Thornton, W.E., Barrile, L., & Seaman, J.M. (1994). *Criminology and justice.* New York: McGraw-Hill.

Warr, M. (1984). Fear of victimization: Why are women and elderly more afraid? *Social Science Quarterly, 65*, 681–702.

Will, J.A., & McGrath, J.H. (1995). Crime, neighborhood perceptions and the underclass: The relationship between fear of crime and class position. *Journal of Criminal Justice, 23* (2), 163–176.

Yin, P. (1982). Fear of crime as a problem for the elderly. *Social Problems, 30*, 240–245.

Chapter 3

Belyea, M.J., & Zingraff, M.T. (1988). Fear of crime and residential location. *Rural Sociology, 53*(4), 473–486.

Bennett, T., & Wright, R. (1984). Constraints to burglary: The offender's perspective. In R. Clarke & T. Hope (Eds.), *Coping With burglary.* Boston: Kluwer-Nijhoff Publishing.

Bennett, T., & Wright, R. (1983). Burglars' perception of targets. *Home Office Research Bulletin, 15.*

Bennett, T., & Wright, R. (1975). The spatial patterning of burglary. *Howard Journal of Penology and Crime Prevention, 14*, 11–24.

Bennett, T., & Wright, R. (1991). Introduction: The dimensions of crime. In P.J. Brantingham & P.L. Brantingham, (Eds.), *Environmental criminology* (pp 7–26). Prospect Heights, IL: Waveland Press, Inc.

Bennett, T., & Wright, R (1990). Situational crime prevention in practice. *Canadian Journal of Criminology, 32*, 17–40.

Brown, B.B., & Altman, I. (1991). Territoriality and residential crime: A conceptual framework. In P.J. Brantingham & P.L. Brantingham (Eds.), *Environmental criminology* (pp. 55–76). Prospect Heights, IL: Waveland Press, Inc.

Conklin, J. (1971). Dimensions of the community response to the crime problem. *Social Problems, 18* (Winter), 373–385.

Covington, J., & Taylor, R.B. (1991). Fear of crime in urban neighborhoods: Implications of between- and within-neighborhood sources for current models. *Sociological Quarterly, 32*(2), 232–249.

Cromwell, P., Olson, J., & Avary, D. (1991). *Breaking and entering: An ethnographic analysis of burglary*. Newbury Park, CA: Sage Publications.

Furstenberg, F. (1971). Public reaction to crime in the streets. *American Scholar, 40*(4), 601–610.

Jacobs, J. (1961). *The death and life of great American cities*. London: Jonathan Cape.

Jeffery, C.R. (1990). *Criminology: An interdisciplinary approach*. Englewood Cliffs, NJ: Prentice Hall.

Jeffery, C.R. (1977). *Crime prevention through environmental design*. Beverly Hills, CA: Sage Publications. (Original work published 1971).

Jeffery, C.R., Hunter, R., & Griswold, J. (1986). Crime prevention and computer analysis of convenience store robberies in Tallahassee, Florida. Paper presented at the annual meeting of the Academy of Criminal Justice Sciences, Orlando, FL.

Lee, G. (1982). Residential location and fear of crime among the elderly. *Rural Sociology, 47*(4), 655–669.

McConnell, E.H. (1996). Students' fear of crime on a southern university campus. Paper presented at the annual meeting of the Academy of Criminal Justice Sciences, Las Vegas, NV.

Nasar, J.L., & Fisher, B. (1992). Design for vulnerability: Cues and reactions to fear of crime. *Sociology and Social Research, 76*(2), 48–60.

Parker, K.D. (1988). Black-white differences in perceptions of fear of crime. *Journal of Social Psychology, 128*(4), 487–494.

Parker, K.D., Morris, B.J., Smith, E., & Murty, K.S. (1993). Fear of crime and the likelihood of victimization: A bi-ethnic comparison. *Journal of Social Psychology, 133*(5), 723–732.

Pearson, F.S., & Toby, J. (1991). Fear of school-related predatory crime. *Sociology and Social Research, 75*(3), 117–119.

Poyner, B. (1983). *Design against crime: Beyond defensible space.* London: Butterworths.

Reaves, B.A., & Goldberg, A.L. (1996). *Campus law enforcement agencies, 1995* [NIJ 161137]. Washington, D.C: U.S. Department of Justice.

Rengert, G.F. (1981). Burglary in Philadelphia: A critique of an opportunity structure model. In P.J. Brantingham & P.L. Brantingham (Eds.), *Environmental criminology* (pp. 189–202). Prospect Heights, IL: Waveland Press, Inc.

Robinson, D.M. (in press). A comparative analysis of environmental characteristics related to criminal victimizations in activity areas of interstate highway interchanges and local highway intersections. *Journal of Security Administration.*

Robinson, D.M. (1996). Interchange activity areas (IAAs): An assessment of environmental characteristics as related to criminal victimizations. Paper presented at the annual meeting of the Southern Criminal Justice Association, Savannah, GA.

Robinson, D.M. (1995). An analysis of the relationship of environmental characteristics to types and rates of criminal victimizations in interchange activity areas surrounding interstate highway interchanges. Doctoral Dissertation, Florida State University, Microfilm, Inc. (AA19612134).

Shipman, M. (1994). Perceptions of campus police: News gathering and access to public records. *Newspaper Research Journal, 15*(2), 1–11.

Stanko, E.A. (1992). The case of fearful women: Gender, personal safety and fear of crime. *Women and Criminal Justice, 4*(1), 117–133.

Warr, M. (1984). Fear of victimization: Why women and elderly are more afraid? *Social Science Quarterly, 56*(4), 681–702.

Winchester, F., & Jackson, H. (1982). Residential burglary: The limits of prevention. *Home Office Research Study, 74.* London: Her Majesty's Stationary Office.

Chapter 4

Bloch, A.M., & Bloch, R. R. (1980). Teachers—A New Endangered Species. In K. Baker & R. J. Rubel (Eds.), *Violence and crime in the schools* (pp. 81–89). Lexington, MA: DC Heath and Company.

Curcio, J. L., & First, P. F. (1993). *Violence in schools.* Newbury Park, CA: Corwin Press, Inc.

Ellis, D. (1992, June 8). Knowledge For Sale. *Time,* 69–71.

Gottfredson, G.D. & Gottfredson, DC (1985). *Victimization in the schools.* New York: Plenum.

Lab, S.P. (1997). *Crime prevention: Approaches, practices and evaluations* (3rd ed). Cincinnati: Anderson Publishing Co.

Lab, S.P., & Clark, R.D. (1997). Crime Prevention in Schools: Individual and Collective Responses. In S.P. Lab (Ed.), *Crime Prevention at a crossroads* (pp. 127–140). Cincinnati: Anderson Publishing Co.

Maguire, K., & Flanagan, T. J. (Eds.). (1991). *Sourcebook of criminal justice statistics 1990* . Washington, DC: U.S. Department of Justice.

Menacker, J., Weldon, W., & Hurwitz, E. (1989). School order and safety as community issues. *Phi Delta Kappan, 71*, 39–40, 55–56.

Metropolitan Life (1993). *Violence in America's public schools*. New York: Louis Harris and Associates.

National Institute of Education. (1978). *Violent schools—Safe schools— The safe school study report to Congress*. Washington, DC: U.S. Government Printing Office.

North Carolina Center for the Prevention of School Violence. (1994). *School violence: Lets get it out of our system*. Raleigh: North Carolina Governor's Crime Commission.

Ogle, L.T. (Ed.). (1990). *The condition of education 1990: Volume 1 elementary and secondary education*. Washington, DC: National Center for Educational Statistics.

Quarles, C. L. (1989). *School violence: A survival guide for school staff*. Washington, DC: National Educational Association.

Toby, J. (1995). The schools. In J.Q. Wilson, & J. Petersilia (Eds.), *Crime*. San Francisco: ICS Press.

Chapter 5

Asmussen, K.J. (1992, Fall). Weapon possession in public high schools. *School Safety*, 28–30.

Bastian, L.D., & Taylor, B.M. (1991). *School crime: A national crime victimization survey report*. Washington, DC: U.S. Department of Justice.

Batsche, G.M., & Knoff, H.M. (1994). Bullies and their victims: Understanding a pervasive problem in the schools. *School Psychology Review, 23*(2), 165–174.

Boulton, M.J., & Underwood, K. (1992). Bully/victims problems among middle school children. *British Journal of Educational Psychology, 62*(1), 73–87.

Christie, D.J., & Toomey, B.G. (1990). The stress of violence: School, community, and world. In L.E. Arnold (Ed.), *Childhood stress* (pp. 297–323). New York: John Wiley & Sons.

Clifford, M.A., & Davis, M. (1991). *Evaluation tests for student assistance programs*. Boulder, CO: National Organization of Student Assistance Programs and Professionals.

Cronbach, L.J. (1970). *Essentials of psychological testing* (3rd ed). New York: Harper & Row.

DuRant, R.H., Cadenhead, C., Pendergrast, R.A., Slavens, G., & Linder, C.W. (1994). Factors associated with the use of violence among urban black adolescents. *American Journal of Public Health*, *84*(4), 612–617.

Elliott, D.S., Huizinga, D., & Ageton, S.S. (1985). *Explaining delinquency and drug use*. Beverly Hills, CA: Sage.

Gaustad, J. (1991). Schools attack the roots of violence. *ERIC Digest*, *63*, 1–2.

Gold, M., & Mann, D.W. (1984). *Expelled to a friendlier place: A study of alternative schools*. Ann Arbor, MI: University of Michigan Press.

Gottfredson, DC (1987). An evaluation of an organizational development approach to reducing school disorder. *Evaluation Review*, *11*(6), 739–763.

Gottfredson, G.D. (1987). *American education—American delinquency*. (Report No. 23). Baltimore: Center for Research on Elementary and Middle Schools.

Jensen, G., & Brownfield, D. (1986). Gender, lifestyles, and victimization: Beyond routine activity theory. *Violence and Victims*, *1*, 85–99.

Johnson, D.W., & Johnson, R.T. (1995a). Why violence prevention programs don't work-and what does. *Educational Leadership*, *52*(5), 63–67.

Johnson, D.W., & Johnson, R.T. (1995b). *Reducing school violence through conflict resolution*. Alexandria, VA: Association for Supervision and Curriculum Development.

Kachur, S.P., Stennies, G.M., Powell, K.E., Modzeleski, W., Stephens, R., Murphy, R., Kresnow, M., Sleet, D., & Lowry, R. (1996). *School-associated deaths in the United States, 1992–1994. Journal of the American Medical Association*, *275*(22), 1729–1733.

Lab, S.P., & Whitehead, J.T. (1992). *The school environment and school crime: Causes and consequences*. Washington, DC: U.S. Department of Justice.

Lane, T.W., & Murakami, J. (1987). School programs for delinquency prevention and intervention. In E.K. Morris & C.J. Braukmann (Eds.), *Behavioral approaches to crime and delinquency* (pp. 305–327). New York: Plenum Press.

Lowry, R., Sleet, D., Duncan, C., Powell, K., & Kolbe, L. (1995). Adolescents at risk for violence. *Educational Psychology Review*, *7*(1), 7–39.

McDermott, J. (1983). Crime in the school and the community: Offenders, victims, and fearful youths. *Crime and Delinquency, 29*(2), 270–282.

McDowall, D. (1995). Firearms and self-defense. *The Annals of The American Academy o Political Science and Social Science, 539*(May), 130–140.

Mulhern, S. (1994). *Preventing youth violence and aggression and promoting safety in schools.* Madison, WI: Wisconsin State Department of Public Instruction.

National Center for School Safety. (1993). *Weapons in schools.* Malibu, CA: Pepperdine University.

National Institute of Education. (1978). *Violent schools-safe schools: The safe schools report to the Congress.* Washington, DC: U.S. Department of Health, Education, and Welfare.

Nolin, M.J., Davies, E., & Chandler, K. (1996). Student victimization at school. *Journal of School Health, 66*(6), 216–221.

Office of Juvenile Justice and Delinquency Prevention. (1996). *Juvenile offenders and victims: 1996 update on violence.* Washington, DC: U.S. Department of Justice.

Olweus, D. (1978). *Aggression in the schools: Bullies and whipping boys.* New York: Wiley.

Pearson, F.S., & Toby, J. (1992). *Perceived and actual risks of school-related victimization.* Washington, DC: U.S. Department of Justice.

Perry, D.G., Kusel, S.J., & Perry, L.C. (1988). Victims of peer aggression. *Developmental Psychology, 24,* 807–814.

Ringwalt, C., Messerschmidt, P., Graham, L., & Collins, J. (1992). *Youths' victimization experiences, fear of attack or harm, and school avoidance behaviors.* Washington, DC: U.S. Department of Justice.

Sheley, J.F., McGee, Z.T., & Wright, J.D. (1995). *Weapon-related victimization in selected inner-city high school samples.* Washington, DC: U.S. Department of Justice.

Tolan, P., & Guerra, N. (1994). *What works in reducing adolescent violence? An empirical review of the field.* Boulder, CO: Center for the Study and Prevention of Violence.

Webster, D.W., Gainer, P.S., & Champion, H.R. (1993). Weapon carrying among inner-city junior high school students: Defensive behavior vs. aggressive delinquency. *American Journal of Public Health, 83*(11), 1604–1608.

Chapter 6

Abbey, A., Ross, L.T., & McDuffie, D. (1996). Alcohol and dating risk factors for sexual assault among college women. *Psychology of Women Quarterly, 20,* 147–169.

Altimore, M. (1991). The social construction of a scientific myth: Pornography and violence. *Journal of Communication Inquiry, 15,* 117–133.

Australian Bureau of Statistics. (1993, April). *Crime and safety, Australia.* Canberra: Australian Bureau of Statistics.

Bausell, R.B., Bausell, C.R., & Siegel, D.G. (1991). *The links among alcohol, drugs and crime on American college campuses: A national followup study.* Towson, MD: Business Publishers, Inc.

Bora, D.J. (1997). Criminal victimization on university campuses. Paper presented at the annual meeting of the Academy of Criminal Justice Sciences, Louisville, KY.

Cohen, L.E., & Felson, M. (1979). Social change and crime rate trends: A routine activities approach. *American Sociological Review, 44,* 588–607.

Engs, R.C., & Hanson, D.J. (1988). University students' drinking patterns and problems: Examining the effects of raising the purchase age. *Public Health Reports, 103*(6), 667–673.

Fox, J.A., & Hellman, D.A. (1985). Location and other correlates of campus crime. *Journal of Criminal Justice, 13*(2), 429–444.

Gonzales, C.E., & Broughton, E.A. (1986). Status of alcohol policies on campus: A national survey. *NASPA Journal, 24*(2), 49–59.

Gottfredson, M.R., & Hirschi, T. (1990). *A general theory of crime.* Stanford: Stanford University Press.

Gusfield, J. (1963). *Symbolic crusade: Status politics and the American temperance movement.* Chicago: The University of Chicago Press.

Hanson, D.J., & Engs, R.C. (1992). College students' drinking problems: A national study, 1982–1991. *Psychological Reports, 71,* 39–42.

Kentucky State Police (1994). *Crime in Kentucky.* Frankfort, KY: Commonwealth of Kentucky.

Kentucky State Police (1995). *Crime in Kentucky.* Frankfort, KY: Commonwealth of Kentucky.

Lederman, D. (1993, January 20). College report 7,500 violent crimes on their campuses in first annual statement required under federal law. *Chronicle of Higher Education,* A32–A43.

Lewis, D.A., & Salem, G. (1986). *Fear of crime: Incivility and the production of a social problem.* New Brunswick, NJ: Transaction Press.

Platt, A. (1977). *The child savers: The invention of delinquency* (2nd ed). Chicago: The University of Chicago Press.

Potter, R.H. (1993). *Reported crimes on Australian university campuses: The 1992 campus crimes survey.* Department of Sociology, The University of New England.

Potter, R.H. (1994). Reported crimes on Australian university campuses: The 1993 campus crimes survey. Department of Sociology, The University of New England.

Potter, R.H. (1995). Reported crimes on Australian university campuses: The 1994 campus crimes survey. Department of Sociology, The University of New England

Potter, R.H. (1996). Reported crimes on Australian university campuses: The 1995 campus crimes survey. Department of Sociology, The University of New England

Potter, R.H., Rambaldi, A.N., Bailey, D., & Upton, E. (1995). Planning campus security: Needs, numbers, and other considerations. *Proceedings of the 2nd Annual Educational Security Conference*. Manly, NSW, Australia.

Rivinus, T.M., & Larimer, M.E. (1993). "Violence, alcohol, other drugs, and the college student. In L.C. Whitaker & J.W. Pollard (Eds.), *Campus violence: Kinds, causes, and cures* (pp. 71–119). New York: The Haworth Press.

Schwartz, M.D., & DeKeseredy, W.S. (1997). *Sexual assault on the college campus: The role of male peer support*. Thousand Oaks, CA: Sage Publications.

Sloan, J.J. (1994). The correlates of campus crime: An analysis of reported crimes on college and university campuses. *Journal of Criminal Justice, 22*, 51–61.

Wechsler, H. (1996, July/August). Alcohol and the American college campus: A report from the Harvard School of Public Health. *Change*, 20–25, 60.

Chapter 7

Bachman, R. (1994). *Violence Against Women*. Washington, DC: U.S. Department of Justice.

Bausell, C., Bausell, B., & Siegel, D. (1991). *The Links Among Drugs, Alcohol, and Campus Crime: Research Results From the Campus Violence Prevention Center's Second Victimization Survey*. Towson, MD: Towson State University, Center for the Study and Prevention of Campus Crime.

Belknap, J., & Erez, E. (1995). The victimization of women on college campuses: Courtship violence, date rape and sexual harassment." In B.S. Fisher & J.S. Sloan (Eds.), *Campus crime: Legal, social and policy perspectives* (pp. 156–178). Springfield, IL: Charles C. Thomas.

Benson, D., Charlton, C., & Coodhart, F. (1992). Acquaintance rape on campus. *Journal of American College Health, 40*(4), 157–165.

Berkowitz, A.(1992). College men as perpetrators of acquaintance rape and sexual assault: A review of current research." *Journal of American College Health, 40*(4), 175–180.

Bishop, M. (1962). *A History of Cornell.* Ithaca, NY: Cornell University Press.

Brantingham, P., Brantingham, P., & Seagrave, J. (1995). Crime and fear of crime at a Canadian University. In B.S. Fisher & J.J. Sloan, (Eds.), *Campus crime: Legal, social and policy perspectives* (pp. 123–155). Springfield, IL: Charles C. Thomas.

Bromley, M. (1995). Securing the Campus: Political and economic forces affecting decision makers. In B.S. Fisher & J.S. Sloan (Eds.), *Campus crime legal, social and policy perspectives* (pp. 214–227). Springfield, IL: Charles C. Thomas.

Bromley, M. (1993). The impact of recently enacted statues in civil law suits on security policies at post-secondary institutions. *The Journal of Police and Criminal Psychology, 9*(2), 46–52.

Bromley, M.L., & Territo, L. (1990). *College crime prevention and personal safety awareness.* Springfield, IL: Charles C. Thomas.

Burd, S. (1992, September 2). Colleges issue federally required reports on campus crime rates, arrests and policies. *The Chronicle of Higher Education,* A-25.

Burling, P. (1991). *Crime on campus: Analyzing and managing the increasing risk of institutional liability.* Washington, DC: National Association of College and University Attorneys.

Burling, P. (1993). *Acquaintance rape on campus: A model for institutional response.* Washington, DC: National Association of College and University Attorneys.

CASA Commission on Substance Abuse at Colleges and Universities (1994). *Rethinking rites of passage: Substance abuse on America's campuses.* New York: Columbia University.

Castelli, J. (1990, November 4). Campus crime 101. *The New York Times Education Life,* 1.

Cerio, N. (1989). Counseling victims and perpetrators of campus violence. In J.N. Sherrill & D.G. Siegel (Eds.), *Responding to violence on campus: New directions for student services.* San Francisco: Jossey-Bass.

Cokey, M., Sherril, J., Cave, R., & Chapman, G.R. (1988). Awareness of campus violence by students and administrators. *Response, 11*(1), 3–6.

Collison, M. (1992, September 23). Four thousand violent crimes occurred on 580 campuses in the past three years: Use of data questioned. *The Chronicle of Higher Education,* A31.

Coulter, E.M. (1951). *College life in the old south.* Athens, GA: University of Georgia Press.

Esposito, D., & Stormer, D. (1989). The multiple roles of campus law enforcement. *Campus Law Enforcement Journal, 19*(3): 26–30.

Fisher, B.S., & Sloan, J. (Eds.) (1995). *Campus crime: Legal, social, and policy perspectives*. Springfield, IL: Charles C. Thomas.

Gordon, N.T., & Riger, S. (1989). *The female fear*. New York: Free Press.

Griffaton, M.C. (1995). State-level initiatives and campus crime. In B.S. Fisher & J.S. Sloan (Eds.), *Campus crime: Legal, social and policy perspectives* (pp. 53–73). Springfield IL: Charles C. Thomas.

Groups Aim Spotlight at Campus Crime (1990). *National On-Campus Report, 18,*1.

Hollis, D.W. (1951). *The University of South Carolina. Vol. I. South Carolina College.* Columbia, SC: University of South Carolina Press.

Humphrey, DC (1976). *From King's College to Columbia 1746–1800.* New York: Columbia University, Press.

International Association of Campus Law Enforcement Administrators (IACLEA). (1997). *Campus crime report, 1994–1995.* Hartford, CT: International Association of Campus Law Enforcement Administrators.

Kaplan, W. A. (1990). *The law of higher education*, 2nd Ed. San Francisco, CA: Jossey- Bassey Publishers.

Kalette, D. (1990, September 14)). Colleges confront liability. *U.S.A. Today*, 6A.

Kirkland, C., & Siegel, D. (1994). *Campus security: A first look at promising practices*. Washington, DC: U.S. Department of Education.

Koss, M.P, Gidycz, C.A., & Wisniewski, N. (1987). The scope of rape: Incidence and prevalence of sexual aggression and victimization in a national sample of higher education students. *Journal of Consulting and Clinical Psychology, 55*(2), 162–170.

Lederman, D. (1993, January 20). Colleges report 7,500 violent crimes on their campuses in first annual statements required under federal law. *The Chronicle of Higher Education*, A32–A43.

Lederman, D. (1994a, February 3). Crime on the campus. *The Chronicle of Higher Education*, A33.

Lederman, D. (1994b, March 9). Weapons on campus. *The Chronicle of Higher Education*, A33.

Lively, K. (1996. April 26). Drug arrests rise again. *The Chronicle of Higher Education*, A37.

Lively, K. (1997, March 21). Campus drug arrests increased 18 percent in 1995: Reports of other crimes fell. *The Chronicle of Higher Education*, A44.

Maloy, C.E. (1991). Paper presented at the Fifth National Conference on Violence, Towson State University, Towson, Maryland.

Mathews, A. (1993, March 7). The campus crime war. *The New York Times Magazine*, 38–47.

McGrane, R.C. (1963). *The University of Cincinnati: A success story in urban higher education.* New York: Harper and Row.

National Center for Educational Statistics. (1997). *Campus crime and security at post-secondary institutions.* Washington, DC: U.S. Department of Education.

Nichols, D. (1986). *The administration of public safety in higher education.* Springfield, IL.: Charles C. Thomas.

Ordovensky, P. (1990, December 3). Students easy "prey" on campus. *U.S.A. Today,* 1A.

Palmer, C. (1993, April 21). Skepticism is rampant about the statistics on campus crime. *The Chronicle of Higher Education,* B1.

Powell, J. (1981) The history and proper role of campus security. *Security World,* 8(1), 18–25.

Powell, J.W., Pander, M.S., & Nielsen, R.C. (1994). *Campus security and law enforcement.* 2nd edition. Boston, MA: Butterworth-Heinemann.

Rape and Assault on Campus Part 1: The Legal and Legislative Response. (1988). *College Security Report, 1,* 2–11.

Reaves, B., & Goldberg, A. (1996). *Campus law enforcement agencies, 1995.* Washington, DC: United States Department of Justice.

Roark, M. (1987). Preventing violence on campus. *Journal of Counseling and Development, 65,* 367–371.

Sellers, C.S., & Bromley, M.L. (1996). Violent behavior in college student dating relationships: Implications for campus service providers. *Journal of Contemporary Criminal Justice,* 12(1), 1–27.

Seng, M.J., & Koehler, N.S. (1993). The crime awareness and campus security act: A critical analysis." *Journal of Crime and Justice,* 16(1), 97–110.

Seng, M. (1995). The crime awareness and campus security act: Some observations, critical comments, and suggestions. In B.S. Fisher & J.J. Sloan (Eds.), *Campus crime: Legal, social and policy perspectives* (pp. 38–52). Springfield, IL: Charles C. Thomas.

Siegel, D., & Raymond, C. (1992). An ecological approach to violent crime on campus. *Journal of Security Administration,* 15(2), 19–29.

Sigler, R., & Koehler, N.S. (1993). Victimization and crime on campus. *International Review of Victimology,* 2(1), 331–343.

Sloan, J.J. (1992). The modern campus police: An analysis of their evolution, structure, and function. *American Journal of Police,* 11(1), 85–104.

Sloan, J.J. (1992). Campus crime and campus communities: An analysis of campus police and security. *Journal of Security Administration,* 15(2), 31–45.

Sloan, J.J. (1994). The correlates of campus crime: An analysis of reported crimes on university campuses. *Journal of Criminal Justice,* 22(1), 51–62.

Sloan, J., & Fisher, B. (1995). Campus crime: Legal, social, and policy contexts. In B.S. Fisher & J.J. Sloan (Eds.) *Campus crime: Legal, so-*

cial, and policy perspectives (pp. 3–19). Springfield, IL: Charles C. Thomas.

Smith, M. (1989) *Campus crime and campus police: A handbook for police officers and administrators*. Asheville, NC: College Administration Publications, Inc.

Smith, M.C. (1995). Vexations victims of campus crime. In B.S. Fisher & J.S. Sloan (Eds.), *Campus crime: Legal, social and policy perspectives* (pp. 25–370). Springfield IL: Charles C. Thomas.

Territo, L., Halsted, J., & Bromley, M. (1998). *Crime and justice in America: A human perspective*. Newton, MA: Butterworth Heinemann.

Tomz, J., & McGillis, D. (1997). *Serving crime victims and witnesses*. Washington, DC: U.S. Department of Justice.

Tuttle, D.F. (1991). Campus crime disclosure legislation. *Campus Law Enforcement Journal, 21*(1), 19–21.

United States Department of Justice (FBI) (1996). *Crime in the United States, 1995, Uniform Crime Report*. Washington, DC: U.S. Government Printing Office.

Ward, S.K., Chapman, S., White, S., & Williams, K. (1991). Acquaintance rape and the college social scene. *Family Relations, 40*(1), 65–71.

Wechsler, H., Davenport, A., Dowdall, G., Moeykens, B., & Lastillo, S. (1994). Health and behavioral consequences of binge drinking in college. *The Journal of the American Medical Association, 272*(21), 1672–1677.

Cases

Duarte v. State of California et al., 151 CAL. RPT. 727 (Cal, App. 1979).

Miller v. State of New York, 62 N.Y.2d 506, 478 N.Y.S.2d 829, 467 N.E.2d 493 (1984); as to damages see 110 A.D.2d 627, 487 N.Y.S.2d 115 (1985).

Mulins v. Pine Manor College et al, 449 NE 2d 331 (Mass. 1983).

Siciliano v. State, NO. 712-95 (Super. Ct. Cal.).

Dixon v. The Alabama Board of Education, 294 F.2d.150 (1961).

Statutes

Cal. Educ. Code Ann., §§ 67380, 67390 to 67393, 94380 (1994).

Conn. Gen. Stat. Ann. §§ 10a-55c (1993).

Del. Code Ann. Title 14, §§ 9001 to 9005 (1993).

Fla. Stat. ch.240.2683 (1993).

La. Rev. Stat. Ann. § 17:3351(3) (1993).

N.Y. Educ. § 6450 (McKinney 1985 and Supp. 1994).

24 Ps. Cons. Stat. § 2501-1 (Purdon 1992).

Student Right-to-Know and Campus Security Act, Public Law No. 101-542 (1990); amended by Public Law No. 102-26, Sec. 10(c) (1991); 20 U.S.C. 1092(f).

Wash. Rev. Code § 28B.10.569 (Supp. 1993).

Wis. Stat. § 36.11(22) (West Supp. 1992).

Chapter 8

American Association of Retired Persons. (1989). *Summary of state legislative action concerning treatment and services for victims of crime with emphasis on older victims 1987–1988*. Washington, DC: AARP Criminal Justice Services Program Department.

Anderson, J.R., & Woodward, P.L. (1985). Victims and witness assistance—New state laws and the system response. *Judicature, 68,* 221–244.

Brown, W.E. (1982). *A new initiative for the Old Dominion: Victim/witness assistance programs in Virginia*. Richmond, VA: Virginia Division of Justice and Crime Prevention

Cronin, R.C., & Bourque, B.B. (1981). *National evaluation program phase I report: Assessment of victim/witness assistance programs*. Washington, DC: U.S. Department of Justice.

Cullen, K. (1991, June 13). Effort continues to save victim aid program. *The Sunday Boston Globe*, A1.

Curriden, M. (1990, April 26). Successful victim-witness program threatened by a lack of funding. *Atlanta Constitution*, XG, 2, 4.

Finn, P., & Lee, B.N. (1987). *Serving crime victims and witnesses*. Washington, DC: National Institute of Justice.

Herrington, L.H. (1985). Victims of crime—Their plight, our response. *American Psychologist, 40,* 99–103.

Jerin, R.A., Moriarty, L.J., & Gibson, M. (1995). Victim service or self service: An analysis of North Carolina prosecution-based victim-witness programs and providers. *Criminal Justice Policy Review, 7*(2), 142–154.

Karmen, A. (1990). *Crime victims: An introduction to victimology*. Pacific Grove, CA: Brooks/Cole Publishing Company.

Legislative Research Committee. (1993). *The rights of victims of crimes: Report to the 1993 General Assembly of North Carolina*. Raleigh, N.C.: North Carolina Vctims Assistance Network.

Roberts, A.J. (1990). *Helping crime victims: Research, policy, and practice*. Newbury Park, CA: Sage.

Rosenblum, R.H., & Blew, C.H. (1979). *Victim/witness assistance*. Washington, DC: Department of Justice.

Sarnoff, S.K. (1994). A national study of policies and administrative methods of state crime victims compensation programs. Doctoral dissertation. Aldephi University.

Tomz, J.E., & McGillis, D. (1997). *Serving crime victims and witnesses* (2nd ed). Washington, DC: U.S. Department of Justice.

Uniform Crime Reports (UCR) (1995). *Crime in the United States, 1995.* Washington, DC: U.S. Government Printing Office

Weigend, T. (1979). Problems of victim/witness assistance programs. *Victimology, 8,* 91–101.

Wisconsin Legislative Audit Bureau. (1989). *An evaluation of crime victim and witness assistance programs.* Madison, WI.

Statutes

G.S. 15A – 824 et Seq. (N.C., 1986).
G.S. 7A – 347 (N.C., 1987).
G.S. 7A – 348 (N.C., 1987).

Chapter 9

Albrecht, S.L., & Green, M. (1977). Attitudes toward the police and the larger attitude complex: Implications for police-community relationships. *Criminology, 15*(1), 67–86.

Belson, W.A. (1975). *The public and the police: An extended summary of the methods and findings of a three part enquiry into relations between the London public and its metropolitan police force.* London: Harper and Row.

Blumstein, A., & Cohen, J. (1980). Sentencing of convicted offenders: An analysis of the public's view. *Law and Society Review, 14*(2), 223–261.

Brandl, S.G., & Horvath, F. (1991). Crime-victim evaluation of police investigative performance. *Journal of Criminal Justice, 19,* 293–305.

Courtis, M.C. (1970). *Attitudes to crime and the police in Toronto.* Centre of Criminology: University of Toronto.

Davis, R.C., Kunreuther, F., & Connick, E. (1984). Expanding the victim's role in the criminal court dispositional process: The results of an experiment. *The Journal of Criminal Law & Criminology, 75*(2), 491–505.

Decker, S.H. (1981). Citizen attitudes toward the police: A review of past findings and suggestions for future policy. *Journal of Police Science and Administration, 9*(1), 80–87.

Doerner, W.G., & Lab, S.P. (1980). The impact of crime compensation upon victim attitudes toward the criminal justice system. *Victimology* , 5(1), 61–67.

Elias, R. (1984). Alienating the victim: Compensation and victim attitudes. *Journal of Social Issues, 40*(1), 103–116.

Erez, E. (1984). Self-defined "desert" and citizens' assessment of the police. *The Journal of Criminal Law & Criminology, 75*(4), 1276–1299.

Erez, E., & Bienkowska, E. (1993). Victim participation in proceedings and satisfaction with justice in the continental systems: The case of Poland. *Journal of Criminal Justice, 21,* 47–60.

Erez, E., & Tontodonato, P. (1992). Victim participation in sentencing and satisfaction with justice. *Justice Quarterly, 9*(3), 393–415.

Hadar, I., & Snortum, J.R. (1975). The eye of the beholder: Differential perceptions of police by the police and the public. *Criminal Justice and Behavior, 2* (1), 37–54.

Hagan, J. (1982). Victims before the law: A study of victim involvement in the criminal justice process. *The Journal of Criminal Law and Criminology, 73* (1), 317–329.

Hagan, J., & Albonetti, C. (1982). Race, class, and the perception of criminal injustice in America. *American Journal of Sociology, 88*(2), 329–355.

Jacob, H. (1971). Black and white perceptions of justice in the city. *Law & Society Review, 6,* 69–89.

Kelly, D.P. (1984). Victims' perceptions of criminal justice. *Pepperdine Law Review, 11*(15), 15–22.

Kidd, R.F., & Chayet, E.F. (1984). Why do victims fail to report? The psychology of criminal victimization. *Journal of Social Issues, 40* (1), 39–50.

Moretz, W.J. (1980). Kids to cops "we think you're important but we're not sure we understand you." *Journal of Police Science and Administration, 8*(2), 220–224.

O'Grady, K., Waldon, J., Carlson, W., Streed, S., & Cannizzaro, C. (1992). The importance of victim satisfaction: A commentary. *The Justice System Journal, 15*(3), 759–764.

Percy, S.L. (1980). Response time and citizen evaluation of police. *Journal of Police Science and Administration, 8*(1), 75–86.

Scaglion, R., & Condon, R.G. (1980a). Determinants of attitudes toward city police. *Criminology, 17*(4), 485–494.

Scaglion, R., & Condon, R.G. (1980b). The structure of black and white attitudes toward police. *Human Organization, 39*(3), 280–283.

Smith, P.E., & Hawkins, R.O. (1973). Victimization, types of citizen-police contacts, and attitudes toward the police. *Law and Society Review, 8*(1), 135–152.

Sullivan, P.S., Dunham, R.G., & Alpert, G.P. (1987). Attitude structures of different ethnic and age groups concerning police. *The Journal of Criminal Law and Criminology*, 78(1), 177–196.

Thomas, C.W., & Hyman, J.M. (1977). Perceptions of crime, fear of victimization, and public perceptions of police performance. *Journal of Police Science and Administration*, 5 (3), 305–317.

Tyler, T.R. (1990). *Why people obey the law.* New Haven, CT: Yale University Press.

Walker, D., Richardson, R.J., Williams, O., Denyer, T., & McGaughey, S. (1972). Contact and support. An empirical assessment of public attitudes toward the police and the courts. *North Carolina Law Review*, 51, 43–79.

Zamble, E., & Annesley, P. (1987). Some determinants of public attitudes toward the police. *Journal of Police Science and Administration*, 15(4), 285–290.

Zevitz, R.G., & Gurnack, A.M. (1991). Factors related to elderly crime victims' satisfaction with police service: The impact of Milwaukee's "Gray Squad." *The Gerontologist*, 31(1), 92–96.

Case

North Carolina v. Alford, 400 U.S. 25, 91 S. Ct. 160 (1970).

Chapter 10

Child Watch, Incorporated. (1981, February). *Advocacy for children in child welfare proceedings*, Raleigh, NC.

Cozort, J., & Nelson, I. (1996, February 9). A report on the status of the guardian ad litem services. Division of the Administrative Office of the Courts by its Director and Administrator.

Cozort, J., & Nelson, I. (1996, January 5). A report on the status of the guardian ad litem services. Division of the Administrative Office of the Courts by its Director and Administrator.

Criminal Justice Research Center. (1996). *Evaluation of the Virginia court-appointed special advocate (CASA) program final report, April 1996*. Richmond, VA.

CRS, Incorporated. (October, 1990). National study of guardian ad litem representation. (Contract 105-89-1727). Washington, DC: Government Printing Office.

CRS, Incorporated. (June, 1988). National evaluation of the impact of guardians ad litem in child abuse or neglect judicial proceedings Volume II: Study findings and recommendations. (Contract 105-86-8123). Washington, DC: Government Printing Office.

CRS, Incorprated. (June, 1988). National evaluation of the impact of guardians ad litem in child abuse or neglect judicial proceedings Volume III: Technical appendices. (Contract 105-86-8123). Washington, DC: Government Printing Office.

Department of Criminal Justice Services. (1996). *Evaluation of the guardian ad litem (GAL) pilot project* (House Document No. 36. Richmond, VA: Commonwealth of Virginia.

Duquette, D., & Ramsey, S. (1987). Representation of children in child abuse and neglect cases: An empirical look at what constitutes effective representation. *Journal of law reform, 20,* 331–409.

Legislative Research Commission. (1997). *Guardian ad litem program report to the General Assembly of North Carolina.* Raleigh, NC: Legislative Research Commission's Committee on GAL Program.

Legislative Research Commission. (1996). *Draft survey results—November 5, 1996 meeting.* Raleigh, NC: Legislative Research Commission.

Nelson, I. (1995, May). *Legal ethics.* Paper presented at the meeting of the Fourteenth Annual Conference of the National CASA Association, Scottsdale, AZ.

Neraas, N. (1983). The non-lawyer guardian ad litem in child abuse and neglect proceedings: The King County, Washington, experience. *Washington law review, 58,* 853–871.

Poertner, J., & Press, A. (1990). Who best represents the interests of the child in court? *Child welfare, LXIX,* 537–549.

Stein, J. (Ed.) (1988). *The random house college dictionary* (Rev. ed.). New York:Random House, Incorporated.

Statutes

N.C. Gen. Stat. Section 7A-485 (1983)
N.C. Gen. Stat. Section 7A-488 (3) (1983)
N.C. Gen. Stat. Section 7A-586 (A) (1983)
N.C. Gen. Stat. Section 7A-586 (1988)
N.C. Gen. Stat. Section 7A-586 (1995)
Va. Code Ann., Section 8.01-1.1 (1978)
Va. Code Ann., Section 8.01-9, Editor's Notes, Supp. (1996)
Va. Code Ann., Section 9-173.8 (A) (1-3), Supp. (1996)
Va. Code Ann., Section 9-173.8 (B), Supp. (1996)
Va. Code Ann., Section 9-173.8 (E), Supp. (1996)
Va. Code Ann., Section 9-173.12, Supp. (1996)
Va. Code Ann., Section 9.174-178 (1981)
Va. Code Ann., Section 16.1–266 (3) (D) (1996)

Va. Code Ann., Section 16.1-266.1 (B) (1995)
Va. Code Ann., Section 16.1-267 (1993)
Va. Code Ann., Section 16.1-267 (A) (1996)
Va. Code Ann., Section 16.1-268 (1977)
Va. Code Ann., Section 63.1-248.8 (1972)

Case

Verrochio v. Verrochio, 16 Va. App. 314 (1993).

Chapter 11

Adams, C.J. (1994). *Woman battering.* Minneapolis: Fortress Press.
Adams, C.J., & Fortune, M.M. (1995). *Violence against women and children.* New York: Continuum.
Barnett, O.W., & Keyson, M. (1996). The relationship between violence, social support, and self blame in battered women. *Journal of Interpersonal Violence, 11*(2), 221–33.
Beane, B. (1997). Balm for the wound. *Jubilee, 4,* 6–13.
Bowker, L.H. (1982). Police services to battered women. *Criminal Justice and Behavior, 9*(4), 476–94.
Bureau of Justice Statistics. (1997). *Criminal victimization 1996.* Washington, DC: U.S. Department of Justice.
Carlson, D. (1997). Healing the hurt. *Jubilee, 4,* 3.
Davis, R.C., & Brickman, E. (1996). Supportive and unsupportive aspects of the behavior of others toward victims of sexual and nonsexual assault. *Journal of Interpersonal Violence, 11*(2), 250–262.
Edleson, J., & Eisikovits, Z. (1996). *Future interventions with battered women and their families.* Thousand Oaks: Sage.
Johnson, K.W. (1997). Professional help and crime victims. *Social Service Review, 3,* 88–109.
Kaniasty, K., & Norris, F.H. (1992). Social support and victims of crime: Matching event, support and outcome. *American Journal of Community Psychology, 20*(2), 211–241.
Kennedy, L.W. (1988). Going it alone: Unreported crime and individual self-help. *Journal of Criminal Justice, 16,* 403–12.
Kuhl, A. F. (1982). Community responses to battered women. *Victimology, 7,* 49–59.
Martin, S.E. (1989). Research note: The response of the clergy to spouse abuse in a suburban county. *Violence and Victims, 4,* 217–225.
Nice, DC (1988). State programs for crime victims. *Policy Studies Journal, 17*(1), 25–41.

Ruback, B. (1994). Advice to crime victims: Effects of crime, victim and advisor factors. *Criminal Justice and Behavior, 21*(4), 423–442.

Sacco, V. F. (1993). Social support and the fear of crime. *Canadian Journal of Criminology, 4,* 187–196.

Survey Research Lab (1997). *A study of Virginia clergy concerning HIV and AIDS.* Richmond, VA: Virginia Commonwealth University.

U.S. Department of Justice. (1983). *The President's Task Force on Victims of Crime.* Washington, DC: Department of Justice.

Chapter 12

Adler, J., with Biddle, N.A., & Shenitz, B. (1995, April 3). Bloodied but unbowed. *Newsweek, 54–56.*

Bureau of Justice Statistics. (1994, March). *Crime victimization in the United States, 1992* (NCJ-145125). Washington, DC: U.S. Department of Justice.

Bureau of Justice Statistics. (1992, December). *Crime victimization in the United States: 1973–90 Trends* (NCJ-139564). Washington DC: U.S. Department of Justice.

Calvi, J.V., & Coleman, S. (1989). *American law and legal systems.* Englewood Cliffs, NJ: Prentice Hall, Inc.

Davis, R.C., & Smith, B.E. (1994a). The effects of victim impact statements on sentencing decisions: A test in an urban setting. *Justice Quarterly, 11,* 453–469.

Davis, R.C., & Smith, B.E. (1994b). Victim impact statements and victim satisfaction: An unfulfilled promise. *Journal of Criminal Justice, 22,* 1–12.

Doerner, W.G., & Lab, S.P. (1995). *Victimology.* Cincinnati, OH: Anderson Publishing Company.

Elias, R. (1990). Which victim movement? The politics of victim policy. In A.J. Lurigio, W.G. Skogan, & R.C. Davis (Eds.), *Victims of crime: Problems, policies, and programs* (pp. 226–250). Newbury Park: Sage Publications.

Erez, E., & Tontodonato, P. (1990). The effect of victim participation in sentencing on sentence outcome. *Criminology, 28,* 451–74.

Friedman, L.M. (1984). *American law.* New York, NY: W.W. Norton & Company.

Gardner, T.J., & Anderson, T.M. (1992). *Criminal law: Principles and cases* (5th ed.). St. Paul, MN.: West Publishing Company.

Glendon, M.A., Gordon, M.W., & Osakwe, C. (1985). *Comparative legal traditions.* St. Paul, MN: West Publishing Company.

Glick, H.R. (1983). *Courts, politics, and justice.* New York City, NY: McGraw-Hill Book Company.

Holman, J.E., & Quinn, J.F. (1996). *Criminal justice: Principles and perspectives.* St. Paul, MN: West Publishing Company.

Karmen, A. (1990). *Crime vctims: An introduction to victimology* (2nd ed.). Belmont, CA: Wadsworth Publishing Company.

Karmen, A. (1984). *Crime victims: An introduction to victimology* . Pacific Grove, CA: Brooks/Cole Publishing Company.

Kelly, D.P. (1990). Victim participation in the criminal justice system. In A.J. Lurigio, W.G. Skogan, & R.C. Davis (Eds.), *Victims of crime: Problems, policies, and programs* (pp. 172–187). Newbury Park: Sage Publications.

Lusk, H.F., Hewitt, C.M., Donnell, J.D., & Barnes, A.J. (1978). *Business law: Principles and cases* (4th ed.). Homewood, IL: Richard D. Irwin, Inc.

Masci, D. (1995, November 18). Mandatory victim restitution OK'd by Senate Judiciary. *Congressional Quarterly Weekly Report, 53,* 3548.

McLeod, M. (1988). *The authorization and implementation of victim impact statements.* Washington, DC: National Institute of Justice.

National Criminal Justice Research Service (1997, April 19). *Civil legal remedies for crime victims* [On-line]. Available: http://www.ncjrs.org/txtfiles/clr.txt.

National Criminal Justice Research Service (1997, April 19 b). *Victims of crime act: Crime victims fund fact sheet* [On-line]. Available: http://www.ncjrs.org/txtfiles/cvfund.txt.

National Victim Center. (1997, April 19). *Rights of crime victims* [On-line]. Available: http://www.nvc.org/ns-search/docs/ddir/info65.htm/NS-search-set=\3357f\s90.57fO9AENS-doc-.

National Institute of Justice. (1996, January). The extent and costs of crime victimization: A new look. *National Institute of Justice Research Preview* (NCJ-155281). Washington, DC: U.S. Department of Justice.

Rand, M.R., Lynch, J.P., & Cantor, D. (1997, April). *Crime victimization, 1973–95, Bureau of Justice Statistics National Crime Victimization Survey* (NCJ-163069). Washington, DC: U.S. Department of Justice.

Reid, S.T. (1997). *Crime and criminology* (8th ed.). Madison, WI: Brown & Benchmark, Publishers.

Roberts, S.V. (1995, April 3). Staring back into the eyes of evil. *U.S. News & World Report,* 8–9.

Samaha, J. (1996). *Criminal procedure* (3rd ed.). St. Paul, MN: West Publishing Company.

Sheley, J.F. (1995). *Criminology* (2nd ed.). Belmont, CA: Wadsworth Publishing Company.

Smith, C.E. (1991). *Courts and the poor.* Chicago, IL: Nelson-Hall Publishers.

Terrill, W. (1992). *World criminal justice systems* (2nd ed.). Chicago, IL: Office of International Justice.

Thigpen, D.E. (1995, April 3). Confronting the killer. *Time*, 50.

Torgia, C.E. (1972). *Wharton's criminal evidence: Volume 1* (13th ed.). Rochester, NY: The Lawyers Co-operative Publishing Company.

Vetter, H.J., & Territo, L. (1984). *Crime and justice in America*. St. Paul, MN: West Publishing Company.

"Victim Justice" (1995, April 17). *The New Republic, 212,* 9.

Weisberg, R. (1995). Victims' rights in criminal trials [Review of the book *With justice for some: Victims' rights in criminal trials*]. *Criminal Justice Ethics, 14,* 56–62.

Cases

Booth v. Maryland, 482 U.S. 496 (1987).

Coy v. Iowa, 487 U.S. 1012 (1988).

Crime Control Act of 1990, 18 U.S. Code 3663 (a).

Hughey v. U.S., 495 U.S. 411 (1990).

Maryland v. Craig, 497 U.S. 836 (1990).

Payne v. Tennessee, 501 U.S. 808 (1991).

United States v. Atkinson, 788 F.2d 900 (2d Cir. 1986).

United States v. Brown, 744 F. 2d. 905 (2d Cir. 1984), *cert. denied* 469 U.S. 1089 (1984).

United States v. Johnson, 816 F.2d 918 (3d Cir 1987).

United States v. Palma, 760 F.2d 475 (3d Cir. 1985).

United States v. Welden, 568 F. Supp. 516 (N.D. Ala., 1983), *aff'd* in part, *rev'd* in part, U.S. v. Satterfield, 743 F.2d 827 (11th Cir. 1984), *cert. denied* 471 U.S. 1117 (1984).

Victim and Witness Protection Act of 1982, 18 U.S. Code 3579.

Violent Crime Control and Law Enforcement Act, Public Law 103-322 (September 13, 1994).

Chapter 13

Anderson, A. (1994, August 15). Demand grows to ID molesters: States weigh children's safety versus offenders' rights. *Chicago Tribune,* 1.

Barrow, J. (1994, August 3). Vigil for slain girl, 7, backs a law on offenders. *New York Times,* B4.

Bernstein, N. (1996, November 18). On prison computer, files to make parents shiver. *New York Times,* 1, B11.

Boerner, D. (1992). Confronting violence: In the act and in the word. 15 U. Puget Sound L. Rev. 525, 525–52.

Donnelly S., & Lieb, R. (1993, December). Community notification: A survey of law enforcement. *Washington State Institute for Public Policy*.

Duda, J. (1988, January 27). Campus notified of local sex offenders. *Wesleyan Argus*, 1–10.

Editorial. (1997, June 25). Kansas sexually violent predator law. *New York Times*, A18.

Fenner, A.E. (1996, March 4). Hotline tracks sex offenders. *New York Daily News*, 1.

Goldstein, H., & Susmilch, C.E. (1982). Repeat sexual offender in Madison—A memorandum on the problem and the community's response, Volume 3. Madison Police Department: University of Wisconsin Law School.

Greenspan, L. (1997, June 24). Likely repeater may stay confined. *New York Times*, B11.

Hanley, R. (1995a, January 4). Judge curbs law on sex offenders. C. Diaz challenges New Jersey's Megan's law. *New York Times*, A1.

Hanley, R. (1995b, March 1). Megan's Law Suffers Setback in Court Ruling. *New York Times*, A1.

Harvard Law Review. (1995). Recent legislation: Criminal law-sex offender notification statute—Washington state community protect act serves as model for other initiatives by lawmakers and communities-1990. Wash. Laws Ch.3, 101–1406 (codified as amended in scattered sections of Wash. Rev.Code). Volume 108: 787–792.

Hopper, J. (1994, August 4). New law is urged on freed sex offenders. *New York Times*, B1.

Hudson, K. (1992, December 13). How outrage sparked law to commit sex predators *Toronto Star*, A1.

Jerome, R., Eftimhades, M., Gallo, N., & Sawicki, S. (1995, March 20). Megan's legacy. *People*, 47–51.

Jerusalem, M.P. (1995). Sex offender framework. *Vanderbilt Law Review*, 48, 219–255.

Klein, L., Luxenburg, J., & Rogers, S. (1990). Not in my backyard: The impact of community sentiment against parolee placement. *Perspectives*, 14(3), 13–17.

Montana, J.A. (1995). An ineffective weapon in the fight against child sexual abuse: New Jersey's Megan's law. *Journal of Law and Policy*, 3, 569–604.

National Center for Missing and Exploited Children. (1995). Listings for states with sex offender registration laws and community notification laws.

Philadelphia Inquirer. (1994, September 2). A rush to respond: More debate is needed on Megan's law. *Philadelphia Inquirer*, A26.

Purdy, M. (1997, June 28). Wave of new laws seeks to confine sexual offender. *New York Times*, 1.

Sagarin, E. 1985. Address at the Annual Conference of the Institute for Criminal Justice Ethics, John Jay College of Criminal Justice, May.

Scott, J. (1994, September 9). Sex offender due for parole, but no place will have him. *New York Times*, A1, B7.

Seattle Times. (1993a, July 13). Vigilante justice is no answer to sex crimes. *Seattle Times*, B4.

Seattle Times. (1993b, July 19). Gallardo again forced to get out of town. *Seattle Times*, B1.

Seminerio, M. (1997, August 15). Megan's law crusade moves to cyberspace. *Microsoft Daily News*, 7.

Siegel, B. (1990, May 10). Locking up "sexual predators." *L.A. Times*, A1.

Simon, J. (1990, January 24). Senate passes a bill on sex offenders. *Seattle Times*, A1.

Smolowe, J. (1994, September 5). Not in my backyard. *Time*, 59.

Song, L., & Lieb, R. (1994). Adult sex offender recidivism: A review of studies. Washington State Institute for Public Policy, January.

Sullivan, J.L. (1994, November 1). Whitman approves stringent restrictions on sex criminals. *New York Times*, B1.

Trelease, F.J. (1997, December 14) "Megan's law" and questions of liability. *New York Times*, 1, 11.

Van Blema, D. (1993, July 26). Burn thy neighbor: Washington community protection act prevents child molester J. Gallardo from returning to Snohomish County." *Time*, 58.

Williams, M. (1996, February 24). Sex offenders law prompts privacy debate in New York. *New York Times*, 1, 26.

Chapter 14

Altman, A. (1996). Making sense of sexual harassment law. *Philosophy and Public Affairs*, 25, 36–64.

Bard, M., & Zacker, J. (1976). How police handle explosive squabbles. *Psychology Today*, 10, 71–74.

Bell, D.J. (1985). A multiyear study of Ohio urban, suburban, and rural police dispositions of domestic disputes. *Victimology*, 10, 301–310.

Berk, S.F., & Loseke, D.R. (1980–1981). "Handling" family violence: Situational determinants of police arrest in domestic disturbances. *Law and Society Review*, 15, 317–346.

Brown, B.B. (1994). Hostile environment sexual harassment: Has Harris really changed things? *Employee Relations Law Journal*, 19, 567–578.

Buzawa, E.S., & Buzawa, C.G. (1993). Introduction: The impact of arrest on domestic violence. *American Behavioral Scientist, 36,* 558–574.

Childers, J. (1993). Is there a place for a reasonable woman in the law? A discussion of recent developments in hostile environment sexual harassment. *Duke Law Journal, 42,* 854–904.

Coleman, F.T. (1993). Creating a workplace free of sexual harassment. *Association Management, 45,* 69–75.

Collinson, D.L. (1992). Mismanaging sexual harassment: Protecting the perpetrator and blaming the victim. *Women in Management Review,* 7, 11–16.

Crawford, S. (1994). A brief history of sexual harassment law. *Training, 31,* 46–49.

Dobash, E., & Dobash, R. (1979). *Violence against wives: A case against patriarchy.* New York: The Free Press.

Echiejile, I. (1993). Dealing with sexual harassment at work. *Employee Counseling Today, 5,* 21–29.

Estrich, S. (1991). Sex at work. *Stanford Law Review, 43,* 813–861.

Ferraro, K.J. (1989). Policing woman battering. *Social Problems, 36,* 61–74.

Flaxman, H.R. (1994). New considerations for hostile working environment. *Human Resource Focus, 71,* 18–19.

Garvin, S.J. (1991). Employer liability for sexual harassment. *Human Resource Magazine, 36,* 101–107.

Gillespie, C.K. (1989). *Justifiable homicide: Battered women, self-defense, and the law.* Columbus, OH: Ohio State University Press.

Goolkasian, G.A. (1986). The judicial system and domestic violence: An expanding role. *Response to the Victimization of Women and Children, 9,* 2–7.

Gragg, E. (1992). Sexual harassment: Confronting the issue of the '90s. *Office Systems, 9,* 33–36.

Greenlaw, P. S., & Kohl, J.P. (1992). Proving Title VII sexual harassment. *Labor Law Journal, 43,* 164–171.

Gutek, B.A. (1992). Responses to sexual harassment. Paper presented at the annual meeting of the Society for Business Ethics Meeting, Las Vegas, NV.

Gutek, B.A., & Morasch, B. (1982). Sex-ratios, sex-role spillover, and sexual harassment of women at work. *Journal of Social Issues, 38,* 55–74.

Hiller, M.D. (1993). Avoiding sexual harassment in the workplace. *Healthcare Executive, 8,* 42.

Husbands, R. (1992). Sexual harassment law in employment: An international perspective. *International Labour Review, 131,* 535–559.

Kaiser, W.H. (1995). Extortion in the workplace: Using civil RICO to combat sexual harassment in employment. *Brooklyn Law Review, 61,* 965–1008.

Karner, J.M. (1995). Political speech, sexual harassment, and a captive workforce. *California Law Review, 83,* 637–691.

Kreps, G.L. (Ed.). (1993). *Sexual harassment: Communication implications.* Cresskill, NJ: Hampton Press.

Kulak, M.S. (1992). Sexual Harassment in the workplace: A claim perspective and interpretation. *CPCU Journal, 45,* 227–233.

Lee, R.D. (1995). The legal evolution of sexual harassment. *Public Administration Review, 55,* 357–364.

Martin, D. 1976. *Battered wives.* San Francisco, CA: Glide Publication.

McCann, N.D., & McGinn, T.A. (1992). *Harassed: 100 women define inappropriate behavior in the workplace.* Homewood, IL: Business One Irwin.

Micklow, P.L. (1988). Domestic abuse: The pariah of the legal system. In V.B. Van Hasset, R.L. Morrison, A.S. Bellack, & M. Hersen (Eds.), *Handbook of family violence* (pp. 407–433). New York: Plenum Press.

O'Leary-Kelly, A.M., Paetzold, R.L., & Griffin, R.W. (1995). Sexual harassment as aggressive action: A framework for understanding sexual harassment. *Academy of Management Journal, Best Papers Proceedings, 38,* 453–457.

Paetzold, R.L. (1994). A postmodern feminist view of 'reasonableness' in hostile environment sexual harassment. *Journal of Business Ethics, 13,* 681–691.

Paetzold, R.L., & O'Leary-Kelly, A.M. (1994). Hostile environment sexual harassment in the United States: Post Meritor developments and implications. *Gender, Work, and Organization, 1,* 50–57.

Payson, M.F. (1992). Avoiding the high costs of sexual harassment. *Credit World, 80,* 28– 30.

Piskorski, T.J. (1993). Reinstatement of the sexual harasser: The conflict between federal labor law and Title VII. *Employee Relations Law Journal, 18,* 617–623.

Quinn, R.E., & Lees, P.L. (1984). Attraction and harassment: Dynamics of sexual politics in the workplace. *Organizational Dynamics, 13,* 35–46.

Sherry, J.E.H. (1995). Employer liability for GMs' sexual harassment: A recurring workplace problem. *Cornell Hotel and Restaurant Administration Quarterly, 36,* 16–17.

Silbergeld, A.F. (1993/1994). *Harris v. Forklift Systems*: The court relaxes the burden of proving sexual harassment claims. *Employment Relations Today, 20,* 465–474.

Simon, H.A. (1991). *Ellison v. Brady*: A 'reasonable woman' standard for sexual harassment. *Employee Relations Law Journal, 17,* 71–80.

Wagner, E.J. (1992). A closer look at hostile environment harassment. *Supervisory Management, 37,* 1, 4.

Wagner, E.J. (1992). *Sexual harassment in the workplace.* New York: AMACOM.

Walker, L.E. (1979). The battered woman. New York: Harper, Colophon, Harper and Row Books.

Wells, D.L. (1993). Justice, sexual harassment, and the reasonable victim standard. *Journal of Business Ethics, 12,* 423–431.

Wilkinson, J.H. (1995). The promise and problems of sexual harassment litigation. *Harvard Journal of Law and Public Policy, 18,* 475–477.

Woods, R.H. (1994). The Supreme Court on gender discrimination: No more "hostile or abusive" work environments. *Cornell Hotel and Restaurant Administration Quarterly, 35,* 20.

Statutes

Equal Employment Opportunity Commission (EEOC). (1993). Guidelines on Harassment Based on Race, Color, Religion, Gender, National Origin, Age, or Disability. 58 Fed. Reg. 51,266 at 29 C.F.R. 1609.

Equal Employment Opportunity Commission (EEOC). (1980). EEOC Guidelines on Discrimination Because of Sex. 29 C.F.R. Section 1604.11.

Cases

Babcock v. Frank 783 F. Supp. 800, S.D.N.Y. 1992.

Barnes v. Costle 561 F.2d 983 DC Circuit, 1977.

Burns v. McGregor Electronic Industries Inc. 989 F.2d 963 8th Circuit, 1993.

Harris v. Forklift Systems 114 S.Ct. 367, 1993.

Highlander v. K.F.C. National Management Co. 805 F.2d 644, 6th Cir, 1986.

Meritor Savings Bank v. Vinson 106 S. Ct. 2399, 1986.

Purrington v. University of Utah, 996 F.2d 1025, 10th Cir. 1993.

Rabidue v. Osceola Refining Company 584 F. Supp. 419, 430, 1984.

Waltman v. International Paper Co., 875 P.2d 468, 474–75, 5th Cir.1989

Chapter 15

Anderson, S.C. (1993). Anti-stalking laws: Will they curb the erotomanic's obsessive pursuit? *Law and Psychology Review*, 17(Spring),
171–191.

Attinello, K.L. (1993). Anti-stalking legislation: a comparison of tradi-
tional remedies available for victims of harassment versus California
Penal Code Section 646.9. (California anti-stalking law). *Pacific Law
Journal*, 24(July), 1945–1980.

Bernstein, S.E. (1993). Living under siege: do stalking laws protect domestic violence victims? *Cardozo Law Review*, 15(October), 525–567.

Buckley, M. (1994). Stalking laws - problem or solution? (Special focus:
Women's health and safety). *Wisconsin Women's Law Journal*, 9
(Winter), 23–66.

Hammell, B.F. (1995). Stalking treatment options program (informational
program material).

Harmon, R.B., Rosner, R., & Owens, H. (1995). Obsessional harassment
and erotomania in a criminal court population. *Journal of Forensic
Sciences*, 40(March), 188–196.

Holden, G.A. (1993). Project to develop a model anti-stalking code for
states (NIJ report 144477). Washington, DC: United States Department of Justice.

Leong, G.B. (1994). DeClerambault syndrome (erotomania) in the criminal justice system: another look at this recurring problem. *Journal of
Forensic Sciences*, 39(March), 378–385.

Lingg, R.A. (1993). Stopping stalkers: a critical examination of anti-
stalking statutes. *St. John's Law Review*, 67(Spring), 347–381.

McAnaney, K.G., Corliss, L.A., & Abetyta-Price, E. (1993). From impru-
dence to crime: anti-stalking laws. *Notre Dame Law Review*, 68,
819–909.

Meloy, J.R. (1995). Stalking (obsessional following): Empirical findings
and object relations theory. Paper presented at the 103rd annual con-
vention of the American Psychological Association. New York, New
York.

Meloy, J.R. (1989). Unrequited love and the wish to kill. *Bulletin of the
Menninger Clinic*, 53, 477–492.

Meloy, J.R., & Gothard, S. (1995). Demographic and clinical comparison of obsessional followers and offenders with mental disorders.
American Journal of Psychiatry, 152, 258–263.

Morville, D.A. (1993). Stalking laws: are they solutions for more problems? *Washington University Law Quarterly*, 71, 921–935.

Patton, E.A. (1994). Stalking laws: in pursuit of a remedy. *Rutgers Law
Journal*, 25, 263–280.

Perez, C. (1993). Stalking: when does obsession become a crime? *American Journal of Criminal Law*, 20, 263–280.

Robinson, A.J. (1984). A remedial approach to harassment. *Virginia Law Review*, 70, 507–535.

Schaum, M., & Parrish, K. (1995). *Stalked: breaking the silence on the crime of stalking in America*. New York: Pocket Books.

Sohn, E.F. (1994). Anti-stalking statutes: Do they actually protect victims? *Criminal Law Bulletin*, 30(May-June), 203–241.

Walker, J.M. (1993). Anti-stalking legislation: Does it protect the victim without violating the rights of the accused? *Denver University Law Review*, 71, 73–302.

Ward, C. (1994). Minnesota's anti-stalking statute: A durable tool to protect victims from terroristic behavior. *Law and Inequality*, 12, 613–647.

Wood, L.T.(1993). Anti-stalker legislation: A legislative attempt to surmount the inadequacies of protective orders. *Indiana Law Review*, 27, 449–473.

Zona, M.A., Sharma, K.K., & Lane, J. (1993). A comparative study of erotomania and obsessional subjects in a forensic sample. *Journal of Forensic Sciences*, 38, 894–903.

Statutes

Arizona Revised Statutes Annotated 13-2905 (1989).

California Penal Code Section 646.9 (1990).

Colorado Revised Statutes Annotated 18-9-112 (West 1990).

Florida Statutes Annotated 810.09 (Supp. 1993).

Kentucky Revised Statutes Annotated 508.050 (Baldwin 1984).

Chapter 525.090 (Baldwin 1984).

Chapter 511.080 (Baldwin 1984).

Montana Code Annotated 45-5-203 (1991).

New Jersey Statutes Annotated 2C:12–3 (1982).

Ohio Revised Code Annotated 2903.21–.22 (Anderson 1993).

Chapter 16

American Psychiatric Association. (1994). *Diagnostic and statistical manual of mental disorders* (4th ed.). Washington, DC: Author.

Bensimon, H. (1994). Violence in the workplace. *Training and Development*, 48, 26–32.

Cassidy, K., McNally, R., & Zeitlin, S. (1992). Cognitive processing of trauma cues in rape victims with post-traumatic stress disorder. *Cognitive Therapy and Research*, 16(3), 283–295.

Davis, G., & Breslau, N. (1994). Post-traumatic stress disorder in victims of civilian trauma and criminal violence. *Psychiatric Clinics of North America, 17*(2), 289–299.

de Becker, G. (1988). Damage control: Managing the violent employee. *Security Management*, September, 70–78.

Einstadter, W., & Henry, S. (1995). *Criminological theory: An analysis of its underlying assumptions.* Fort Worth, TX: Harcourt Brace College Publishers.

Franks, L. (1994, November 14). The judge and I. *New York*, 40–46.

Hanson, R., Saunders, B., & Lipovsky, J. (1992). The relationship between self-reported levels of distress of parents and victims in incest families. *Journal of Child Sexual Abuse, 2*, 49–60.

Hanson, R., Kilpatrick, D., Falsetti, S., & Resnick, H. (1995). Violent crime and mental health. In J. Freedy & S. Hobfoll (Eds.), *Traumatic stress: From theory to practice* (pp. 129–156). New York: Plenum Press.

Henry, S. (Ed.). (1990). *Degrees of deviance: Student accounts of their deviant behavior.* Salem, WI: Sheffield.

Hunzeker, D. (1992) Stalking laws. *National Conference of State Legislatures' State Legislative Report, 17*(19), 1–6.

Kaniasty, K., & Norris, F. (1992). Social support and victims of crime. *American Journal of Community Psychology, 20*, 211–241.

Kolarik, G. (1992). Stalking laws proliferate. *ABA Journal*, 35–36.

Kruttschnitt, C. (1993). Gender and interpersonal violence. In A.J. Reiss, & J. Roth (Eds.), *Understanding and preventing violence: Vol 3. Social influences* (pp. 293–376). Washington, DC: National Academy Press.

Lott, L.D. (1995, November). Violence in the police family. *FBI Law Enforcement Bulletin*, 12–16.

Lowney, K.S., & Best, J. (1995). Stalking strangers and lovers: Changing media typifications of a new crime. In J. Best (Ed.), *Images of issues* (2nd ed.) (pp. 33–57). New York: Aldine de Gruyter.

Meloy, R. (1996). Stalking (obsessional following): A review of some preliminary studies. *Aggression and Violent Behavior, 1*, 147–162.

Meloy, R. (1992). *Violent attachments.* Northvale, NJ: Jason Aronson.

Meloy, R., & Gothard, S. (1995). Demographic and clinical comparisons of obsessional followers and offenders with mental disorders. *American Journal of Psychiatry, 152*, 258–263.

Moscarello, R. (1991, Summer). Posttraumatic stress disorder after sexual assault: Its psychodynamics and treatment. *Journal of the American Academy of Psychoanalysis, 19*, 235–253.

Nadelson, C., & Notman, M. (1979). Psychoanalytic considerations of the response to rape. *International Review of PsychoAnalysis, 6*, 97–103.

Perez, C. (1993). Stalking: When does obsession become a crime? *American Journal of Criminal Law*, *20*, 263–280.

Reiss, A.J., & Roth, J. (1993). Patterns of violence in American society. In A.J. Reiss, & J. Roth (Eds.), *Understanding and preventing violence: Vol 1* (42–97). Washington, DC: National Academy Press.

Resnick, H., Kilpatrick, D., Dansky, B., Saunders, B., & Best, C. (1993, December). Prevalence of civilian trauma and posttraumatic stress disorder in a representative national sample of women. *Journal of Consulting and Clinical Psychology*, *6*, 984–991.

Resnick, P. (1993, June). The psychological impact of rape. Special Section: Rape. *Journal of Interpersonal Violence*, *8*, 223–255.

Saldana, T. (1986). *Beyond survival*. New York: Bantam.

Sampson, R.J., & Laub, J.H. (1993). Crime in the making: Pathways and turning points through life. Cambridge, MA: Harvard University Press.

Sohn, E. (1994). Anti-stalking statutes: Do they actually protect victims? *Criminal Law Bulletin*, *30*, 203–241.

U.S. Department of Justice. (1996). *Domestic violence, stalking, and antistalking legislation: Annual report to Congress*. Washington, DC: Government Printing Office.

U.S. Department of Justice. (1993). *Project to develop a model antistalking code for States*. Washington, DC: U.S. Government Printing Office.

Winkel, F., Denkers, A., & Vrij, A. (1994, May). The effects of attributions on crime victims' psychological readjustment. *Genetic, Social, and General Psychology Monographs*, *120*, 145–168.

Winter, P.D. (1983, January). Notes on a death threat. *Ms. Magazine*, *8*, 60–65. Zona, M., Sharma, K., & Lane, J. (1993, July). A Comparative Sample of Erotomanic and Obsessional Subjects in a Forensic Sample. *Journal of Forensic Sciences*, *39*, 894–903.

Contributors

Lisa Bozenhard is a Master of Science degree candidate in Criminal Justice at Westfield State College where she holds the position of graduate research assistant and has served as an adjunct faculty member. Ms. Bozenhard also serves as an instructor at the Springfield (MA) Police Academy. She plans to pursue a doctorate in the field of criminal justice/criminology.

Max L. Bromley is an Associate Professor in the Department of Criminology at the University of South Florida. He has previously served as the Associate Director of Public Safety at the University of South Florida and worked in the criminal justice field for almost 25 years. He is the senior co-author of *College Crime Prevention and Personal Safety Awareness*, has co-edited a volume entitled *Hospital and College Security Liability Awareness*, and is co-author of the 5th Edition of *Crime and Justice in America*. In addition, he has written numerous scholarly articles on campus crime and policing as well as technical documents on a variety of criminal justice topics. Dr. Bromley also wrote *Department Self-Study: A Guide for Campus Law Enforcement Administrators* used at over 1,000 institutions of higher education.

Timothy S. Bynum is a Professor in the School of Criminal Justice at Michigan State University. He also serves as an Associate Director of the Institute for Public Policy and Social Research where he formerly directed the Evaluation Research Division. Dr. Bynum has been the principal investigator in a wide range of criminal justice public policy areas including the exclusionary rule, community corrections, prison overcrowding, narcotics enforcement, policing innovations, sentencing guidelines, juvenile justice, alternative schools, delinquency prevention, and drug treatment. He has published in a variety of criminal justice journals and has co-authored a monograph on evaluating juvenile justice programs. Dr. Bynum is currently involved in the evaluation of community based programs for delinquent youth and is a co-principal investigator of an NIJ funded evaluation of a conflict resolution program for middle school students.

Richard D. Clark received his Ph.D. in Criminal Justice from the State University of New York at Albany and is currently an Assistant Professor at John Carroll University. His research interests include families and delinquency, school crime, and reactions to victimization. He is currently engaged in several research projects including an assessment of a violence prevention project in public schools, and the extent and impact of harassment received by environmental activist. He has published numerous articles and book chapters.

Stephen M. Cox received his Ph.D. in 1995 from the School of Criminal Justice at Michigan State University and is currently an Assistant Professor in the Department of Sociology/Criminal Justice at Central Connecticut State University. His current work involves investigating the mitigating factors of school violence, evaluating education-based interventions, methods of community crime control, and community policing initiatives. In the past, Dr. Cox has participated in research projects in the following areas: community policing, alternative education programs for delinquent youth, community corrections, special alternatives to incarceration (prison boot camps), and substance abuse programs for parolees.

William S. Davidson is a Professor in the Psychology Department and Chair of the Ecological Psychology Department at Michigan State University. He has been the principal investigator in several community based research projects involving juvenile diversion programs, community corrections, prison boot camps, substance abuse programs for prisoners, and day treatment programs for delinquent youth. Dr. Davidson is currently the co-principal investigator of an NIJ funded evaluation of a school violence reduction program.

M.A. DuPont-Morales earned her doctorate at Northeastern University in Boston, MA in Law, Policy, and Society. As an Assistant Professor in the School of Public Affairs at Penn State, Harrisburg, she conducts research in victimology, predatory violence, stalking, and accountability in corrections. Dr. DuPont-Morales has worked with violent crime victims for twenty years. She completed the first Commonwealth of Pennsylvania Victimization Survey in 1997 and is working on the second stage of the survey. She was selected by the Secretary of Defense to participate in the Joint Civilian Orientation Conference for the Department of Defense in May 1997. She has presented papers at the Academy of Criminal Justice Sciences, the National Public Sector Productivity Improvement Conference, The Critical Perspective on Accounting Symposium for the Public Interest Section of the American Accounting Association, and the Institute for Women's Policy Research.

Patricia H. Grant is a programmer analyst in the President's Office at Virginia Commonwealth University. She has a Master of Science in Criminal Justice from VCU and is currently pursuing a Ph.D. in Public Policy. Mrs. Grant is an adjunct professor with the Department of Criminal Justice at VCU.

James L. Hague has a JD degree from the University of Richmond and an LLM degree. He is a Professor in the Department of Criminal Justice at Virginia Commonwealth University. Professor Hague provides professional training and development for many law enforcement agencies throughout the state of Virginia.

Robert A. Jerin is the Chair of the Law and Justice Department at Endicott College and serves as the faculty athletic representative. He has a BS in Criminal Justice from the University of New Haven, a Master of Science in Criminology from Florida State University, and a Ph.D. in Criminal Justice from Sam Houston State University. He has previously taught at North Georgia College, Salem State College, and Appalachian State University. He has published articles in the *American Journal of Police* and *Criminal Justice Policy Review*. Additionally, he has had chapters published in edited volumes on *Media and Crime, Crime in the 21st Century, Crime Victims Services*, and the *Juvenile Justice System*. He has published a textbook with Dr. Laura J. Moriarty entitled *Victims of Crime*. Dr. Jerin is a former juvenile detention officer for the State of Connecticut and is currently involved in research on restorative justice and crime prevention.

Peggy L. Kenworthy received a Bachelor of Liberal Studies in Political Science from Mary Washington College located in Fredericksburg, Virginia. She received a Master of Science in Criminal Justice from Virginia Commonwealth University located in Richmond, Virginia. She is currently employed as a paralegal for an attorney in Fredericksburg. She, her husband, and their son live in Stafford, Virginia.

Nicholas N. King is an adjunct faculty member at the University of Louisville, School of Law. He is a former member of the Kentucky Supreme Court, and former Commonwealth's Attorney for Jefferson County, Kentucky.

Lloyd Klein is an Assistant Professor of Sociology at Medgar Evers College, City University of New York. His research concentrates on victimology and criminal justice policy. He has authored professional papers and published in the areas of crime prevention and peacemaking criminology. He is also involved in the Restorative Justice movement through active participation with the UN Working Party on Restorative Justice (affiliated with the Alliance of NGOs on Crime Prevention and Criminal Justice). His participation includes active organizational work with the Campaign for Equity-Restorative Justice (CERJ). In addition, he is author of *It's in the Cards: Consumer Credit and the American Experience* (Praeger, 1998) and another forthcoming edited volume on daytime television talk programs.

Steven P. Lab holds a Ph.D. in Criminology from Florida State University and is presently Professor and Director of Criminal Justice at Bowling Green State University. He is author of *Crime Prevention: Approaches,*

Practices and Evaluations, 3rd edition, 1997, Juvenile Justice: An Intro-duction, 2nd edition (with John Whitehead, 1996), and *Victimology* (with W.G. Dorner, 1995), the editor of *Crime Prevention at a Cross-roads* (1997), and has written numerous articles. His current research fo-cuses on crime, victimization, and crime prevention activity in secondary school settings.

David L. Mitchell received his Ph.D. from the University of Florida in So-ciology. He is owner of Mitchell Training, Inc., a Florida-based training and consulting company.

Darin K. Moore is a Graduate Student in the Department of Justice Ad-ministration at the University of Louisville. He holds a B.S. in Justice Ad-ministration from the University of Louisville. His research centers on HIV/AIDS and the legal system, judicial processing of child sexual abuse offenders, and rural criminal justice.

Laura J. Moriarty is an Associate Professor in the Department of Crimi-nal Justice and Assistant Dean, College of Humanities and Science at Vir-ginia Commonwealth University. She has a Ph.D. in Criminal Justice from Sam Houston State University. Her primary research interests include vic-timology, violent crime, and theory testing. She is the co-author (with Robert A. Jerin) of the textbook, *Victims of Crime* (1998, Nelson Hall). Her work has appeared in the *Journal of Criminal Justice Education, Criminal Justice Policy Review, Criminal Justice Review, American Jour-nal of Criminal Justice*, among others. In addition, she is the author of many book chapters and technical reports. Dr. Moriarty is currently co-editing (with David L. Carter) a book entitled "Criminal Justice Technol-ogy in the 21st Century" (Charles C. Thomas, in press).

Bernadette T. Muscat is a Doctoral Candidate (A.B.D.) in Public Admin-istration in the School of Public Affairs at Penn State, Harrisburg. Her primary research interests are in criminal justice, public policy, and vio-lence against women specifically domestic violence, sexual harassment, and stalking. She has presented her research findings at national confer-ences and is published in the journal *Women & Criminal Justice*.

Gregory P. Orvis, is a member in good standing of the Louisiana State Bar Association and an Associate Professor in the Department of Social Sci-ences at the University of Texas at Tyler, where he teaches law courses in the Criminal Justice and Master of Public Administration programs. Dr. Orvis received his Juris Doctorate from Tulane School of Law in 1978 and his Doctor of Philosophy from the University of Houston in 1988. He has published articles in the *American Journal of Criminal Justice, Bridges, Forensic Science Review, Harvard Law and Policy Review, Jus-*

tice Quarterly, as well as several chapters in several books. Dr. Orvis' research interests focus primarily on constitutional law issues particularly as they impact the workplace and the courtroom.

William V. Pelfrey, Sr. is Professor of Criminal Justice at Virginia Commonwealth University. He has researched and published on topics such as fear of crime, victimization, patterns and trends in violent crime, and the causes of crime and delinquency. He received his Ph.D. from Florida State University.

William V. Pelfrey, Jr. is a member of the faculty of the College of Criminal Justice, University of South Carolina. Previously, he was a researcher in the Center for Public Policy at Temple University while completing his coursework for the Ph.D. in Criminal Justice, Temple University. His major research and publishing interests include spatial analysis of crime, GIS, policing, and public policy evaluation methods. He holds a masters degree in Clinical Psychology.

Roberto Hugh Potter is a native of Florida. He received his education at the University of South Florida (B.A., 1975) and the University of Florida (M.A., 1977 and Ph.D., 1982). He has worked as a Criminal Justice Planner, Founding Director of the Florida Juvenile Justice Institute, Training and Research Director for the Florida Runaway Shelters, and Director of Evaluation Research and Information Systems for Families First in Atlanta. His academic career has spanned five and one-half years teaching Sociology and Criminology in Australia (University of New England), and more recently as Director of the Institute for Correctional Research and Training at Morehead State University (Kentucky). His applied research interests center on justice and community welfare issues, including crime on university campuses. Publications in this area include studies on juvenile justice system decision-making, net-widening, and campus crime. On the academic side, he is interested in behaviors and products at the margins of society, as reflected in the 1996 publication, *Pornography: Group Pressures and Individual Rights*, a study of the X-rated video industry and consumers in Australia. Somewhere in all of this were a couple of mis-spent years in computer training management.

Deborah Mitchell Robinson is Assistant Professor of Criminal Justice at Valdosta State University. She received her Ph.D. from Florida State University, School of Criminology and Criminal Justice in 1995. Her major areas of research and publication include crime prevention, environmental criminology, and victimology.

Anne Sullivan is an Assistant Professor of Criminal Justice at Salem State College. She received her Ph.D. in Law, Policy, and Society at Northeastern University in 1994. Her research and teaching interests include environmental crime, domestic violence, hate crime, and community policing.

Richard Tewksbury is an Associate Professor in the Department of Justice Administration at the University of Louisville. Currently he serves as Editor of the *American Journal of Criminal Justice*. His recent publications include *Introduction to Corrections* (Glencoe/McGraw-Hill, 1997) and *A Manual for Evaluating Child Advocacy Centers* (National Network of Child Advocacy Centers, 1997).

Alban L. Wheeler is a native of Miami, Florida. He received his higher education at Mississippi College (B.A., 1963, M.A., 1964) and Mississippi State University (Ph.D., 1972). His academic career extends over a period of 32 years during which time he has served as Professor of Sociology, Dean of Students, Department Head, Program Director, School Dean, and Member of the Board of Regents. Professor Wheeler's research interests are in violence and health related issues. His current research is focused on crime, victimization, and fear of crime in educational settings and small communities

Authors Index

Subject Index